Knowing Him

Discovering God through His Names and Attributes

DAVID A. CANTER

SPECIAL THANKS to the following:

Baker Books, Grand Rapids, Michigan for pemission to quote from *Thayer's Greek-Hebrew Lexicon.*

HarperCollins Publishers, Inc. for permission to quote from *The Knowledge of the Holy, The Attributes of God: Their Meaning in the Christian Life*, Copyright © 1961 by Aiden Wilson Tozer.

Lifeway Christian Resources for permission to quote from *Word Pictures in the New Testament*, by A.T. Robertson; and *Holman Bible Dictionary.*

Loizeaux Brothers, Inc., Neptune, New Jersey for permission to quote from *The World's Greatest Name*, by Charles J. Rolls.

Tyndale House Publishers, Inc., Wheaton Illinois for permission to quote from *Life Application Study Bible* copyright © 1988. All rights reserved.

Dedication

I dedicate this book to my wife and children

Linda
David, Jr.
Nichole

I pray that the great I AM will continually be in me and make me the husband my wife needs and the father my children and grandchildren need as well.

I also dedicate this book to the memory of

Derek Anthony Canter

My first grandchild, age five, was struck by a car on December 26, 1997, and went to be with the Lord. At the throne of grace Derek talks face-to-face with the God I love to contemplate through His revealed names and attributes. "For now we see in a mirror, dimly, but then face to face. Now I know in part, but then I shall know just as I am known" (1 Corinthians 13:12, *NKJV*).

Contents

Contents (continued)

Preface

Written for Christians, this book is not for the unbeliever or the scoffer. If you have been a Christian for any length of time you have faced trials that seemed more than you could handle—even with the help of a loving God. We tend to think of Him as being like us—only bigger, wiser and stronger.

But He is not a super-human being, *He is God*! He is not limited to our concept of time and space. Nor is He limited to a finite body, finite knowledge or finite strength. God is *infinite* in every way.

There is no place where He is not present. There is nothing one can know or think that He is not aware of. He can meet every need and answer every desire. God loves without measure, and He wants only the best for His creation. God is only good; there is no evil in Him. He puts His desires in the hearts of those who receive and respond to Him.

He is willing to do signs, wonders and miracles in answer to our prayers. He heals and delivers the oppressed. Through the blood of Jesus, we are born again when we put our faith in His work on the cross. He is the God of new beginnings.

Christians do not realize how great God is. Consequently, believers often behave like spiritual paupers, rarely appropriating the goodness and grace He offers. We need to develop a closer relationship with Him by spending time in God's Word, and in prayer and fellowship with Him. First John 2:12-14, *NKJV*, describes three maturity levels of a Christian:

> I write to you, little children, because your sins are forgiven you for His name's sake. I write to you, fathers, because you have known Him who is from the beginning. I write to you, young men, because you have overcome the wicked one. I write to you, little children, because you have known the Father. I have written to you, fathers, because you have known Him who is from the beginning. I have written to you, young men, because you are strong, and the word of God abides in you, and you have overcome the wicked one.

The "little child" is a Christian who knows that his sins are forgiven. The "young man" is a Christian who has grown and is strong in the Lord and in the knowledge of the Word. The "father" is a Christian who "has known Him who is from the beginning."

A sign of maturity in the believer is knowing God. Knowing Him, then, should be the priority of all Christians. The principal purpose in life is to know God, to glorify Him, to enjoy His presence, and to introduce others to Him. We need more fathers in the faith to win the lost, to train the "children" effectively, and to teach the younger men to overcome the evil one.

Acknowledgments

Many people deserve credit for encouraging me to complete this work. When I would set it aside and consider quitting the endless hours of research, a phone call from someone wanting to know what God had shown me lately through my studies always spurred me on.

Linda Canter, my wife, believes in me and in the God I serve. Over the past 10 years, many hours were spent away from her during the preparation of this book. But she wouldn't let me quit or put the work aside until it was completed. I am grateful.

David Brown met with me weekly in a Bible study group I led while using these materials. Many times he encouraged me to dig deeper; and it is largely his prompting that has put this book into the hands of the publisher.

Two Promise Keeper's groups that meet weekly and use these materials have encouraged and challenged me, as they "chewed" on every word. Devotional thoughts concerning one of God's names or attributes often came to me during one of these accountability group meetings.

Helen Boucher and H. Dennis (Denny) Bates are dear friends who have spent countless hours reading, rereading, editing and re-editing the contents of this book. This final product is largely a result of their willingness to labor and serve.

Key To Studying the Names of God

SAMPLE

16. I Am – *Hayah*

"And God said unto Moses, I AM THAT I AM: and he said, Thus shalt thou say unto. . . .

Definition: *Hayah* (haw-yaw') [1961]; a primitive root [compare *hava'*)]; to exist, i.e. be or . . . . (S)

(*See #21.*)

KEY

16. I Am: This is the equivalent of God's name in English.

Hayah (**haw-yaw'**): This is a transliteration of this particular Hebrew word with its phonetic pronounciation in English. Names of God may also be in Greek or Aramaic.

[1961]: This is the code number linked to *Strong's Hebrew and Greek Dictionary of the Bible.*

(S): This abbreviation identifies *Strong's Hebrew and Greek Dictionary of the Bible* as the source for the definition.

See #21: This refers to Bible study number 21 in this book.

Introduction

The Bible admonishes us to know our God. "In every place where I record My name [or cause My name to be remembered] I will come to you, and I will bless you" (Exodus 20:24, *NKJV*).

"I will bow toward Your holy temple and will praise Your name for Your love and Your faithfulness, for You have exalted above all things Your Name and Your Word" (Psalm 138:2, *NIV*).

"I know whom I have believed, and am convinced that He is able to guard that which I have entrusted to Him for that day" (2 Timothy 1:12, *NIV*).

"And this is eternal life, that they may know You, the only true God, and Jesus Christ whom You have sent" (John 17:3, *NKJV*).

Throughout the Bible, God revealed Himself to people through many manifestations. Each time He appeared to them, they recorded His revealed name or attribute. The name often described an aspect of the Godhead.

As a jeweler holds an expensive diamond to a light and turns it to allow himself to study each facet, so the light of God's revelation comes to us through our knowledge of Him. As we know more about Him we know more about living the Christian life. We cannot appropriate gifts and blessings we do not know about. So we must know God, and how to pray according to His will!

God is present in the Father, Son and Holy Spirit. Manifested in different forms, they are of a single character and essence. The Father is God; the Son is God; the Holy Spirit is God. Together they are one God. As we study the nature of God, we increase our faith in His ability to meet our needs.

"Jesus Christ is the same yesterday and today and forever" (Hebrews 13:8, *NIV*). "God is not a man, that he should lie, nor a son of man, that he should change his mind. Does he speak and then not act? Does he promise and not fulfill?" (Numbers 23:19, *NIV*).

May your faith increase as you allow God to reveal Himself to you through His Word. The scripture references are, to the best of my knowledge, the first mention of each name in the Bible. The attributes give the accepted proof texts for each. I pray with Paul:

> that the God of our Lord Jesus Christ, the Father of Glory, may give to you the spirit of wisdom and revelation in the knowledge of Him, the eyes of your understanding being enlightened; that you may know what is the hope of His calling, what are the riches of the glory of His inheritance in the saints, and what is the exceeding greatness of His power toward us who believe, according to the working of His mighty power (Ephesians 1:17-19, *NKJV*).

I have emphasized words in their Scriptural context throughout, to help identify those applicable to the study. When a paraphrase is used, it is noted for its clarity and consistency. May God richly bless you as you learn more about Him!

PART 1

THE TRIUNE GOD

PART 1
The Triune God

His Hebrew Names in
GENESIS

1. God – *'Elohiym*

"In the beginning *God* created the heaven and the earth" (Genesis 1:1).

> **Definition:** *'Elohiym* (el-o-heem) [430]; plural of *'elowahh*; gods in the ordinary sense; but specifically used (in the plural thus, especially with the article) of the supreme God; occasionally applied by way of deference to magistrates; and sometimes as a superlative: – angels, X exceeding, God (gods) (-dess, -ly), X (very) great, judges, X mighty. (S)

'Elohiym is a uni-plural noun meaning God. It is used as a name for other gods, as well as Jehovah. This, the first name used for God in the Bible, speaks of His being the one true God and indicates that He is plural in nature. Like the nouns, "deer" or "moose," it is used in the same form whether referring to God

in the singular or God in three persons, as in the Trinitarian view of the Godhead. (*See #6, #7, #58.*)

2. Light Giver – *Ma'owr*

"Then *God made two great lights*: the greater light to rule the day, and the lesser light to rule the night. He made the stars also" (Genesis 1:16, *NKJV*).

> **Definition:** *Ma'owr* (maw-ore') [3974]; or *ma'or* (maw-ore'); also (in plural) feminine *me'owrah* (meh-o-raw'); or *meorah* (meh-o-raw'); from *'owr*, properly, a luminous body or luminary, i.e. (abstractly) light (as an element): figuratively, brightness, i.e. cheerfulness; specifically, a chandelier: – bright, light. (S)

As you can see from Strong's definition, this application of the word *ma'owr* refers to God as the source of light or brightness. In the proper sense, He brings physical illumination. In the abstract sense, He brightens up otherwise gloomy situations in life. On the first day of creation God said, "Let there be light" and light was (Genesis 1:3). During the fourth creation day God chose to make the sun and moon, along with other heavenly structures, which He placed in the sky for us to ponder.

❑ According to Revelation 21:22-27, the New Jerusalem will have neither sun nor moon to brighten the sky. The presence of God the Father and His Son, Jesus Christ, will bring illumination to every part of the City.

❑ When God appeared to Moses, He came as a shimmering light that looked like a fire, but it did not consume the bush that it surrounded.

❑ When God directed the Israelites through the wilderness, He appeared as a pillar of cloud by day and fire (shimmering light) by night.

❑ God's glory caused Moses' face to shine (Exodus 34:29), and filled the tabernacle (Exodus 40:35).

Where God is, there is light! There is a sense, though, in which God illuminates things around us right now, without artificial light sources or the need for the sun or moon. He shows us our sins and failures. He shows us truth in the midst of a lie and gives revelation to those willing to receive it. This too is the light of God. He truly is our Light Giver. (*See #63, #121, #173, #184, #271.*)

3. LORD – *YHVH* (*Yehovah*)

"This is the account of the heavens and the earth when they were created, in the day that the *Lord* God made earth and heaven" (Genesis 2:4, *NASB*).

> **Definition:** *Yehovah* (yeh-ho-vaw') [3068]; from *hayah* [1961]; (the) self-Existent or Eternal; Jehovah, Jewish national name of God: Jehovah, the Lord. (S)

Yehovah, or Jehovah, is the proper name of God. In the Old Testament, the name was so holy that the Israelites would not pronounce it for fear of breaking the fourth commandment (see Exodus 20:7). In the King James version of the Bible, this name for God is always written in capital letters to set it apart from any other name used. (*See #4, #5, #8, #25, #61.*)

4. Jehovah – *YHWH* (*Yahweh*)

"These are the generations of the heavens and of the earth when they were created, in the day that the *Lord* God made the earth and the heavens" (Genesis 2:4).

> **Definition:** *Yehovah* (yeh-ho-vaw') [3068]; from *hayah* [1961]; (the) self-Existent or Eternal; Jehovah, Jewish national name of God: – Jehovah, the Lord. (S)

Vowels were not used in the original Hebrew manuscripts, so pronunciation was assumed through tradition. Unfortunately, *YHWH* was never pronounced (see #3), so there was no way to transliterate this name. Jehovah is the modern pronunciation of this word. This name for

God was actually derived by using the consonants from the name *Yahweh*, and the vowels from the name *Adonai*.

An interesting thing about the history of this name is that the Jehovah's Witnesses have been so adamant about "Jehovah" being the only name for God. But *Jehovah* is not even used in the original manuscripts. *YHWH* is the name to which they are referring; Jehovah is the modern day pronunciation used for it. The full truth from Scripture sometimes contradicts our religions. (*See #3, #5, #8, #57, #61, #70*.)

5. Lord God – *Yehovah- 'Elohiym*

"These are the generations of the heavens and of the earth when they were created, in the day that the *Lord God* made the earth and the heavens" (Genesis 2:4).

Definition: '*Elohiym* (el-o-heem') [430]; (*see #1*)

In the second chapter of the Bible, we find this name used to describe the Lord God. It refers to the self-existence of God, and His character as the Eternal Creator. The self-existence of God implies that He does not need anything or anyone to make Him complete.

We will see later that one of the names of God is "I Am." *He is* when we acknowledge Him and when we don't, when we believe in Him and when we don't. He is Lord, whether we recognize Him as such or not. Accepting Him as Lord, we assume a proper position under His lordship.

The eternal Creator does not change; He is always the same. This means that He is still in the business of creating today. We were made in His image, and we cannot be content unless we are involved and active in His creation. We were not created to sit and watch the world move around us. It was not the purpose of God for us to stop all activity when we get older, or to be idle and unproductive when we are healthy and able to be productive in society. Work keeps us mentally, physically and spiritually healthy. It keeps us balanced. Retirement should not be a time of inactivity. It can be a period in life when one is able to devote more time and energy to God's kingdom. (*See #3, #4, #8, #57, #61, #70.*)

6. God – *'El*

"And Melchizedek king of Salem brought forth bread and wine: and he was the priest of the most high *God*" (Genesis 14:18).

> **Definition:** *'El* – (ale) [410]; shortened from Hebrew *'ayil*; *strength*; as adjective *mighty*; especially the *Almighty* (but used also of any *deity*) :– God (god), X goodly, X great, idol, might (-y one), power, strong. Compare names in "-el."

El is a common adjective or prefix, meaning "God." The word implies "to be strong or extend control over." It is a prefix to many words that help to define our God. It is sometimes used alone, and at such times it is translated "God" meaning our supreme Maker, or "god" meaning some lower authority. Several hyphenated names of God use *El* as their root. (*See #1, #7, #58.*)

7. God of Gods (Most High God) – *'El 'Elyown*

"And Melchizedek king of Salem brought forth bread and wine: and he *was* the priest of the *most high God*" (Genesis 14:18).

"He hath said, which heard the words of God, and knew the knowledge of the *most High*, which saw the vision of the Almighty, falling into a trance, but having his eyes open" (Numbers 24:16).

"For the Lord your God is *God of gods*, and Lord of lords, a great God, a mighty, and a terrible, which regardeth not persons, nor taketh reward" (Deuteronomy 10:17).

> **Definition:** *'Elyown*, (el-yone') [5945]; from *'alah*; an *elevation*, i.e. (adjective) *lofty* (comparative); as title, the Supreme: - (Most, on) high (-er, -est), upper (-most). (S)

Our God is the "God of gods." He is the supreme God; no other god can contend with Him. Satan is not a god. He is not equal with *El Elyon.* At times Satan may seem very powerful and in control of the circumstances of our lives, but that is a lie from the pit of hell. Jesus bound Satan when He entered into hell after His crucifixion, and He was raised again because Satan had no right to hold Him.

Jesus was human like us, but without sin. Therefore, when He rose from the grave He rose as, "the Living One; I was dead, and behold I am alive for ever and ever! And I hold the keys of death and Hades" (Revelation 1:18, *NIV*). He won the victory and gave all of us access to all the rewards of Christians.

In spite of this, we need to respect powers and principalities. Jude said in verse 9 of his letter, "Yet Michael, one of the mightiest of the angels, when he was arguing with Satan about Moses' body, did not dare to accuse even Satan, or jeer at him, but simply said, 'The Lord rebuke you'" (*TLB*). We need Jesus Christ and His power to stand up to any of the demonic hosts. Our God is King of kings and Lord of lords. We are able to do all things through Him who gives us strength, but we are nothing without Him. (*See #1, #6, #58.*)

8. Lord – *Adonay*

"And Abram said, *Lord* God, what wilt thou give me, seeing I go childless, and the steward of my house is this Eliezer of Damascus?" (Genesis 15:2).

> **Definitions:** *Adonay* (ad-o-noy') [136]; an emphatic form of '*adown*; the *Lord* (used as a proper name of God only) :- (my) Lord. (S)
>
> *Adonay-* 1. My lord; lord (a) used of men (b) used of God.
> 2. Lord (a title) spoken instead of *Yahweh* as a Jewish display of reverence (*Briggs Hebrew-English Lexicon*).

The Israelites used this name most frequently when referring to their God in conversation. *Adonai* speaks more of the title as Lord than the proper name *Jehovah*. The Israelites considered it a more personal revelation of God, and less formal. Also, they felt they could use this name without breaking the commandments. This name "Lord" is spelled with a capital L; the remainder of the letters are in lowercase in most translations. (*See #3, #4, #5, #57, #61, #70.*)

9. God Who Sees – *'El Ro'iy*

"Then she called the name of the Lord who spoke to her, 'Thou art a God who sees'; for she said, 'Have I even remained alive here after seeing Him?'" (Genesis 16:13, *NASB*).

> **Definition:** Ro'iy (*ro-ee'*) [7210]; from (*ra'ah*); *sight*, whether abstract (*vision*) or concrete (a *spectacle*): - gazingstock, look to, (that) see (-th). (S)

When Hagar was running from Sarah, Abraham's wife, an angel of the Lord met her and assured her that "He saw" her and knew her needs. There is not a situation in our lives, nor a need, that Jesus is not fully aware of. In fact, He always has better understanding of the true source of the problem than we have.

A silly song we sing at Christmastime says that Santa Claus knows when you've been sleeping, and he knows when you're awake. He even knows when you've been good or bad. The author of this song attributes to a fictitious character the understanding and insight that only God has. But there is only one God in the universe with this kind of understanding: He is Father, Son and Holy Spirit, not Santa Claus. This attribute of God is perfectly illustrated in Psalm 139:1-12:

> O Lord, you have examined my heart and know everything about me. You know when I sit or stand. When far away you know my every thought. You chart the path ahead of me, and tell me where to stop and rest. Every moment, you know where I am. You know what I am going to say before I even say it. You both precede and follow me, and place your hand of blessing on my head.

This is too glorious, too wonderful to believe! I can never be lost to your Spirit! I can never get away from my God! If I go up to heaven, you are there; if I go down to the place of the dead, you are there. If I ride the morning winds to the farthest oceans, even there your hand will guide me, your strength will support me. If I try to hide in the darkness, the night becomes light around me. For even darkness cannot hide from God; to you the night shines as bright as day. Darkness and light are both alike to you (*TLB*).

(*See #45, #293.*)

10. Almighty – *Shaddai*

"And when Abram was ninety years old and nine, the Lord appeared to Abram, and said unto him, I am the *Almighty God*; walk before me, and be thou perfect" (Genesis 17:1).

> **Definitions:** *Shadday* (shad-dah'ee) [7706]; from *shadad*; the Almighty : - Almighty. (S)

Hebrew *Shad* is translated "breast" or "mountain." This name implies that God is like a mountain. He is almighty and capable of supplying our needs. In much the same way, a mother provides all that her child needs for life and growth. The name is used frequently in Job. (*See #11, #107, #257, #291.*)

11. God Almighty – *'El Shaddai*

"When Abram was ninety-nine years old, the LORD appeared to him and said, "I am *God Almighty*; walk before me and be blameless" (Genesis 17:1, *NIV*).

> **Definition:** *'El* (ale) [410]; shortened from *'ayil*; strength; as adjective, mighty; especially the Almighty (but used also of any deity): – *God (god), X goodly, X great, idol, might (-y one), power, strong. Compare names in "-el."*
>
> *Shaddai* – the Omnipotent, the name of God in frequent use in Hebrew Scriptures, generally translated 'the Almighty.' (E)

This name refers to the power and provision of God in the lives of His people. The God of the mountains is also the sustainer of life.

The "breasted God" is the literal meaning of this phrase. The word *Shad*, commonly translated "breast," evokes the mental picture of a baby nursing at the breast of its mother and drawing its strength and nourishment from her. Everything a newborn baby requires for life is in mother's milk. In the same way, God is everything we need for the Christian life. To me, this as a greater revelation of the provision of God in our lives than the name *Jehovah-jireh* from Genesis 22:14.

"And God said unto him, I am *God Almighty*: be fruitful and multiply; a nation and a company of nations shall be of thee, and kings shall come out of thy loins" (Genesis 35:11).

"And *God Almighty* give you mercy before the man, that he may send away your other brother, and Benjamin. If I be bereaved of my children, I am bereaved" (Genesis 43:14).

"And Jacob said unto Joseph, *God Almighty* appeared unto me at Luz in the land of Canaan, and blessed me" (Genesis 48:3). (*See #10, #13, #291.*)

12. Eternal God – *'El 'Owlam*

"Abraham planted a tamarisk tree in Beersheba, and there he called upon the name of the Lord, the *Eternal God*" (Genesis 21:33, *NIV*).

> **Definition:** '*Owlam* (o-lawm'); or '*olam* (o-lawm') [5769]; from '*alam*; properly, concealed, i.e. the vanishing point; generally, time out of mind (past or future), i.e. (practically) eternity; frequently adverbial (especially with prepositional prefix) always: Always: alway (-s), ancient (time), any more, continuance, eternal, (for, [n-]) ever (-lasting, -more, of old), lasting, long (time), (of) old (time), perpetual, at any time, (beginning of the) world (+without end). (S)

Jesus said, "He is not the God of the dead, but of the living" (Mark 12:27, *NASB*). Jesus was referring to the fact that all of us are eternal creatures. We have been made in the likeness of God, and

God is eternal. Adam was created to have eternal fellowship with the Father, but because of sin, he was separated from God. From that moment he was dead in the truest meaning of the word. Through rebirth, however, the believer can again be ushered into eternal life through the Son and receive the full benefits of that relationship.

"Before the mountains were brought forth, or ever thou hadst formed the earth and the world, even from everlasting to everlasting, thou art God" (Psalm 90:2). (*See #46.*)

13. Lord It Shall Be Seen – *Jehovah-Jireh*

"And Abraham called the name of that place Jehovah-jireh: as it is said to this day, in the mount of the *Lord it shall be seen*" (Genesis 22:14).

> **Definition:** *Jehovah-jireh*, (yeh-ho-vaw' yir-eh'), [3070]; from *Yehovah* and *ra'ah*; Jehovah will see (to it); *Jehovah-Jireh*, a symbolical name for Mt. Moriah: - Jehovah-Jireh. (S)

Abraham gave this name to the altar he erected on Mt. Moriah after the Lord provided a ram as a substitute sacrifice for his son, Isaac. The place on Mt. Moriah where Abraham offered up Isaac is the same place where, about 2,000 years later, God provided the final provision for all believers when Jesus Christ gave His all.

Most modern language versions of the Bible have translated this phrase as "The Lord will provide," but the root word, *Jireh*, is always interpreted in the Hebrew as "will see" or "has seen." In the eternal heavenly realm, our God is not limited to time and space. He is omniscient and omnipresent.

Jesus said that His Father was not the God of the dead, but of the living. In the eternal present tense of God, everything that will ever be, is; and everything that ever was, is as well. Therefore, what God has seen is a certainty. What He has spoken will be. When God created the heavens and the earth, He spoke them into existence. His voice has the power to create all that we see in this universe from nothing at all. God told Abraham that his offspring would be as numerous as the sands of the seashore or the stars in the heavens.

Abraham believed that if God spoke it, in Him it already was. Therefore, he (Abraham) did not have to worry about making things happen. All he had to do was to believe God and wait on Him for the promise. When God told Abraham to offer up the sacrifice of his only son, Isaac, Abraham held to the word that God had spoken over his life and believed Him.

"By faith, Abraham, at the time of testing, offered Isaac back to God. Acting in faith, he was as ready to return the promised son, his only son, as he had been to receive him—and this after he had already been told, 'Your descendants shall come from Isaac.' Abraham figured that if God wanted to, he could raise the dead. In a sense, that's what happened when he received Isaac back, alive from off the altar" (Hebrews 11:17-19, *TM*).

We all could benefit by adopting some of Abraham's faith. There are many illustrations throughout the Bible that declare the goodness and provision of God. Think about God's abundance and His willingness to let us share with Him.

When Israel was in the wilderness, God rained down manna from heaven, so the people could eat bread. He caused birds to fall out of the sky, so they would have meat. God caused water to come forth from a rock (enough for every man, woman and child, as well as their animals). The Lord kept their shoes and clothing from wearing out for the entire 40 years.

In the Old Testament, God fed a prophet by sending a raven to him with meat (1 Kings 17:6). The Lord supernaturally multiplied a barrel of meal and a bottle of oil (vv. 14-16). He caused a strange noise to scare off an entire army and leave enough spoils for the Israelites to feed an entire city (see 2 Samuel 7).

In the New Testament, Jesus turned water into wine, brought money to Peter in the mouth of a fish, and fed two multitudes of people on different occasions using just a few fish and some small loaves of bread. (*See #9, #11.*)

14. God, the God of Israel – *'El 'Elohey Yisra'el*

"And he erected there an altar, and called it El-elohe-Israel" (Genesis 33:20).

> **Definition:** 'El 'Elohey Yisra'el (*ale el-o-hay' yis-raw-ale'*); from *'el* and *'elohiym* and *Yisra'el*; the *mighty God of Jisrael; El-Elohi-Jisrael*, the title given to a consecrated spot by Jacob : - *El-elohe-israel*. (S)

Jehovah is the God of Abraham. Abraham represents those of us who are, and have been, faithful. Jehovah is also the God of Isaac. Isaac represents those who are wimpy or lighthearted. Jehovah is the God of Jacob, and Jacob represents the worldly-wise people.

Jacob, a conniving man, would say and do whatever promised to work for his good at the time. His moral attitude is called "situational ethics" today. *Jacob* means "supplanter," "deceitful," or "twister" (literally, one who takes the heel).

After he wrestled with the angel, his name was changed to *Israel*, which means, "Prince with God." He walked with a limp and was never the same after his encounter with the Lord. We worship the Lord, the God of Israel who is able to humble us and get our attention. He truly turns everything around and makes a difference.

The list of blessings in Psalm 146:5-9 shows the benefits of a proper relationship with the God of Jacob: "Blessed is he whose help is the God of Jacob, whose hope is in the Lord his God, the Maker of heaven and earth, the sea, and everything in them—the Lord, who remains faithful forever" (Psalm 145:5, 6, *NIV*).

He upholds the cause of the oppressed and gives food to the hungry. The Lord sets prisoners free, gives sight to the blind, lifts up those who are bowed down, and loves the righteous. The Lord watches over the alien and sustains the fatherless and the widow; but He frustrates the ways of the wicked.

May our ambition be to walk in the fullness of the benefits of our relationship with the Most High God. We must put our faith in Him, not in our own abilities or attributes. He is able to watch over us and protect us; He can change us every time we encounter Him. Like Israel, we may walk with a limp, but we will eat at the table of the King. (*See #75.*)

15. Mighty God – *'Abiyr*

"But his bow abode in strength, and the arms of his hands were made strong by the hands of the *mighty God* of Jacob; (from thence is the shepherd, the stone of Israel)" (Genesis 49:24).

"Until I find out a place for the Lord, an habitation for the *mighty God* of Jacob" (Psalm 132:5).

"And I will feed them that oppress thee with their own flesh; and they shall be drunken with their own blood, as with sweet wine: and all flesh shall know that I the Lord am thy Savior and thy Redeemer, the *mighty One* of Jacob" (Isaiah 49:26).

Definition: *'Abiyr* (aw-beer'); *mighty* (spoken of God): - mighty (one). (S)

An undercurrent of belief in today's world holds that the God of the Christians is wimpy. Satan is thought to have more influence in the real world. At least that's the way it sounds, even in some Christian circles.

Artistic portrayals of God throughout the ages have pictured Him as an old man in most paintings. These depictions make it seem that God is beyond His prime years of effectiveness. The truth is that our God is mighty and powerful, and not to be easily reckoned with or taken for granted. (*See #10, #11.*)

PART 1
The Triune God

His Hebrew Names in

EXODUS – PSALMS

---

16. I Am – *Hayah*

"And God said unto Moses, I AM THAT I AM: and he said, Thus shalt thou say unto the children of Israel, I AM hath sent me unto you" (Exodus 3:14).

> **Definition:** *Hayah* (haw-yaw') [1961]; a primitive root [compare *hava'*)]; to exist, i.e. be or become, come to pass (always emphatic, and not a mere copula or auxiliary) : - beacon, X altogether, be (-come), accomplished, committed, like), break, cause, come (to pass), do, faint, fall, + follow, happen, X have, last, pertain, quit (oneself-), require, X use. (S)

God revealed Himself to Moses as "I AM that I AM." He is the eternal, self-existent God who was, and is, and is to come. He needs nothing to complete or finish Him. He said of Himself, "I am Alpha and Omega, the beginning and the ending, saith the Lord, which is, and which was, and which is to come, the Almighty" (Revelation 1:8). We are not self-existent; only God is. We require Him to complete us; we have a God-sized hole in our being that only He can fill.

When Moses asked God to tell him who he should proclaim had sent him, the Lord told Moses to tell the Israelites that "I AM" sent him. In the New Testament Jesus asked whether his listeners had read in the Bible where the Lord said, "'I am the God of Abraham, and the God of Isaac, and the God of Jacob?' He is not the God of the dead, but of the living" (Matthew 22:32, *NASB*).

When we tell others about Jesus, we are not just telling them about a great historic figure who lived long ago. We are telling the world about a Savior that, "is the same yesterday, today, and forever" (Hebrews 13:8). (*See #186.*)

17. Lord Who Heals – *Jehovah-Rapha'*

"And said, If thou wilt diligently hearken to the voice of the Lord thy God, and wilt do that which is right in his sight, and wilt give ear to his commandments, and keep all his statutes, I will put none of these diseases upon thee, which I have brought upon the Egyptians: for I am the *Lord that healeth* thee" (Exodus 15:26).

> **Definition:** *Rapha'* (raw-faw') [7495]; or *raphah* (raw-faw'); a primitive root; properly to mend (by stitching), i.e. (figurative) to cure : - cure, (cause to) heal, physician, repair, X thoroughly, make whole. (raphah). (S)

The Lord showed Moses His mighty power to heal when He sweetened the bitter waters of Marah. God also gave the promise to Moses that He would keep all the diseases of the Egyptians from the Israelites, if only they would follow His commands. The Bible gives repeated testimony of God's dominion over sickness and death.

"But you shall serve the Lord your God, and He will bless your bread and your water; and I will remove sickness from your midst" (Exodus 23:25, *NASB*).

He who dwells in the shelter of the Most High will abide in the shadow of the Almighty. I will say to the Lord, "My refuge and my fortress, My God, in whom I trust!" For it is He who delivers you from the snare of the trapper, and from the deadly pestilence. He will cover you with His pinions, and under His wings you may seek refuge; His faithfulness is a shield and bulwark. You will not be afraid of the terror by night, or of the arrow that flies by day; of the pestilence that stalks in darkness, or of the destruction that lays waste at noon. A thousand may fall at your side, and ten thousand at your right hand; but it shall not approach you. You will only look on with your eyes, And see the recompense of the wicked" (Psalm 91:1-8, *NASB*).

"He forgives your sins—every one. He heals your diseases—every one" (Psalm 103:3, *TM*).

"He spoke, and they were healed—snatched from the door of death" (Psalm 107:20 *TLB*).

"He heals the brokenhearted, And binds up their wounds" (Psalm 147:3, *NKJV*).

"Do not let kindness and truth leave you; Bind them around your neck, Write them on the tablet of your heart. So you will find favor and good repute In the sight of God and man. Trust in the Lord with all your heart, And do not lean on your own understanding. In all your ways acknowledge Him, And He will make your paths straight. Do not be wise in your own eyes; Fear the Lord and turn away from evil. It will be healing to your body, And refreshment to your bones" (Proverbs 3:3-8, *NASB*).

"My son, give attention to my words; Incline your ear to my sayings. Do not let them depart from your sight; Keep them in the midst of your heart. For they are life to those who find them, And health to all their whole body" (Proverbs 4:20-22, *NASB*).

"Surely he took up our infirmities and carried our sorrows, yet we considered him stricken by God, smitten by him, and afflicted.

But he was pierced for our transgressions, he was crushed for our iniquities; the punishment that brought us peace was upon him, and by his wounds we are healed. We all, like sheep, have gone astray, each of us has turned to his own way; and the Lord has laid on him the iniquity of us all" (Isaiah 53:4-6, *NIV*).

"You know of Jesus of Nazareth, how God anointed Him with the Holy Spirit and with power, and how He went about doing good, and healing all who were oppressed by the devil; for God was with Him" (Acts 10:38, *NASB*).

"Is anyone among you sick? Let him call for the elders of the church, and let them pray over him, anointing him with oil in the name of the Lord; and the prayer offered in faith will restore the one who is sick, and the Lord will raise him up, and if he has committed sins, they will be forgiven him. Therefore, confess your sins to one another, and pray for one another, so that you may be healed. The effective prayer of a righteous man can accomplish much" (James 5:14-16, *NASB*).

"And He Himself bore our sins in His body on the cross, that we might die to sin and live to righteousness; for by His wounds you were healed" (1 Peter 2:24, *NASB*).

"We're the best of friends, and I pray for good fortune in everything you do, and for your good health—that your everyday affairs prosper, as well as your soul!" (3 John 1:2, *TM*).

Repeatedly, God has demonstrated His authority over sickness and death. I have seen the power of God restore others and have experienced the same grace of God in my own life. He does not heal as I would like Him to every time I pray, but I have learned from Scripture that our part in the plan is to be obedient to His command to pray for the sick (James 5:13-16). We cannot know God's will completely for every situation of life. But I do know what He told us in His Word, and I am convinced that we should pray for the sick and expect to see miracles. (*See #128, #168.*)

18. Lord Our Banner – *Yehovah-Nissi*

"And Moses built an altar, and called the name of it Jehovah-Nissi" (Exodus 17:15).

> **Definition:** *Yehovah Nic*c*iy* (yeh-ho-vaw' nis-see') [3071]; from *Yehovah* and *nec** with pronoun suffix; Jehovah (is) my banner; *Jehovah-Nissi*, the symbolical name of an altar in the desert: - *Jehovah-Nissi*. (S)

Moses gave this name to the altar he erected in the wilderness to commemorate the defeat of the Amalekites. Aaron and Hur went up on the hillside during the battle and stood with Moses, helping to hold up his hands and staff. As long as the staff of God was held up, Israel was victorious; when Moses let his hands fall, the Israelites suffered loss. The Lord was, in fact, their banner, or the standard under which they did battle.

> Then they set out from Mount Hor by the way of the Red Sea, to go around the land of Edom; and the people became impatient because of the journey. And the people spoke against God and Moses, "Why have you brought us up out of Egypt to die in the wilderness? For there is no food and no water, and we loathe this miserable food." And the Lord sent fiery serpents among the people and they bit the people, so that many people of Israel died.
>
> So the people came to Moses and said, "We have sinned, because we have spoken against the Lord and you; intercede with the Lord, that He may remove the serpents from us." And Moses interceded for the people. Then the Lord said to Moses, "Make a fiery serpent, and set it on a standard; and it shall come about, that everyone who is bitten, when he looks at it, he shall live." And Moses made a bronze serpent and set it on the standard; and it came about, that if a serpent bit any man, when he looked to the bronze serpent, he lived (Numbers 21:4-9, *NASB*).

Jesus said, "And as Moses lifted up the serpent in the wilderness, even so must the Son of Man be lifted up" (John 3:14). Jesus was saying He would have to be put on a standard and placed as a banner before all who were afflicted physically or spiritually, so that they can look on Him and be made whole.

No matter how badly the serpent bites or where he bites us, all we have to do is look on Jesus for healing and forgiveness. "And I, if I be lifted up from the earth, will draw all men to Myself" (John 12:32, *NASB*). Thus Jesus pointed to the cross upon which He would have to hang in order for us to have access to the Father.

A man decorated for bravery during the Civil War was flagbearer for a Union Army unit that charged a Confederate position. As they closed in, all of his comrades were wounded or killed by the Confederates. He never let the flag drop, however, and he never swayed or turned away from the enemy. As he neared their lines, his foes began to shout and cheer him on. He was taken prisoner of war amid an outcry of praise and awe for his bravery.

He was released from a prisoner of war camp shortly after the war, and the men who took him prisoner petitioned the Union Army to award him the highest medal that could be awarded to any soldier, the Medal of Honor, for his bravery and valor.

The story challenged my heart with thoughts of those entrusted with *Jehovah-Nissi*, the Lord who is our banner, but who have let the banner suffer reproach while under attack by the Enemy of our souls. We do not serve a God unable to help us in time of need. Yet we act as if He were powerless to change circumstances in our lives.

Christianity is not a religion for weak-hearted wimps. Christianity is a relationship with the Creator of the universe, well able to move mountains and change lives. Hold the standard of our faith, Jesus Christ our Lord, high for all the world to see, even if you have to take a few shots along the way.

> Let this mind be in you, which was also in Christ Jesus: Who, being in the form of God, thought it not robbery to be equal with God: but made himself of no reputation, and took upon him the form of a servant, and was made in the likeness of

men: and being found in fashion as a man, he humbled himself, and became obedient unto death, even the death of the cross. Wherefore God also hath highly exalted him, and given him a name which is above every name: that at the name of Jesus every knee should bow, of things in heaven, and things in earth, and things under the earth; and that every tongue should confess that Jesus Christ is Lord, to the glory of God the Father (Philippians 2:5-11).

(*See #112.*)

19. Lord Thy God – *Jehovah-'Eloheka*

"I am the Lord thy God, which have brought thee out of the land of Egypt, out of the house of bondage" (Exodus 20:2).

"Thou shalt not bow down thyself to them, nor serve them: for I the Lord thy God am a jealous God, visiting the iniquity of the fathers upon the children unto the third and fourth generation of them that hate me" (Exodus 20:5). "Thou shalt not take the name of the Lord thy God in vain; for the Lord will not hold him guiltless that taketh his name in vain" (Exodus 20:7).

> Strong's uses only *'Elohiym*, the root word, not the actual word used in the text.

Moses had a personal experience with God, not a distant relationship. When God came to Moses on the mount, God told him that He considered the people of Israel to be His personal possession and Himself to be the property of this people. When He referred to Himself as "The Lord thy God," He was stating the terms of His relationship with the people of His chosen nation, Israel. (*See #34, #47, #60.*)

20. Lord Our Sanctification – *Yehovah-Qadash*

"But as for you, speak to the sons of Israel, saying, 'You shall surely observe My sabbaths; for this is a sign between Me and you throughout your generations, that you may know that I am the Lord who sanctifies you" (Exodus 31:13, *NASB*).

> **Definition:** *Qadash*, (kaw-dash') [6942]; a primitive root; to *be* (causat. *make, pronounce or observe* as) *clean* (ceremonially or morally) : - appoint, bid, consecrate, dedicate, defile, hallow, (be, keep) holy (-er, place), keep, prepare, proclaim, purify, sanctify (-ied one, self), X wholly. (S)

Moses received the law concerning the Sabbath, but was assured that following the law would not make anyone holy. Only God can make us holy; He is "our sanctification." To be sanctified means to be set apart by God for His purposes. "Now do you see it? No one can ever be made right in God's sight by doing what the law commands. For the more we know of God's laws, the clearer it becomes that we aren't obeying them; his laws serve only to make us see that we are sinners" (Romans 3:20, *TLB*).

> It is clear, then, that God's promise to give the whole earth to Abraham and his descendants was not because Abraham obeyed God's laws but because he trusted God to keep his promise. So if you still claim that God's blessings go to those who are 'good enough,' then you are saying that God's promises to those who have faith are meaningless, and faith is foolish. But the fact of the matter is this: when we try to gain God's blessing and salvation by keeping his laws we always end up under his anger, for we always fail to keep them. The only way we can keep from breaking laws is not to have any to break! (4:13-15, *TLB*).

Paul also said, "The Ten Commandments were given so that all could see the extent of their failure to obey God's laws. But the more we see our sinfulness, the more we see God's abounding grace forgiving us" (5:20, *TLB*).

God has sanctified us positionally in Christ; He is sanctifying us progressively through all the events of life. (*See #124, #295.*)

21. Jealous – *Qanna'*

"For thou shalt worship no other god: for the Lord, whose name is *Jealous*, is a jealous God" (Exodus 34:14).

"Thou shalt not bow down thyself to them, nor serve them: for *I the Lord thy God am a jealous God,* visiting the iniquity of the fathers upon the children unto the third and fourth generation of them that hate me" (Exodus 20:5).

> **Definition:** *Qanna'* (kan-naw') [7067]; from *qana'*; jealous: – jealous. Compare *Qannow'*. (S)

Though the two words seem almost alike, there is a vast difference between jealousy and envy. Both are wrong for a Christian from an earthly point of view. To envy is to desire something that another has in a sinful, covetous way. Jealousy is expressed when we hold onto something in a way that selfishly guards it against any other person's use (or against its use by God).

In this passage of Scripture, God is portrayed as One who jealously holds onto what is His. He does not share His possessions with others. Moses spoke this word to the Israelites when he came down from the mount with the second set of tablets containing the Ten Commandments. God foresaw the iniquity of His people and warned them against the adulterous activities in which He knew they would partake.

They were warned against making covenants with the people who inhabited the Promised Land they were preparing to conquer. They were to honor the Lord through their observance of the Sabbath and all other holy days as defined by His servant, Moses. They were warned about disobeying God's laws, and told of His punishment if they should fail.

Some find the word calling God "jealous" a bit unnerving. Those who have the Spirit of Christ should find tremendous comfort, however. We do not have to worry about holding ourselves in the will of God; He will keep us in the midst of trials. He is a jealous God and will not allow any other power, principality or ruler to have us. This should give all Christians assurance and confidence in their Maker. (*See #28.*)

22. Most High – *Qodesh 'Elyown*

"He hath said, which heard the words of God, and knew the knowledge of the *most High*, which saw the vision of the Almighty, falling into a trance, but having his eyes open" (Numbers 24:16).

Definition: '*Elyown* (el-yone') [5945]; from '*alah*; an elevation, i.e. (adjective) lofty (comparative); as title, the Supreme: – (Most, on) high (-er, -est), upper (-most). (S)

Nothing—and no one—has preeminence over our God. Rate everything that has ever been, that is now, or that ever will be, and our Lord is more important, bigger and better. God has preeminence over the sum total of everything in all creation, because the Creator must have more value than His creation. (*See #29, #300.*)

23. Lord Is Peace – *Yehovah-Shalowm*

"And the Lord said to him, 'Peace to you, do not fear; you shall not die.' Then Gideon built an altar there to the Lord and named it The Lord is Peace" (Judges 6:23, 24, *NASB*).

Definition: *Yehovah Shalowm* (yeh-ho-vaw' shaw-lome') [3073]; from *yehovah* and *shalowm*; Jehovah (is) peace; *Jehovah-Shalom*, a symbolical name of an altar in Palestine: - *Jehovah-Shalom*.

When the Lord came to Gideon and commissioned him to lead the forces of Israel against the Midianites, he built an altar to "The Lord who is Peace." Many other Scriptural references indicate how much of our lives God wants to affect with His peace.

"For a child will be born to us, a son will be given to us; And the government will rest on His shoulders; And His name will be called Wonderful Counselor, Mighty God, Eternal Father, *Prince of Peace*" (Isaiah 9:6, *NASB*).

"You will keep in perfect *peace* him whose mind is steadfast, because he trusts in you" (Isaiah 26:3, *NIV*).

"And the work of righteousness will be *peace*; And the effect of righteousness will be quietness and assurance forever" (Isaiah 32:17).

"He arose, and rebuked the wind, and said unto the sea, Peace, be still. And the wind ceased, and there was a great calm" (Mark 4:39).

"*Peace* I leave with you; My *peace* I give to you; not as the world gives, do I give to you. Let not your heart be troubled, nor let it be fearful" (John 14:27, *NASB*).

"But the fruit of the Spirit is love, joy, *peace*, patience, kindness, goodness, faithfulness, gentleness and self-control. Against such things there is no law" (Galatians 5:22, 23, *NIV*).

"And having shod your feet with the preparation of the gospel of *peace*" (Ephesians 6:15, *NKJV*).

"Be anxious for nothing, but in everything by prayer and supplication with thanksgiving let your requests be made known to God. And the *peace* of God, which surpasses all comprehension, shall guard your hearts and your minds in Christ Jesus" (Philippians 4:6, 7, *NASB*).

The peace of God surpasses understanding or comprehension. His peace does not depend on pleasant circumstances for its manifestation. The Lord's peace reaches into our innermost being in the midst of the good times, as well as the times of trials and tribulations. God's peace is an active, vital, life-changing, effective power that tears down strongholds; not a passive, ineffective philosophy of making the best out of bad things and circumstances.

Reading the Psalms early one morning, I was deeply moved by the implications of the subtle words David wrote:

> Lord, my heart is not haughty [*proud*], Nor my eyes lofty [*arrogant*]. Neither do I concern myself with great matters, Nor with things too profound [*difficult*] for me. Surely I have calmed and quieted my soul, Like a weaned child with his mother; Like a weaned child is my soul within me. O Israel, hope in the Lord from this time forth and forever (Psalm 131:1-3, *NKJV, clarifying words added*).

Many times I have been consumed by thoughts too big or profound for me. I have worried about events in life over which I have absolutely no control. We are all guilty of this kind of soulish activity at times in our lives. The average family cannot afford to miss more than two or three paychecks or everything would fall apart around them. Many are not covered by health or life insurance policies and, consequently, suffer in fear and trembling, worrying about health and other feared setbacks. Perhaps the future of your loved ones and family, both young and old. Sometimes it bothers you.

David instructs us to calm and quiet our souls. We are not to be ruled by our feelings, our emotions, our fears or triumphs. He evokes the image of a child weaned from its mother. A nursing mother's life is controlled and ruled over by the child she nurses. Her husband cannot relieve her responsibility for more than a short time, and she is constantly at the beck and call of the baby. This is the natural order of things until it is time to wean. When the mother weans her child, she takes on the role of controlling her child. She can discipline and rule over the child to a much greater degree.

So it is with our souls. We must wean them, rule over them, and stop the out-of-order control that has ruled so much of life. When we trust in God and not our own understanding, He will make our paths straight, and lead us in paths of righteousness for His name's sake. (*See #109, #213, #220.*)

24. Lord of Hosts – *Jehovah-Tsaba'*

"And this man went up out of his city yearly to worship and to sacrifice unto the *Lord of hosts* in Shiloh" (1 Samuel 1:3).

> **Definition:** *Tsaba'* (tsaw-baw) [6635]; or (feminine) *tseba'ah* (tseb-aw-aw'); from tsaba; a mass of persons (or figuratively, things), especially reg. organized for war (an army); by implication, a campaign, literally or figuratively (specifically, hardship, worship): – appointed time, (+)army, (+)battle, company, host, service, soldiers, waiting upon, war (-fare). (S)

Elkanah and his wife Hannah went to Shiloh to worship Jehovah-Sabbaoth under Eli's ministry (1 Samuel 1:3). David often refers to

Jehovah-Sabbaoth in the Psalms. The name could be rendered "Jehovah who is the Commander-in-chief of all the angelic armies."

A story in 2 Kings 6:15-17 tells of the Elisha and his servant: "When the attendant of the man of God had risen early and gone out, behold, an army with horses and chariots was circling the city. And his servant said to him, 'Alas, my master! What shall we do?' So he answered, 'Do not fear, for those who are with us are more than those who are with them.' Then Elisha prayed and said, 'O Lord, I pray, open his eyes that he may see.' And the Lord opened the servant's eyes, and he saw; and behold, the mountain was full of horses and chariots of fire all around Elisha" (*NASB*).

When Elisha's servant's eyes were opened by the Spirit of The Lord, he could see angelic armies that were there all the time. God demonstrated to Elisha's servant His dominion over the armies of the earth, those in the heavenlies, and even the demonic armies of Satan.

In his books *This Present Darkness* and *Piercing The Darkness*, Frank Peretti tells stories in ways that seem to reveal the realities of powers and principalities in our everyday world. The key to all this is that our God is King of kings and Lord of lords. He is well able to lead His army of angelic hosts to victory. (*See #82.*)

25. God – *'Elahh*

"Then ceased the work of the house of God which is at Jerusalem. So it ceased unto the second year of the reign of Darius king of Persia" (Ezra 4:24).

Definition: *'Elahh* (el-aw) [426]; corresponding to *'Elowahh*; God: – God, god. (S)

This name for God appears only in the books of Ezra and Daniel. It is a word of Aramaic origin, which explains why these two men would have used it to describe their God. The Book of Daniel deals with the time of the Babylonian captivity of the Hebrew people, and the Book of Ezra recounts the early days of the return to Israel from the Persian captivity. Both of these world powers were of Chaldean descent and influence. The definition for this word describes it as having a similar meaning to the Hebrew words *El* and *Elohim*. (*See #1, #6, #7, #58*.)

26. Redeemer – *Ga'al*

"For I know that my *redeemer* liveth, and that he shall stand at the latter day upon the earth" (Job 19:25).

> **Definition:** *Ga'al* (gaw-al') [1350]; a primitive root, to redeem (according to the Oriental law of kinship), i.e. to be the next of kin (and as such to buy back a relative's property, marry his widow, etc.): – X in any wise, X at all, avenger, deliver, (do, perform the part of near, next) kinsfolk (-man), purchase, ransom, redeem (-er), revenger. (S)

Somewhere in America a company produces a peculiar item called "green stamps." The stamps must be special to those who make them because the manufacturer goes to great lengths to make them different from other trading stamps. And they do strange things to hold the customers who trade them. When you buy merchandise in certain stores, you are given green stamps proportionate to the size of your purchase. Save them until you have an ample supply and you can lick these foul-tasting stamps and put them into books.

People with odd values want those stamps back so much that they provide a catalog of gifts they are willing to give you in exchange for specified numbers of stamps arranged in books. When you have collected a lot of books of stamps, you take them to the redemption store and the green stamp people redeem (or buy back) those stamps—even after they have been licked, put into books, stacked in boxes and made of little value to anyone but their makers.

See the analogy? God made us unique in His creation. He looked at His finished work and said that it was good. Satan came to deceive Eve and cause Adam to fall, and humanity was given over to Satan's possession because of Adam's sin. God's crowning glory of creation seemed to have been licked, put away, stacked up and made of little value to anybody but the Creator. God wanted us back, but because of the legal right Satan had to us, God had to purchase or redeem us from the hands of the apparent master.

God sent His Son, Jesus, to pay the ultimate price for our redemption—His own blood. He bought us back at a great price. Considering who we are and what intrinsic value we have, I see no reason for God to go to such great lengths to get us back. From His perspective, however, God sees a tremendous value in us because He is the one who made us. He loved us and redeemed us for His good works, which He has prepared in advance for us to do.

The story of redemption is played out in the Book of Hosea when, after the prophet's wife played the harlot and made him look like a fool, Hosea buys back his own wife from the public auction block. The Book of Ruth dramatizes the story of redemption when the kinsman-redeemer, Boaz, marries Ruth and buys back Naomi's land as an inheritance for her family. Studying both of these books carefully gives one a fuller understanding of the doctrine of redemption.

Another common practice in ancient Israel helps to illustrate the principle of redemption. If a person was a poor steward of his possessions and fell into debt beyond his ability to pay, he could claim bankruptcy, but the process was done differently than it is now. If you were unable to pay your debtors, you could make that fact public in a humiliating way by posting a list of your debts on the doorpost of your home. Everyone who passed by could look at that list and see the financial condition you were in.

The hope was that perhaps a person would pass by who would agree to be your benefactor. Should that happen, the benefactor would fold the list and sign his name across it. This meant that every bill or encumbrance the debtor had listed would become the responsibility of the person signing the note. Thus the benefactor became the "double" for the person in debt, because he had doubled over, or folded, the list and signed it as his own.

"Comfort ye, comfort ye my people, saith your God. Speak ye comfortably to Jerusalem, and cry unto her, that her warfare is accomplished, that her iniquity is pardoned: for she hath received of the Lord's hand double for all her sins" (Isaiah 40:1, 2). This is our story. God became our double when He redeemed us by the blood of His Son Jesus. Every debt we had—or will ever accrue—was paid at Calvary by Jesus. (*See #123.*)

27. God My Maker – '*Elowahh 'Asah*

"But no one says, 'Where is *God my Maker*, Who gives songs in the night' " (Job 35:10, *NKJV*).

> **Definition:** '*Elowahh* (el-o'-ah) [433]; rarely (shortened) '*eloahh* (el-o'-ah); probably prolonged (emphatic.) from *El*; a deity or the Deity: – God, god. See '*Elohiym*. (S)
>
> '*Asah* (aw-saw') [6213]; a primitive root; to do or make, in the broadest sense and widest application (as follows): – accomplish, advance, appoint, apt, be at, become, bear, bestow, bring forth, bruise, be busy, X certainly, have the charge of, commit, deal (with), deck, + displease, do, (ready) dress (-ed), (put in) execute (-ion), exercise, fashion, + feast, [fighting-] man, + finish, fit, fly, follow, fulfill, furnish, gather, get, go about, govern, grant, great, + hinder, hold ([a feast]), X indeed, + be industrious, + journey, keep, labour, maintain, make, be meet, observe, be occupied, offer, + officer, pare, bring (come) to pass, perform, praise, prepare, procure, provide, put, requite, X sacrifice, serve, set, shew, X sin, spend, X surely, take, X thoroughly, trim, X very, + vex, be [warr-] ior, work (-man), yield, use. (S)

Elihu finally stands up and contradicts Job's three friends: Eliphaz the Temanite, Bildad the Shuhite, and Zophar the Naamathite. Elihu shows that Job has been wrong in his complaint about God's treatment of him. In Job 35, Elihu is building a case against Job, because he spoke self-righteously in his own defense during his time of trial. At this point Elihu refers to the Creator as "God my Maker," and goes on to point out that this same God "gives songs in the night."

Elihu had a grasp of the sovereignty of God that far exceeded Job's or his friends'. In Job 36, Elihu goes on in his speech to point out that God is good in all His ways, and there is no unrighteousness in Him. (*See #33, #41.*)

28. Righteous God – *Tsaddiyq*

"Let the wickedness of the wicked come to an end; but establish the just: for the *righteous God* trieth the hearts and reins" (Psalm 7:9).

> **Definition:** *Tsaddiyq* (tsad-deek') [6662]; from *Tsadaq*; just: – just, lawful, righteous (man). (S)

There is no unrighteousness in God. All of His ways are lawful, just and righteous. In a sense this is a frightening thought for one who has come in contact with the blinding light of God's holiness. You see, we all have sinned and have come short of obeying the law (see Romans 3:23). Therefore we deserve nothing but the wrath of a holy, just and lawful God. Our only hope is the mercy of God, which caused Him to send His Son. He took upon Himself the punishment due to you and me. Psalm 7:9 says that God establishes the just believers by trying or testing our hearts.

The Bible says, "No temptation has seized you except what is common to man. And God is faithful; he will not let you be tempted beyond what you can bear. But when you are tempted, he will also provide a way out so that you can stand up under it" (1 Corinthians 10:13, *NIV*). There will be tests, but God will never test you beyond His provision to keep you. (*See #42, #78.*)

29. Lord Most High – *Jehovah- 'Elyown*

"I will praise the Lord according to His righteousness, and will sing praise to the name of the *Lord most high*" (Psalm 7:17, *NKJV*).

"For the *Lord most high* is terrible; he is a great King over all the earth" (Psalm 47:2).

"For thou, Lord, art high above all the earth: thou art exalted far above all gods" (Psalm 97:9).

> **Definition:** '*Elyown* (el-yone') [5945]; from '*alah*; an elevation, i.e. (adj.) lofty (comparative); as title, the Supreme: – (Most, on) high (-er, -est), upper (-most). (S)

Landowners, elders, teachers, business leaders and scribes all used "lord" as a title during the days of Christ. The title, *Lord Most High*, implies that His transcendent nature is bigger than creation. He is Lord of lords and King of kings. Jesus demonstrated His authority over the wind, the waves, sickness, death, the flesh and Satan while on earth, and He is still in charge today! (*See #22.*)

30. Strength – '*Eyaluwth*

"But be not thou far from me, O Lord: O my *strength*, haste thee to help me" (Psalm 22:19).

> **Definition:** '*Eyaluwth* (eh-yaw-looth') [360]; feminine of '*eyal*; power; by implication, protection: – strength. (S)

This is the only place in the Bible where this Hebrew word is used. By Strong's definition, it is the feminine form of another Hebrew word. While this may not seem to be a significant issue to some, I think we need to consider the implications of that revelation. A colloquial expression describes a person as "madder than a she-bear separated from her cubs." An unbelievable power of protection is bred into most of the females of God's creation. In most species there is a total commitment by a mother to protect her young. This trait is also present in the human female. This scripture demonstrates this same kind of tenacious care and protection in our Father God.

The strength of God to watch over and protect that which is His is unconquerable. It is a strength we can depend on, even when we believe that we are unworthy of His concern. He created us; therefore He will watch over and protect us. (*See #48, #51, #77, #81, #113, #114, #208, #245, #246, #247.*)

31. Lord Our Shepherd – *Jehovah-Rohi* or *Ra'ah*

"The Lord is my shepherd; I shall not want" (Psalm 23:1).

Definition: Ra'ah (*raw-aw*) [7462]; a primitive root; to tend a flock; i.e. pasture it; intransitively, to graze (literally or figuratively); generally to rule; by extension, to associate with (as a friend): – X break, companion, keep company with, devour, eat up, evil entreat, feed, use as a friend, make friendship with, herdman, keep [sheeper]-), pastor, + shearing house, shepherd, wander, waste. (S)

David saw the Lord as a shepherd who loved His sheep dearly and cared for them. We are the sheep of God's pasture. An Eastern shepherd is quite different from an American sheepherder in the way he cares for his sheep. Sheep are both an investment and friends to the shepherd. The shepherd knows his sheep and has a pet name for each of them. When going from a pasture or fold to another, the shepherd walks ahead of his sheep. They gladly follow his voice because they are familiar with it. He inspects and cares for them daily. He personally sees to their physical needs.

Psalm 23 was written to people who understood shepherds to be men who loved and cared for their sheep as we might care for our families. These shepherds would literally give their lives in service to their master's flocks. David told Saul that he had killed both the lion and the bear while protecting his father's flock. When he wrote Psalm 23, David was writing it from the perspective of this kind of shepherd.

In contrast, the American sheepherder may use dogs or motorcycles to drive his sheep wherever he wants them to go. Few, if any, would develop a personal relationship with the individuals within their flock. They have a monetary investment in their sheep, so they watch over them, but rarely do you hear of one endangering himself over a few sheep.

"All we like sheep have gone astray; we have turned every one to his own way; and the Lord hath laid on him the iniquity of us all" (Isaiah 53:6).

"For thus saith the Lord God; Behold, I, even I, will both search my sheep, and seek them out" (Ezekiel 34:11).

"I am the good shepherd: the good shepherd giveth his life for the sheep" (John 10:11).

When Jesus called Himself a good shepherd, He was letting His people know that He would lay His life down for even one of His flock. He did this on Calvary and made the way for each of us to have a relationship with the Master of the flock. If you are following the Good Shepherd, you will normally sense His peace and care over your circumstances.

When things on earth seem difficult, you won't feel that there is a sheepdog nipping at your heels, driving you along the path. Jesus will lead you by the desires of your heart (Psalm 37:4); He will gently draw you where He wants you to go. It will always be for your good to follow Him. He always will lead you down the right path. The Twenty-third Psalm is a beautiful song of life with the Good Shepherd. Unfortunately, you hear it most when you go to funerals. I have made some minor adjustments in the wording and have appropriated this psalm as a prayer that ministers to me frequently:

> You, O Lord, are *my* Shepherd; *I* shall not want. *You* make *me* lie down in green pastures. *You* lead *me* beside still waters. *You* restore *my* soul. *You* lead *me* in the paths of righteousness for *Your* Name's sake. Even though *I* walk through the valley of the shadow of death *I* will fear no evil, for *You* are with *me. Your* rod and *Your* staff, they comfort *me. You* have prepared a table before *me* in the very presence of *my* enemies. *You* anoint *my*

head with oil; *my* cup overflows. Surely goodness and mercy will follow *me* all the days of *my* life and *I* will dwell in the house of *the Lord* forever (my paraphrase).

(*See #76, #187, #249.*)

32. King of Glory – *Melek Kabowd*

"Lift up your heads, O ye gates; and be ye lift up, ye everlasting doors; and the *King of glory* shall come in. Who is this King of glory? The Lord strong and mighty, the Lord mighty in battle. Lift up your heads, O ye gates; even lift them up, ye everlasting doors; and the King of glory shall come in. Who is this King of glory? The Lord of hosts, he is the King of glory. Selah" (Psalm 24:7-10).

> **Definition:** *Melek* (meh'-lek) [4428]; from *malak*; a king: – king, royal. (S)
>
> *Kabowd* (kaw-bode') [3519]; rarely *kabod* (kaw-bode'); from *kabad*, properly, weight, but only figuratively in a good sense, splendor or copiousness: - glorious (-ly), glory, honour (-able). (S)

In Hebrew the word *glory* speaks of God's "weight or presence" in a tangible way. In these verses God is called "the King of Glory." He is "the sovereign master of spiritual weight and presence." When one has an encounter with the Lord, he or she will be changed. It happened to the prophet in Isaiah 6, and it has happened to every other person who has seen God's glory.

The glory of the Lord was so strong upon Moses that his face shone with God's presence. "When Aaron and all the children of Israel saw Moses, behold, the skin of his face shone; and they were afraid to come nigh him" (Exodus 34:30).

It is common today to hear someone talk about a meaningful experience as "heavy." To meet the risen Lord of glory is truly a *heavy* experience. It brings a feeling of the imminent weight and fear of His presence to the believer and unbeliever alike.

Sometimes God's glory was seen as coming to His people; at other times the glory was seen departing. In every case the presence of the glory of the Lord revealed His power and His presence in a way that had a profound impact upon people's lives. In these verses the historical record of what happened when people saw the glory of the Lord unfolds to us.

The glory of the Lord directed Israel through the wilderness. "And it came to pass, as Aaron spake unto the whole congregation of the children of Israel, that they looked toward the wilderness, and, behold, the glory of the Lord appeared in the cloud" (Exodus 16:10).

When Israel saw God's glory, the people were afraid. "And the sight of the glory of the Lord was like devouring fire on the top of the mount in the eyes of the children of Israel" (Exodus 24:17).

When Moses dedicated the Tabernacle, the glory of the Lord so filled the place that no one could enter. "Then a cloud covered the tent of the congregation, and the glory of the Lord filled the tabernacle. And Moses was not able to enter into the tent of the congregation, because the cloud abode thereon, and the glory of the Lord filled the tabernacle" (Exodus 40:34, 35).

When Solomon dedicated the Temple, the glory of the Lord filled the place and no one could enter. "So that the priests could not stand to minister because of the cloud: for the glory of the Lord had filled the house of the Lord" (1 Kings 8:11).

We are told to arise and shine forth with the glory of the Lord upon us. "Arise, shine; for thy light is come, and the glory of the Lord is risen upon thee" (Isaiah 60:1).

Ezekiel saw the glory of the Lord depart from the Temple, and eventually from the city of Jerusalem. "And the glory of the Lord went up from the midst of the city, and stood upon the mountain which *is* on the east side of the city" (Ezekiel 11:23).

There will come a day when the knowledge of God's glory will fill the earth. "For the earth shall be filled with the knowledge of the glory of the Lord, as the waters cover the sea" (Habakkuk 2:14).

When Jesus came in the flesh, the glory of the Lord was revealed. "And, lo, the angel of the Lord came upon them, and the glory of the Lord shone round about them: and they were sore afraid" (Luke 2:9).

The glory of the Lord has the ability to change lives today as it did in Paul's time. "But we all, with open face beholding as in a glass the glory of the Lord, are changed into the same image from glory to glory, even as by the Spirit of the Lord" (2 Corinthians 3:18). (*See #87, #91.*)

33. Lord Our Maker – *Jehovah-'Asah*

"Oh come, let us worship and bow down; let us kneel before the Lord our Maker" (Psalm 95:6, *NKJV*).

"Know that the Lord, He is God; It is He who has made us, and not we ourselves; We are His people and the sheep of His pasture" (Psalm 100:3, *NKJV*).

Definition: *'Asah* (aw-saw') [6213]; a primitive root; to do or make, in the broadest sense and widest application (as follows): – accomplish, advance, appoint, apt, be at, become, bear, bestow, bring forth, bruise, be busy, X certainly, have the charge of, commit, deal (with), deck, + displease, do, (ready) dress (-ed), (put in) execute (-ion), exercise, fashion, + feast, [fighting-] man, + finish, fit, fly, follow, fulfill, furnish, gather, get, go about, govern, grant, great, + hinder, hold ([a feast]), X indeed, + be industrious, + journey, keep, labour, maintain, make, be meet, observe, be occupied, offer, + officer, pare, bring (come) to pass, perform, practise, prepare, procure, provide, put, requite, X sacrifice, serve, set, shew, X sin, spend, X surely, take, X thoroughly, trim, X very, + vex, be [warr-] ior, work (-man), yield, use. (S)

There is comfort in knowing that God made us. The Lord is familiar with our weaknesses, our capacity to fail or let Him down. He created us in Adam to have fellowship with Himself, and to glorify Him in all we do; yet, we have the free will to fall and to fail. It did not surprise God when Adam fell, and it does not startle Him when we do the same.

Jesus, a man like us, came in the flesh; yet, He did not sin. The same power that was in Him is available to every believer who trusts in His name and trusts in Him. (*See #27, #41.*)

34. Lord Our God – *Jehovah-'Elheenu*

"Exalt ye the *Lord our God*, and worship at his footstool; for he is holy.... Thou answeredst them, O *Lord our God*: thou wast a God that forgavest them, though thou tookest vengeance of their inventions. Exalt the *Lord our God*, and worship at his holy hill; for the *Lord our God* is holy" (Psalm 99:5, 8, 9).

Strong's lists only *'Elohiym*, the root word, not the actual word used in the text.

Like you and me, David was imperfect. From the Scriptural accounts it seems that every time he messed up, he was caught. Confronted by God's prophets, he had no delusions about his own purity. Yet, at the end of life he declared his understanding that the Lord was still his personal possession, and that he belonged to God in an intimate way. (*See #19, #47, #60.*)

35. God Who Forgives – *'El Nasa'*

"O Lord our God, you answered them; you were to Israel a forgiving God, though you punished their misdeeds" (Psalm 99:8, *NIV*).

Definition: *Nasa'* (naw-saw') [5375]; or *nacah* (Psalm 4:6 [7]) (naw-saw'); a primitive root; to lift, in a great variety of applications, literal and figurative, absolute and relative (as follows): – accept, advance, arise, (able to, [armor], suffer to) bear (-er, up), bring (forth), burn, carry (away), cast, contain, desire, ease, exact, exalt (self), extol, fetch, forgive, furnish, further, give, go on, help, high, hold up, honorable (+man), lade, lay, lift (self) up, lofty, marry, magnify, X needs, obtain, pardon, raise (up), receive, regard, respect, set (up), spare, stir up, + swear, take (away, up), X utterly, wear, yield. (S)

When we look into the perfect law of God, it is obvious how far we have missed the mark. At times, sin weighs heavily upon us, like an anchor around our necks. If Satan could, he would defeat Christians by making them feel totally beyond the redemptive work of the Cross. During these times it is good to know that our God is a God who forgives. David saw this truth and wrote Psalm 51:

Have mercy upon me, O God, according to Your loving-kindness; according to the multitude of Your tender mercies, blot out my transgressions. Wash me thoroughly from my iniquity, and cleanse me from my sin. For I acknowledge my transgressions, and my sin is always before me. Against You, You only, have I sinned, and done this evil in Your sight—that You may be found just when You speak, and blameless when You judge. Behold, I was brought forth in iniquity, and in sin my mother conceived me. Behold, You desire truth in the inward parts, and in the hidden part You will make me to know wisdom.

Purge me with hyssop, and I shall be clean; wash me, and I shall be whiter than snow. Make me hear joy and gladness, that the bones You have broken may rejoice. Hide Your face from my sins, and blot out all my iniquities. Create in me a clean heart, O God, and renew a steadfast spirit within me. Do not cast me away from Your presence, and do not take Your Holy Spirit from me. Restore to me the joy of Your salvation, And uphold me by Your generous Spirit. Then I will teach transgressors Your ways, and sinners shall be converted to You.

Deliver me from the guilt of bloodshed, O God, the God of my salvation, and my tongue shall sing aloud of Your righteousness. O Lord, open my lips, and my mouth shall show forth Your praise. For You do not desire sacrifice, or else I would give it; You do not delight in burnt offering. The sacrifices of God are a broken spirit, a broken and a contrite heart—these, O God, You will not despise (vv. 1-17 *NKJV*).

David knew the love and forgiveness of *'El Nasa'*! (*See #21.*)

PART 1
The Triune God

His Hebrew Names in

ISAIAH – MALACHI

---

36. Lord Our Judge – *Jehovah-Shaphat*

"For the *Lord is our judge*, the Lord is our lawgiver, the Lord is our king; he will save us" (Isaiah 33:22, *NASB*).

> **Definition:** *Shaphat* (shaw-fat') [8199]; a primitive root; to judge, i.e. pronounce sentence (for or against); by implication, to vindicate or punish; by extenssion, to govern; passively, to litigate (literally or figuratively): – + avenge, X that condemn, contend, defend, execute (judgment), (be a) judge (-ment), X needs, plead, reason, rule. (S)

A day of judgment is coming for all the people of the earth. The God who is omniscient will be our judge, and there is nothing about us that He does not know perfectly. No evidence will be thrown out of court as inadmissible, because He acquired it honestly. He knows us perfectly and has known us from the beginning. The hope of a

Christian is in the Cross. Although we have been found guilty, God has imputed the righteousness of Christ to provide payment for our sins. Woe be to the person who stands before our Righteous Judge trusting in his or her own merit. "For all have sinned, and come short of the glory of God" (Romans 3:23). (*See #197, #226.*)

37. Lord Our Lawgiver – *Jehovah-Chaqaq*

"For the Lord is our judge, the *Lord is our lawgiver*, the Lord is our king; he will save us" (Isaiah 33:22, *NASB*).

Definition: *Chaqaq* (khaw-kak') [2710]; a primitive root; properly, to hack, i.e. engrave (Judges 5:14, to be a scribe simply); by implication, to enact (laws being cut in stone or metal tablets in primitive times) or (gen.) prescribe: -appoint, decree, governor, grave, lawgiver, note, portray, print, set. (S)

At the center of this revelation of God is the understanding that He is not only the God of Moses, through whom the law was given, but He is the God who is still imparting the light of His law upon our hearts today. He who gave life is well qualified to give us the law. In infinite compassion and love, God made the law for us. Jeremiah said:

> But this is the covenant that I will make with the house of Israel after those days, says the Lord: I will put My law in their minds, and write it on their hearts; and I will be their God, and they shall be My people. No more shall every man teach his neighbor, and every man his brother, saying, "Know the Lord," for they all shall know Me, from the least of them to the greatest of them, says the Lord. For I will forgive their iniquity, and their sin I will remember no more (31:33, 34, *NKJV*).

Ezekiel also saw this and recorded it in his prophecies.

> For I will take you from the nations, gather you from all the lands, and bring you into your own land. Then I will sprinkle clean water on you, and you will be clean; I will cleanse you from all your filthiness and from all your idols. Moreover, I will give you a new heart and put a new spirit within you; and I will remove the heart of stone from your flesh and

give you a heart of flesh. And I will put My Spirit within you and cause you to walk in My statutes, and you will be careful to observe My ordinances (36:24-27, *NASB*).

In the Sermon on the Mount, Jesus told us that He required more of us than the law of Moses required. "The laws of Moses said, 'You shall not commit adultery.' But I say: Anyone who even looks at a woman with lust in his eye has already committed adultery with her in his heart" (Matthew 5:27, 28 *TLB*). Jesus puts His law in the hearts of each of His believers. The Lord truly is the Lawgiver to those who allow Him access to their hearts. With His law always comes the power of God to obey.

38. Lord Our King – *Jehovah-Melek*

"For the Lord is our judge, the Lord is our lawgiver, the *Lord is our king*; he will save us" (Isaiah 33:22).

"Rejoice greatly, O daughter of Zion! Shout, O daughter of Jerusalem! Behold, your *King* is coming to you; He is just and having salvation, Lowly and riding on a donkey, A colt, the foal of a donkey" (Zechariah 9:9, *NKJV*).

Definition: *Melek* (meh'-lek) [4428]; from *malak*; a king: – king, royal. (S)

The history of the Israelites had shown that Jehovah was their King. The Book of Judges recounts the struggles the Israelites faced with this relationship early in their existence. They made the mistake of asking for a king like all the other nations, and God gave them Saul even though His desire for Israel was for it to be His personal kingdom. You and I gain much when we learn from their error. We need to come under God's dominion instead of seeking the covering of a person or a big-name ministry.

It is enough to know that Jehovah is our King. This is not a word against church authority; I am merely calling for us to keep God in the place of ultimate authority.

The founding fathers chose to form three branches of government in this country: the judicial, the congressional and the executive branches. They were set up as checks and balances to protect us from the influence of power-hungry individuals who might try to take over the nation from within. Isaiah 33:22 shows that Jehovah holds these three important roles in the life of a believer. He is our judge (judicial); He is our lawgiver (the congressional branch); and He is our king (the executive branch). In a proper relationship with God there is no fear, because He will never harm us or misuse His authority in our lives. (See #224, #225.)

39. Way Maker – *Yehovah Derek Nathan*

"Thus says the Lord, who makes a way in the sea And a path through the mighty waters" (Isaiah 43:16, *NKJV*).

Definition: *Derek* (deh'-rek) [1870]; from *darak*; a road (as trodden); figuratively, a course of life or mode of action, often adverb: – along, away, because of, + by, conversation, custom, [east-] ward, journey, manner, passenger, through, toward, [high-] [path-] way [-side], whither [-soever]. (S)

Nathan (naw-than') [5414]; a primitive root; to give, used with greatest latitude of application (put, make, etc.): – add, apply, appoint, ascribe, assign, X avenge, X be ([healed]), bestow, bring (forth, hither), cast, cause, charge, come, commit, consider, count, + cry, deliver (up), direct, distribute, do, X doubtless, X without fail, fasten, frame, X get, give (forth, over, up), grant, hang (up), X have, X indeed, lay (unto charge, up), (give) leave, lend, let (out), + lie, lift up, make, + O that, occupy, offer, ordain, pay, perform, place, pour, print, X pull put (forth), recompense, render, requite, restore, send (out), set (forth), shew, shoot forth (up), + sing, + slander, strike, [sub-] mit, suffer, X surely, X take, thrust, trade, turn, utter, + weep, + willingly, + withdraw, + would (to) God, yield. (S)

There are many examples of our Lord as a "way maker" for those who are His children. Scripture implies God's intervention and leadership in the life of His people. This is true in both the Old and New Testaments.

"But he said to me, 'The Lord, before whom I walk, will send His angel with you and prosper your way; and you shall take a wife for my son from my family and from my father's house" (Genesis 24:40, *NKJV*).

"Then let us arise and go up to Bethel; and I will make an altar there to God, who answered me in the day of my distress and has been with me in the way which I have gone" (Genesis 35:3, *NKJV*).

"And the Lord went before them by day in a pillar of cloud to lead the way, and by night in a pillar of fire to give them light, so as to go by day and night" (Exodus 13:21, *NKJV*).

"Behold, I send an Angel before you to keep you in the way and to bring you into the place which I have prepared" (Exodus 23:20, *NKJV*).

"As for God, His way is perfect; the word of the Lord is proven; He is a shield to all who trust in Him. God is my strength and power, and He makes my way perfect" (2 Samuel 22:31, 33, *NKJV*).

"Yet in Your manifold mercies You did not forsake them in the wilderness. The pillar of the cloud did not depart from them by day, To lead them on the road; Nor the pillar of fire by night, To show them light, And the way they should go" (Nehemiah 9:19, *NKJV*).

"Lead me, O Lord, in Your righteousness because of my enemies; Make Your way straight before my face" (Psalm 5:8, *NKJV*).

"As for God, His way is perfect; The word of the Lord is proven; He is a shield to all who trust in Him" (Psalm 18:30, *NKJV*).

"I will instruct you and teach you in the way you should go; I will guide you with My eye" (Psalm 32:8, *NKJV*).

"That the Lord your God may show us the way in which we should walk and the thing we should do" (Jeremiah 42:3, *NKJV*).

"As it is written in the book of the words of Isaiah the prophet, saying: 'The voice of one crying in the wilderness: *Prepare the way of the Lord; make His paths straight*'" (Luke 3:4, *NKJV*).

"Jesus said to him, 'I am the way, the truth, and the life. No one comes to the Father except through Me'" (John 14:6, *NKJV*).

"Now may our God and Father Himself, and our Lord Jesus Christ, direct our way to you" (1 Thessalonians 3:11, *NKJV*).

The Lord has not changed or weakened through the years. We can still expect Him to lead us and guide us along the paths of life. Our Lord is still a way maker today! (*See #190.*)

40. First and the Last – *Ri'shown 'Acharown*

"Thus says the Lord, the King of Israel, And his Redeemer, the Lord of hosts: 'I am the First and I am the Last; Besides Me there is no God'" (Isaiah 44:6, *NKJV*).

> **Definition:** *Ri'shown* (ree-shone') [7223]; or *ri'shon* (ree-shone'); from *ri'shah*; first, in place, time or rank (as adjective or noun): – ancestor, (that were) before (-time), beginning, eldest, firstfore, [-father] (-most), former (thing), of old time, past. (S)
>
> *'Acharown* (akh-ar-one') [314]; or (shortened) *'acharon* (akh-ar-one'); from *'achar*; hinder; generally, late or last; specifically (as facing the east) western: – after (-ward), to come, following, hind (-er, -ermost, -most), last, latter, rereward, ut (ter) most. (S)

"I am the First and I am the Last." Through Isaiah, God was speaking to an idolatrous nation that had frequently slipped into adulterous relationships with other gods. In the first 39 chapters of Isaiah, the prophet warns the Israelites of their impending fall. They had gone too far . . . for too long. In the last 27 chapters, we hear something of the grace, peace and hope from God. Instead of denying the existence of other gods, the Lord assures His people that before any other gods were, He was; and after they are gone, He will still be.

We benefit from a proper understanding of this attribute of the Lord. Though we are plagued with trials and tribulations, God is bigger than our problems. There is nothing we can face that the

Lord has not already faced and overcome. Before our problems ever materialized, God was the answer. After we have gone through our trials, He will still be there for us. The Creator is bigger than His creation. (*See #254, #256, #258.*)

41. Our Potter – *Yatsar*

"But now, O Lord, thou art our father; we are the clay, and thou *our potter*; and we all are the work of thy hand" (Isaiah 64:8).

> **Definition:** *Yatsar* (yaw-tsar') [3335]; probably identical with *yatsar* (through the squeezing into shape); ([compare *yatsa'*]); to mold into a form; especially as a potter; figuratively, to determine (i.e. form a resolution): – X earthen, fashion, form, frame, make (-r), potter, purpose. (S)

Many stories illustrate how God works in the life of a believer as a potter works with a lump of clay. At times in my life I have felt like a piece of clay that the great Potter had put on His wheel to mold and squeeze into the likeness of Christ. I have felt the hand of God pushing me from the inside out; and at the same time, pressing me from the outside in. A good potter gets all the imperfections out of the clay before he forms it into a vessel fit for use and ready to go through the fire. If a piece of clay is subjected to the heat of the furnace before the imperfections are removed, it is usually destroyed. Air pockets cause the clay to explode. In much the same way, God lovingly works out the imperfections and weaknesses in the lives of believers so that when the heat is applied, they will stand up in the day of testing.

> This is the word that came to Jeremiah from the Lord: "Go down to the potter's house, and there I will give you my message." So I went down to the potter's house, and I saw him working at the wheel. But the pot he was shaping from the clay was marred in his hands; so the potter formed it into another pot, shaping it as seemed best to him. Then the word of the Lord came to me: "O house of Israel, can I not do with you as this potter does?" declares the Lord.

"Like clay in the hand of the potter, so are you in my hand, O house of Israel" (Jeremiah 18:1-6, *NIV*).

(*See #33.*)

42. Lord Our Righteousness – *Yehovah Tsidqenuw*

"In his days Judah shall be saved, and Israel shall dwell safely: and this is his name whereby he shall be called, The Lord our righteousness" (Jeremiah 23:6; see 33:16).

Definition: *Yehovah Tsidqenuw* (ye-ho-vaw' tsid-kay'-noo) [3072]; from *Yehovah* and *tsedeq* with pronominal suffix; Jehovah (is) our right; *Jehovah-Tsidkenu*, a symbolical epithet of the Messiah and of Jerusalem: – the Lord our righteousness. (S)

Jeremiah refers to the future Davidic king as *Jehovah-Tsidqenuw*, the Lord our righteousness. In 33:16, he gives this same name to the city of the Davidic king. Jesus is the promised Davidic king, and we are the city of the Davidic king (the New Jerusalem).

The righteousness of God implies right standing with God, not perfection of the saints on earth. While we are exhorted to be perfect as He is perfect, we are also told that none are righteous, at least not in our own strength. The righteousness of God is imputed to us when we believe on the One whom He has sent.

This phenomenon is illustrated in the Scriptural account of the first Passover. Moses told each family to slay a lamb and cook it a certain way. Then they were to apply the blood of the lamb to the doorposts and lintels of their houses.

They were to stay in their houses after dark so that the angel of death might pass over and spare the firstborn within. It didn't matter who was under the roofs of these houses. Some say that many Egyptians who believed the warnings of Moses came and stayed with the Hebrews to avoid the plague, and were spared by the same blood that saved the Jews.

God knows all we have ever done and all we are yet to do. He looks for the blood of the Passover Lamb on the doorposts of our hearts and lintels of our lives. Wherever He finds the blood He imputes the righteousness of Jesus and we are spared. It makes no difference how bad we've been, if God has imputed the righteousness of Christ to us, we are clean in His sight.

"For he hath made him to be sin for us, who knew no sin; that we might be made the righteousness of God in him" (2 Corinthians 5:21).

An African tribe punished murderers by strapping the body of the victims on their backs. Gradually, the corruption and death of the corpse would steal the life of the one who bore the deadly load.

Before I knew Christ as Savior, I felt I was carrying around a dead man on my back. There was no way to be released from the burden of guilt and shame that Satan often reminded me of. Now God has clothed me in His righteousness and has released me from the law of sin and death. In effect, He removed the dead man I carried.

Imagine a courtroom scene. God is judge; Jesus, the Advocate (lawyer); and you are on trial for your sins. Since "all have sinned, and come short of the glory of God" (Romans 3:23), you could not be found innocent if you are exposed for your sins.

God already knows your sins and has declared you guilty. Yet, His Son died on the cross to make payment for us. Although the Judge found you guilty, the Advocate (Jesus) took the punishment that you deserved. (*See #28, #78.*)

43. Lord God of Recompenses – *Yehovah 'El Gemuwlah*

"Because the spoiler is come upon her, even upon Babylon, and her mighty men are taken, every one of their bows is broken: for the *Lord God of recompenses* shall surely requite" (Jeremiah 51:56).

> **Definition:** *Yehovah* (yeh-ho-vaw') [3068]; from *Hayah*; (the) self-Existent or Eternal; Jehovah, Jewish national name of God: – Jehovah, the Lord. Compare *Yahn, Yehovih* (S)
>
> *'El* (ale) [410]; shortened from *'Ayil*; strength; as adjective, mighty; especially the Almighty (but used also of any deity): – God (god), X goodly, X great, idol, might (-y one), power, strong. Compare names in "-el." (S)
>
> *Gemuwlah* (ghem-oo-law') [1578]; feminine of *gemuwl*; meaning the same: – deed, recompense, such a reward. (S)

Much of what Jeremiah, the weeping prophet, said was rejected by the people of Israel. He knew that judgment was coming and tried to warn his people to flee from the wrath of God. In chapters 50 and 51, the prophet turns to those through whom the punishment of God came, the Babylonians. He assured those whom God would use to chastise Israel that they would not get away with anything. Habakkuk saw this day coming and was amazed that God would use a more wicked Babylon to chastise a less wicked Israel (see Habakkuk 1:5-7).

This name of God implies that a reward can be earned by actions on our part. While that may be true in some instances, we must keep in mind that God looks at the heart of a man, not just the outward appearances (see 1 Samuel 16:7). God sovereignly rewards those with whom He is pleased and punishes those with whom He is displeased. No believer can manipulate or coerce God into any course of action by doing or saying anything. God knows our hearts and our motives and will reward believers accordingly. (*See #44.*)

44. Lord That Smiteth – *Yehovah Nakah*

"And mine eye shall not spare, neither will I have pity: I will recompense thee according to thy ways and thine abominations that are in the midst of thee; and ye shall know that I am the *Lord that smiteth*" (Ezekiel 7:9).

Definition: *Yehovah* (yeh-ho-vaw') [3068]; from *Hayah*; (the) self-Existent or Eternal; Jehovah, Jewish national name of God: – Jehovah, the Lord. Compare *Yahn, Yehovih*. (S)

Nakah (naw-kaw') [5221]; a primitive root; to strike (lightly or severely, literally or figuratively): – beat, cast forth, clap, give [wounds], X go forward, X indeed, kill, make [slaughter], murderer, punish, slaughter, slay (-er, -ing), smite (-r, -ing), strike, be stricken, (give) stripes, X surely, wound. (S)

In Proverbs, many references suggest that God smites or chastens those whom He loves and treats them as a father would treat his son or daughter. The topic is not popular in most Christian circles, but this revelation of God is well documented throughout the Bible. It cannot be ignored or glossed over.

"My son, do not despise the chastening of the Lord, nor detest His correction; for whom the Lord loves He corrects, just as a father the son in whom he delights" (Proverbs 3:11, 12, *NKJV*).

"The fear of the Lord is the beginning of wisdom, and the knowledge of the Holy One is understanding" (Proverbs 9:10, *NKJV*).

"He who disdains instruction despises his own soul, but he who heeds rebuke gets understanding" (Proverbs 15:32, *NKJV*).

"If you say, 'Surely we did not know this,' Does not He who weighs the hearts consider it? He who keeps your soul, does He not know it? And will He not render to each man according to his deeds?" (Proverbs 24:12, *NKJV*). (*See #43.*)

45. Lord Is There – *Jehovah-Sham*

"The city shall be 18,000 cubits round about; and the name of the city from that day shall be, '*The Lord is there*'" (Ezekiel 48:35, *NASB*).

Definition: *Sham* (shawm) [8033]; a primitive particle [rather from the relative pronoun, '*aher*]; there (transferring to time) then; often thither, or thence: – in it, + thence, there (-in, + of, + out), + thither, + whither. (S)

After giving the plans for the construction of the "New Jerusa-lem," Ezekiel proclaimed that the presence of the Lord would never depart from His people in that day. We, the church, are "The Bride of Christ," and the "New Jerusalem" manifest in the earth today. The Lord is present in His church!

David spoke of this in Psalm 139 when he wrote,

> Where can I go from your Spirit? Where can I flee from your presence? If I go up to the heavens, you are there; if I make my bed in the depths, you are there. If I rise on the wings of the dawn, if I settle on the far side of the sea, even there your hand will guide me, your right hand will hold me fast (vv. 7-10, *NIV*).

There is no place where God is not present. There is no place you can go to get away from Him, and no place you have ever gone that He has not been before you! (*See #9, #292.*)

46. Ancient of Days – '*Attiyq Yowm*

"I beheld till the thrones were cast down, and the *Ancient of days* did sit, whose garment was white as snow, and the hair of his head like the pure wool: his throne was like the fiery flame" (Daniel 7:9).

"I saw in the night visions, and, behold, one like the Son of man came with the clouds of heaven, and came to the *Ancient of days*, and they brought him near before him" (Daniel 7:13).

"Until the *Ancient of days* came, and judgment was given to the saints of the most High; and the time came that the saints possessed the kingdom" (Daniel 7:22).

Definition: '*Attiyq* (Aramaic) (at-teek') [6268]; corresponding to *attiyq*; venerable: – ancient. (S)

Yowm (Aramaic) (yome) [3118]; a day: – day (by day), time. (S)

Daniel used this name to describe the God who judges all the great world empires. Some countries looked like they were all-powerful and secure enough to stand the test of time; but in reality, none of the nations that Daniel saw made it through the test of time and history. Only the Lord has remained the same. The things of this world will one day pass away, but God's kingdom will never perish. (*See #12.*)

47. Lord My God – *Jehovah-Elohay*

"Thus saith the Lord my God; Feed the flock of the slaughter" (Zechariah 11:4).

"And ye shall flee to the valley of the mountains; for the valley of the mountains shall reach unto Azal: yea, ye shall flee, like as ye fled from before the earthquake in the days of Uzziah king of Judah: and the Lord my God shall come, and all the saints with thee" (Zechariah 14:5).

In the three places where this name is mentioned—*the Lord thy God* (#19), *the Lord our God* (#34), and *the Lord my God* (#47)—I see three distinct areas of relationship. The first is a positional relationship. God declared to Moses that He Himself was "the Lord thy God." He was proclaiming that He was Israel's God and they were His people.

This relationship was not be taken lightly for it placed the Lord in an area of responsibility and authority over their lives. No other people group had this relationship with God. It is important to note that we, as Christians, are the new recipients of this same promise.

The second area of our relationship with God is a corporate one. David wrote Psalm 99 at the end of his life and declared Jehovah to be "the Lord our God." It is one thing for God to proclaim that He is someone else's God. It is another to realize, as David did, a relationship with God that is personal despite failures and shortcomings. David saw himself and the people of Israel in a close relationship with their Maker; not because of anything that they did or did not do, but because of who He was and is.

Zechariah prophesied during the rebuilding of the temple, after the captivity of the Assyrians, Babylonians and Persians. He spoke on behalf of "the Lord my God." He knew his God so well that he referred to Him in a personal and possessive way.

Zechariah saw himself as the possession of Jehovah and, at the same time, in possession of all the benefits of the inheritance that relationship might bring. He related to God as a son relates to his father.

We must see ourselves as God sees us: as His possession and personal property. *We are His, and He is ours.* (*See #19, #34, #60.*)

The Triune God

Hebrew Names That Signify

GOD'S PROTECTION

"The Lord is my *rock* and my *fortress* and my *deliverer;* The God of my *strength,* in whom I will trust; my *shield* and the *horn of my salvation,* my *stronghold* and my *refuge;* my *Savior,* You save me from violence" (2 Samuel 22:2, 3, *NKJV*).

"The Lord is my *rock,* and my *fortress,* and my *deliverer;* my God, my *strength,* in whom I will trust; my *buckler,* and the *horn of my salvation,* and my *high tower*" (Psalm 18:2).

These names of the triune God are intimate and caring, yet have powerful implications. The Lord is our rock, fortress and deliverer. He is our strength, shield and high tower. He is our refuge, our Savior, and the horn of our salvation. Consider carefully the wonderful protection of our mighty God.

Psalm 18:2, like 2 Samuel 22:2, 3, is the testimony of an old man who has learned what it is to be kept from harm's way and held in the hands of a loving God. David wrote these words shortly before his death. Both references show the same progression of praise.

The song is sung to give thanks for all that God had done in David's life. There is significance in the fact that few portions of Scripture are repeated in such detail and length. David knew the protection and keeping power of his Lord in a way that few have understood. Look at each of the words that define the protective attributes and character of God.

48. Rock – *Cela'*

"For You are my *rock* and my fortress; therefore, for Your name's sake, lead me and guide me" (Psalm 31:3, *NKJV*).

"He also brought me up out of a horrible pit, out of the miry clay, and set my feet upon a *rock*, and established my steps" (Psalm 40:2, *NKJV*).

"Be my strong refuge, to which I may resort continually; You have given the commandment to save me, for You are my *rock* and my fortress" (Psalm 71:3, *NKJV*).

"Let the wilderness and its cities lift up their voice, the villages that Kedar inhabits. Let the inhabitants of *Sela* sing, let them shout from the top of the mountains" (Isaiah 42:11, *NKJV*).

"The pride of your heart has deceived you, you who dwell in the clefts of the *rock*, whose habitation is high; you who say in your heart, 'Who will bring me down to the ground?'" (Obadiah 1:3, *NKJV*).

> **Definition:** *Cela'* (seh'-lah) [5553]; from an unused root meaning to be lofty; a craggy rock, literally or figuratively (a fortress): – (ragged) rock, stone (-ny), strong hold.

Our God is likened to a lofty, or craggy, rock or stone. He is a fortress high above the earth and all that's in it.

Nothing can get to you unless it comes through the Lord first. (*See #51, #77, #81, #113, #114, #208, #214, #245, #246, #247.*)

49. Fortress – *Matsuwd*

"Since you are my rock and my fortress, for the sake of your name lead and guide me" (Psalm 31:3, *NIV*).

"Be my rock of refuge, to which I can always go; give the command to save me, for you are my rock and my fortress" (Psalm 71:3, *NIV*).

"I will say of the LORD, 'He is my refuge and my fortress, my God, in whom I trust'" (Psalm 91:2, *NIV*).

> **Definition:** *Matsuwd* (maw-tsood') [4686]; or (feminine) *metsuwdah* (mets-oo-daw'); or *metsudah* (mets-oo-daw'); for *metsowd*; a net, or (abstractly) capture; also a fastness; – castle, defense, fort (-ress), (strong) hold, be hunted, net, snare, strong place. (S)

A fortress is a place of security surrounded by high walls. It has a very strong gate to protect you from the outside world. Paul wrote in Colossians 3:3, "For you died, and your life is hidden with Christ in God" (*NKJV*). This places us in the center of a fortress of love and mercy. (*See #55.*)

50. Deliverer – *Palat*

"But I am poor and needy; yet the Lord thinketh upon me: thou art my help and my *deliverer*; make no tarrying, O my God" (Psalm 40:17).

> **Definition:** *Palat* (paw-lat') [6403]; a primitive root; to slip out, i.e. escape; causatively, to deliver: – calve, carry away safe, deliver, (cause to) escape. (S)

This action word describes God's activity in our lives to move us aggressively through circumstances that are more than we can handle. We are to pray about trials and tribulations, but God has never said that He would deliver us *out of them*. It is more accurate to say that the Lord delivers us *in* our trials and tribulations. Paul writes,

> No temptation has overtaken you but such as is common to man; but God is faithful, who will not allow you to be tempted beyond what you are able, but with the temptation will also make the way of escape, that you may be able to bear it (1 Corinthians 10:13, *NKJV*).

God is our Deliverer! (*See #202.*)

51. Strength/Rock – *Tsuwr*

"No one is holy like the Lord, For there is none besides You, Nor is there any *rock* like our God" (1 Samuel 2:2, *NKJV*).

"The Lord lives! Blessed be my *Rock*! Let God be exalted, The *Rock* of my salvation!" (2 Samuel 22:47, *NKJV*).

"Let the words of my mouth, and the meditation of my heart, be acceptable in thy sight, O Lord, my *strength*, and my redeemer" (Psalm 19:14).

"Be to me a great protecting *Rock*, where I am always welcome, safe from all attacks. For you have issued the order to save me" (Psalm 71:3, *TLB*).

Definition: *Tsuwr* (tsoor) [6697]; or *Tsur* (tsoor); from *tsuwr,* properly, a cliff (or sharp rock, as compressed); generally, a rock or boulder; figuratively, a refuge; also an edge (as precipitous): – edge, X (mighty) God (one), rock, X sharp, stone, X strength, X strong. See also *Beyth Tsuwr.* (S)

David isn't referring to a piece of sandstone that can be easily broken. The solid stone he talks about has stood the test of time, heat and pressure, much like volcanic rock. The strength of God is the impenetrable strength and protection we depend on. (*See #30, #48, #77, #71, #113, #114, #208, #214, #245, #246, #247.*)

52. Shield/Buckler – *Magen*

"After these things the word of the Lord came to Abram in a vision, saying, 'Do not be afraid, Abram. I am your *shield*, your exceedingly great reward'" (Genesis 15:1, *NKJV*).

"You have also given me the *shield* of your salvation; your gentleness has made me great" (2 Samuel 22:36, *NKJV*).

"But You, O Lord, are a *shield* for me, my glory and the One who lifts up my head" (Psalm 3:3, *NKJV*).

"The Lord is my strength and my *shield*; My heart trusted in Him, and I am helped; Therefore my heart greatly rejoices, And with my song I will praise Him" (Psalm 28:7, *NKJV*).

"For the Lord God is a sun and *shield*; The Lord will give grace and glory; no good thing will He withhold from those who walk uprightly" (Psalm 84:11, *NKJV*).

Definition: *Magen* (maw-gane') [4043]; also (in plural) feminine *meginnah* (meg-in-naw'); from *ganan*; a shield (i.e. the small one or buckler); figuratively, a protector; also the scaly hide of the crocodile: – X armed, buckler, defence, ruler, + scale, shield. (S)

An incident happened when I was working at a car dealership that reminds me of this particular revelation of God. I had spent some time with an elderly man, trying to help him choose the right vehicle. When he came to buy the car, he was so unsure of himself that he brought along a friend to make sure we were giving him a good deal and selling him a quality vehicle.

The friend went on the test drive. After another hour of conversation, the man decided to purchase the car. As we negotiated the trade-in and sale price, the friend was consulted at every step. I explained to the finance and insurance agent that the purchaser wanted a friend along when he made his decisions, the agent said, "So he's got his *magen* with him."

I had never heard the term, so I asked what he meant. He said, "I mean he has his counselor with him and this could make for a very difficult sale."

As time went by, I saw what he meant. Nothing could be done to consummate the sale until both parties felt secure in the purchase. The friend felt he had to offer some resistance at every turn of events in order to validate his being there. We could not get to the customer without first going through his counselor.

Now I see the value of having a shield, a buckler, a counselor or a protector with me everywhere I go. There is nothing that can come to me that does not first have to go through my "*magen*."

God is my shield and my buckler, and I can trust Him for sound advice and protection wherever I go and whatever I do. Nothing is too small for God to care about, and nothing is too big for the Lord to handle. (*See #86.*)

53. Horn of My Salvation – *Yesha' Qeren*

"The Lord is . . . the *horn of my salvation*" (Psalm 18:2).

Definitions: *Yesha'* (yeh'-shah) [3468]; or *yesha'* (yay'-shah); from *yasha'*; liberty, deliverance, prosperity: – safety, salvation, saving. (S)

Qeren (keh'-ren) [7161]; from *qaran*; a horn (as projecting); by implication, a flask, cornet; by resemblance an elephant's tooth (i.e. ivory), a corner (of the altar), a peak (of a mountain), a ray (of light); figuratively, power: – X hill, horn. (S)

This horn is not a musical instrument; it is a projection, like an antler or tusk. This kind of horn always denotes power and dominance. It also typifies male prowess and virility. Our God is a powerful and virile being who actively watches over His own. (*See #162.*)

54. High Tower/Refuge/Defense – *Misgab*

"The Lord also will be a *refuge* for the oppressed, a refuge in times of trouble" (Psalm 9:9).

"The Lord of hosts is with us; the God of Jacob is our *refuge*. Selah" (Psalm 46:7).

"He only is my rock and my salvation; he is my *defense*; I shall not be greatly moved" (Psalm 62:2, *NKJV*).

> **Definition:** *Misgab* (mis-gawb') [4869]; from *sagab*; properly, a cliff (or other lofty or inaccessible place); abstractly, altitude; figuratively, a refuge: – defence, high fort (tower), refuge, Misgab, a place in Moab: Misgab. (S)

This word is translated "high tower, refuge or defense." God is more that a person; He is a place of shelter in the time of storms or battles. We can run to God and hide under His wings of protection and find comfort with the One who is better and much more dependable than a big brother.

A minister went to a farm after a fire had destroyed it and found none of the beautiful farm buildings left. Debris was scattered everywhere; animals stood stunned and confused by the destruction and turmoil. Debris that looked like a pile of burnt rags smoldered in the middle of the yard.

Absently, the minister kicked the pile of rubbish and several small chicks came chirping and scampering from under it. Looking closer, the man saw that what appeared to be a pile of rags was really a dead hen that had spread her wings to shelter her chicks during the fire. She refused to leave them and the fire killed her. This is what God did when He came as a Man and spread His arms on the cross of Calvary. All who come under His wings find shelter and defense from life's trials and tribulations. (*See #93, #97.*)

55. Refuge – *Manowc*

"My God is my rock, in whom I take refuge, my shield and the horn of my salvation. He is my stronghold, my *refuge* and my savior—from violent men you save me" (2 Samuel 22:3, *NIV*).

"I will sing of your strength, in the morning I will sing of your love; for you are my fortress, my *refuge*" (Psalm 59:16, *NIV*).

"Lord, my strength and my fortress, my *refuge* in time of distress, to you the nations will come from the ends of the earth and say, 'Our fathers possessed nothing but false gods, worthless idols that did them no good'" (Jeremiah 16:19, *NIV*).

Definition: *Manowc* (maw-noce') [4498]; from *nuwc*; a retreat (literally or figuratively); abstractly, a fleeing: – X apace, escape, way to flee, flight, refuge. (S)

This refuge is not a physical place as much as it is a spiritual place of escape. At times the world seems to be crushing and pressing in from every direction. During those times there is a place of rest within the Godhead where you can find peace in the midst of conflict.

In the privacy of a prayer closet or in the silence of the early morning hours, He will meet with you and become a hiding place and a source of unmerited peace and joy. These are some of the most precious moments in the life of a believer. (*See #49.*)

56. Savior – *Yasha'*

"The Lord lives! Praise be to my Rock! Exalted be God, the Rock, my *Savior*!" (2 Samuel 22:47, *NIV*).

"He will receive blessing from the Lord and vindication from God his *Savior*" (Psalm 24:5, *NIV*).

"Guide me in your truth and teach me, for you are God my *Savior*, and my hope is in you all day long" (Psalm 25:5, *NIV*).

"Come quickly to help me, O Lord my *Savior*" (Psalm 38:22, *NIV*).

"Praise be to the Lord, to God our *Savior*, who daily bears our burdens. Selah" (Psalm 68:19, *NIV*).

"They forgat God their *savior*, which had done great things in Egypt" (Psalm 106:21).

"And it shall be for a sign and for a witness unto the Lord of hosts in the land of Egypt: for they shall cry unto the Lord because of the oppressors, and he shall send them a *savior*, and a great one, and he shall deliver them" (Isaiah 19:20).

"For I am the Lord, your God, the Holy One of Israel, your *Savior*; I give Egypt for your ransom, Cush and Seba in your stead" (Isaiah 43:3, *NIV*).

Definition: *Yasha'* (yaw-shah') [3467]; a primitive root; properly, to be open, wide or free, i.e. (by implication) to be safe; causatively, to free or succor: – X at all, avenging, defend, deliver (-er), help, preserve, rescue, be safe, bring (having) salvation, save (-iour), get victory. (S)

The word "Savior" is both a name and title for God in a triune sense. It is a name and title of Jesus, the Son of God. By this I mean that God was, is, and shall be a Savior to all those who look to Him.

Historically, the Book of Judges shows that the people of Israel needed a Savior many times, even before Jesus came. God was a Savior to them every time they cried out to Him for help.

Sometimes He came quickly, sometimes He tarried; but the Lord always came in His perfect time.

Prophesies in the Old Testament use this name to refer to God's Son, Jesus Christ, as the soon-coming King and Savior. God is and always has been, the Rock of salvation in whom we can find safety.

In the New Testament, the Greek word *soter* is translated as Savior in much the same way. Sometimes it refers to God in a general sense, and sometimes it is used as a specific title of Jesus Christ. (*See #122, #161, #181 #235.*)

PART 1
The Triune God

Greek Names in

THE NEW TESTAMENT

---

57. Lord – *Kurios*

"But while he thought on these things, behold, the angel of the *Lord* appeared unto him in a dream, saying, Joseph, thou son of David, fear not to take unto thee Mary thy wife: for that which is conceived in her is of the Holy Ghost" (Matthew 1:20).

"The *Lord* is risen indeed, and hath appeared to Simon" (Luke 24:34).

> **Definition:** *Kurios* (koo'-ree-os) [2962]; from *kuros* (supremacy); supreme in authority, i.e. (as noun) controller; by implication, Mr. (as a respectful title): – God, Lord, master, Sir. (S)

This name (or title) is used in Scripture to refer to both the Father and the Son (see John 20:18; 21:20). The Greek word *Kurios* has at its core the same meaning that we found for the

the Hebrew name *Adonai*, which is more a title than a name. It refers to God as our Master and heavenly Ruler, our Sovereign Lord. It can be likened to the way we speak of the president of the United States.

As I write these words, our nation's leader is President Bill Clinton. The title of "president" before his name has much the same meaning as the title "Lord" or *Kurios*. Both God the Father and God the Son (Jesus Christ) are referred to by this title. (*See #3, #4, #5, #8, #61, #70.*)

58. God – *Theos*

"Behold, a virgin shall be with child, and shall bring forth a son, and they shall call his name Emmanuel, which being interpreted is, *God* with us" (Matthew 1:23).

> **Definition:** *Theos* (theh'-os) [2316]; of uncertain affinity; a deity, especially (with *ho*) the supreme Divinity; figuratively, a magistrate; by Hebraism, very: – X exceeding, God, god [-ly, -ward]. (S)

This name emphasizes His self-sufficiency and self-determination. The word is used frequently throughout the New Testament when speaking of God in any of His triune forms. Here it refers to the Father being manifest to us through His Son Jesus Christ. It has much the same meaning as "Jehovah" in the Hebrew. (*See #1, #6, #7.*)

59. Highest – *Hupsistos*

"And the multitudes that went before, and that followed, cried, saying, Hosanna to the Son of David: Blessed is he that cometh in the name of the Lord; Hosanna in the *highest*" (Matthew 21:9).

> **Definition:** *Hupsistos* (hoop'-sis-tos) [5310]; superlative from the base of *hupsos*; highest, i.e. (masculine singular) the Supreme (God), or (neuter plural) the heavens: – most high, highest. (S)

The people in the world recognized many gods at the time of Christ. Here the angels are proclaiming that the God of Israel is God *most high*. There is none like Him. He is Lord of lords and King of kings. (*See #22, #29, #300.*)

60. My God – *Eli*

"And about the ninth hour Jesus cried with a loud voice, saying, *Eli, Eli,* lama sabachthani? that is to say, My God, my God, why hast thou forsaken me?" (Matthew 27:46).

> **Definition:** *Eli* (ay-lee') or *Eloi* (ay-lo'-ee) [2241]; of Hebrew origin [*anegkletos* with pronominal suffix]; my God: – Eli. (S)

This is the personal name for God that Jesus called as He experienced separation from the Father at Calvary. He had walked with the Father in a daily, intimate way. The knowledge that the time of death was before Him brought Jesus to His knees in the Garden of Gethsemane.

Imagine the inner pain of knowing God as intimately as Jesus did and having to face separation from Him. This was what drew the sweat-drops of blood from Jesus in the Garden, not just the fear of the cross.

Not knowing what was ahead, the disciples did not experience the visible anguish that Jesus exhibited in the Garden. Jesus had never known a time when He was not in communion with the Father, nor has He ever known a time of broken communion since. (*See #19, #34, #47.*)

61. Lord – *Despotes*

"*Lord,* now You are letting Your servant depart in peace, According to Your word" (Luke 2:29, *NKJV*).

> **Definition:** *Despotes* (des-pot'-ace) [1203]; perhaps from *deo* and *posis* (a husband); an absolute ruler ("despot"): – Lord, master. (S)

This Greek word is used four times in the New Testament. Twice it refers to Jehovah-God, and twice it refers to Jesus. The first mention of God as *despotes* is when the baby Jesus was presented in the temple at His dedication. Simeon saw the fulfillment of a prophetic word and sang with excitement the "Song of Simeon."

The word "despot" has negative connotations for most American minds. We automatically think of a tyrant who leads a nation in total, self-centered autonomy.

But Simeon worshiped the Lord when he referred to God as *despotes.* He was acknowledging God's sovereignty and infinite authority. In Simeon's mind the Lord had proven Himself to be everything He ever claimed to be; and in so doing, God was demonstrating His omnipotence, omniscience and omnipresence. Here are other usages:

"So when they heard that, they raised their voice to God with one accord and said: 'Lord, You are God, who made heaven and earth and the sea, and all that is in them'" (Acts 4:24, *NKJV*).

"For certain men have crept in unnoticed, who long ago were marked out for this condemnation, ungodly men, who turn the grace of our God into lewdness and deny the only Lord God and our Lord Jesus Christ" (Jude 1:4, *NKJV*).

"They called out in a loud voice, 'How long, Sovereign *Lord*, holy and true, until you judge the inhabitants of the earth and avenge our blood?'" (Revelation 6:10, *NIV*). (*See #3, #4, #5, #8, #57 #70.*)

62. Godhead – *Theotes*

"For in him dwelleth all the fulness of the *Godhead* bodily" (Colossians 2:9).

Definition: *Theotes* [2320] - deity, the state of being God, Godhead (*Thayers Greek-English Lexicon*).

The fullness of the triune God dwelt in Jesus. He was not inferior to the Father or the Holy Spirit, He was equal in authority and power. But Jesus had a different purpose in God's plan.

The word *Godhead* can be used of any of the parts that make up the whole. Although separate in purpose and anointing, each is due the respect and adoration deserved by the Lord God of the universe. (*See #1, #301.*)

63. Light – *Phos*

"This then is the message which we have heard of him, and declare unto you, that *God is light*, and in him is no darkness at all" (1 John 1:5).

Definition: *Phos* (foce) [5457]; from an obsolete *phao* (to shine or make manifest, especially by rays; compare *phaino, phemi*); luminousness (in the widest application, nat. or artificial, abstract or concrete, literal or figurative): – fire, light. (S)

This is a revelation of one of the attributes of God. He is light! Everything we know about light is wrapped up in who God is. Light is one of the ways to define Him. God's presence brings illumination and makes the darkness go away. Psalm 139:11, 12 says,

If I say, Surely the darkness shall cover me; even the night shall be light about me. Yea, the darkness hideth not from thee; but the night shineth as the day: the darkness and the light are both alike to thee.

Light is an active energy that always dispels darkness. You do not make a thing darker, you turn down the light and allow the darkness to take over. Darkness never overpowers light, it is merely the passive result of the absence of light.

I have heard that when tourists were taken to the bottom of Carlsbad Caverns in New Mexico in years past, at one point the tour guides would turn off all the lights. At first the darkness was frightening; most had never seen that kind of pure darkness. After the eyes became accustomed to the total darkness, the guide would light a match and hold it up over his or her head.

The effect was amazing. That little match would produce enough light to see hundreds of feet down the cavern. You could almost read a newspaper by that small light 25 or 30 feet away. The light of God dispels darkness. Only His brightness can make the blinding light of the sun seem dull and dim by comparison. (*See #2, #121, #173, #184, #271.*)

64. Love – *Agape*

"Beloved, let us love one another: for love is of God; and every one that loveth is born of God, and knoweth God. He that loveth not knoweth not God; for *God is love*" (1 John 4:7, 8).

> **Definition:** *Agape* (ag-ah'-pay) [26]; from *agapao*; love, i.e. affection or benevolence; specially (plural) a love-feast: – (feast of) charity ([-ably]), dear, love. (S)
>
> "God is love (*ho theos agape estin*). John does not say that love is God, but only that God is love. The two terms are not interchangeable. God is also light (1 John 1:5) and spirit (John 4:24)" (*Word Pictures in the New Testament*).

"Love is patient, love is kind. It does not envy, it does not boast, it is not proud. It is not rude, it is not self-seeking, it is not easily angered, it keeps no record of wrongs. Love does not delight in evil but rejoices with the truth. It always protects, always trusts, always hopes, always perseveres" (1 Corinthians 13:4-7, *NIV*).

Everyone believes that love is important, but love is usually thought of as a feeling. In reality, love is a choice and an action, as 1 Corinthians 13:4-7 shows. God is the source of our love: he loved us enough to sacrifice his Son for us. Jesus is our example of what it means to love; everything he did in life and death was supremely loving. The Holy Spirit gives us the power to love; he lives in our hearts and makes us more and more like Christ. God's love always involves a choice and an action, and our love should be like his (*Life Application Study Bible*).

Agape is love as God loves. His love does not depend on our performance or merit; it is undeserved and beyond our ability to manipulate or control.

Phileo, a Greek word translated "love," speaks of brotherly love or friendship, not the kind of love Jesus wanted from Peter in John 21:15-17.

So when they had dined, Jesus saith to Simon Peter, Simon, son of Jonas, lovest (*agape*) thou me more than these? He saith unto him, Yea, Lord; thou knowest that I love (*phileo*) thee. He saith unto him, Feed my lambs. He saith to him again the second time, Simon, son of Jonas, lovest (*agape*) thou me? He saith unto him, Yea, Lord; thou knowest that I love (*phileo*) thee. He saith unto him, Feed my sheep. He saith unto him the third time, Simon, son of Jonas, lovest (*phileo*) thou me? Peter was grieved because he said unto him the third time, Lovest (*phileo*) thou me? And he said unto him, Lord, thou knowest all things; thou knowest that I love (*phileo*) thee. Jesus saith unto him, Feed my sheep.

This conversation came after Peter had denied Jesus. I believe that if Jesus had asked Peter prior to his denial, Peter probably would have assured Jesus that he did indeed love (*agape*) Him. But at this conversation, Peter was aware of his own inability to live for Jesus or love Him in the same way that Jesus loved him. Peter was broken and aware of human weakness. It is interesting to note that Jesus still told Peter to feed His lambs. You will not be disqualified because you are unable to live the Christian life in your own strength.

To the contrary, only when you are aware of your inability to live the Christian life can Christ come in and live His life through you. The Lord uses only broken vessels, so feed His sheep! Don't tell Him why you are unable to do it; He already knows all about your weaknesses. He is waiting for you to cease striving and know that He is God. Let Him live His life through you.

Other words are translated "love" from the Greek, but *eros* describes the emotion most in our culture identify as love. *Eros* describes the kind of love that manifests itself in lust and self-serving emotionalism.

This word is not used in the text of the New Testament, but it does rather accurately describe what Hollywood tries to sell as love.

> Who shall separate us from the love of Christ? Shall tribulation, or distress, or persecution, or famine, or nakedness, or peril, or sword? As it is written: 'For Your sake we are killed all day long; We are accounted as sheep for the slaughter.' Yet in all these things we are more than conquerors through Him who loved us. For I am persuaded that neither death nor life, nor angels nor principalities nor powers, nor things present nor things to come, nor height nor depth, nor any other created thing, shall be able to separate us from the love of God which is in Christ Jesus our Lord (Romans 8:35-39, *NKJV*).

"So now I am giving you a new commandment: Love each other. Just as I have loved you, you should love each other. Your love for one another will prove to the world that you are my disciples" (John 13:34, 35, *NLT*).

"Jesus said to him, 'You shall love the Lord your God with all your heart, with all your soul, and with all your mind.' This is the first and great commandment. And the second is like it: 'You shall love your neighbor as yourself.' On these two commandments hang all the Law and the Prophets" (Matthew 22:37-40, *NKJV*). (*See #98.*)

65. Jasper Stone – *Iaspis*

"Immediately I was in the Spirit; and behold, a throne set in heaven, and *One* sat on the throne. And He who sat there was like a *jasper* and a sardius stone in appearance; and there was a rainbow around the throne, in appearance like an emerald" (Revelation 4:2, 3, *NKJV*).

> **Definition:** *Iaspis*; of Phoenician origin; *jasper* (a translucent stone) :- jasper(4).

In several verses of Revelation, the author uses stones, gems, precious metals and pearls to describe what he saw in heaven. John had no other point of reference from which to explain the things he saw. He did the best he could but was forced to use things known to the people he wrote to, in order to explain the visions.

In many ways God is like the jasper stone John used to describe Him. Jasper is a transparent gem. So is God in a unique way.

Jesus spoke in parables, and the people who heard Him often found them difficult to understand. But the Father sent the Holy Spirit to open the eyes of our understanding, so that we might have insight into the mysteries of God. There is no guile in our Lord, He comes to us openly and in the light of day.

> His countenance was like a jasper and a sardine-stone;
> he is not described by any human features, so as to be

89

represented by an image, but only by his transcendent brightness. This jasper is a transparent stone, which yet offers to
the eye a variety of the most vivid colors, signifying the
glorious perfections of God; the sardine-stone is red, signifying the justice of God, that essential attribute of which he
never divests himself in favor of any, but gloriously exerts
it in the government of the world, and especially of the
church, through our Lord Jesus Christ. This attribute is displayed in pardoning as well as in punishing, in saving as
well as in destroying sinners. (*Holman Bible Dictionary*)

Jasper is seen in many colors. This may be stretching the
illustration a bit, but I do not see our God as the white man's
Lord any more than He is the black man's, red man's, or
yellow man's Lord. The salvation that Jesus wrought is available to all people everywhere. No single color can describe
Him or His people. (*See #66.*)

66. Sardius Stone – *Sardios*

"Immediately I was in the Spirit; and behold, a throne
set in heaven, and One sat on the throne. And He who sat
there was like a jasper and a *sardius stone* in appearance;
and there was a rainbow around the throne, in appearance
like an emerald" (Revelation 4:2, 3, *NKJV*).

Definition: *Sardios* (sar'-dee-os) [4556]; properly, an adjective from an uncertain base; sardian (*leethos* being
implied), i.e. (as noun) the gem so called: – sardius. (S)

Matthew Henry said in the previous reference, "The sardine-stone is red, signifying the justice of God." Red is also
symbolic of the color of blood which represents life. God is
described as a sardis stone in appearance. Sardis is a precious stone, common enough to be familiar to the author
and his readers, but rare enough to establish its value as
greater than that of most stones of the area. (*See #65.*)

OUR FATHER GOD

PART 2
Our Father God

Hebrew, Greek and Aramaic Names of

OUR FATHER GOD

---

67. Father – *'Ab*

"Do you thus deal with the Lord, O foolish and unwise people? Is He not your *Father*, who bought you? Has He not made you and established you?" (Deuteronomy 32:6, *NKJV*).

"A *father* of the fatherless and a judge for the widows, is God in His holy habitation" (Psalm 68:5, *NASB*).

But now, O Lord, *thou art our father*; we are the clay, and thou our potter; and we all are the work of thy hand" (Isaiah 64:8).

> **Definition:** *'Ab* (awb) [1]; a primitive word; father, in a literal and immediate, or figurative and remote application): – chief, (fore-) father ([-less]), X patrimony, principal. Compare names in "Abi-". (S)

Without God we are like orphan children without any hope of breaking the bonds of poverty and despair. Jesus, the firstborn of many brethren, made the way for us to have access to the Father. Through faith in Jesus we have all the rights and privileges of a full-fledged heir as sons of God. He is King of kings and this makes us princes in His kingdom. Amen! (*See #69, #71.*)

68. Everlasting Father – *'Ad 'Ab*

"For unto us a child is born, unto us a son is given: and the government shall be upon his shoulder: and his name shall be called Wonderful, Counsellor, The mighty God, The everlasting Father, The Prince of Peace" (Isaiah 9:6).

> **Definition:** *'Ad* – (ad) [5703]; from (`adah); properly a (peremptory) terminus, i.e. (by implication) duration, in the sense of advance or perpetuity (substantially as a noun, either with or without a preposition): – eternity, ever (-lasting, -more), old, perpetually, + world without end. (S)

Not only is God our father, but He is our everlasting Father. Many of today's fathers seem to think of the position as a temporary state, or something that can be avoided when things get uncomfortable. God has demonstrated His immutable nature throughout history: He does not change. Humanity has often proven to be unworthy of God's love and care, but He never changes in His character or demeanor.

The everlasting Father has chosen us to be recipients of His inheritance as coheirs with Jesus. (*See #108, #289.*)

NEW TESTAMENT REFERENCES

69. Father – *Pater*

"Whosoever therefore shall confess me before men, him will I confess also before my *Father* which is in heaven'" (Matthew 10:32).

"And he said unto them, 'How is it that ye sought me? wist ye not that I must be about my *Father's* business?" (Luke 2:49).

"But Jesus answered them, My *Father* worketh hitherto, and I work" (John 5:17).

> **Definition:** *Pater* (pat-ayr') [3962]; apparently a primary word; a "father" (literally or figuratively, near or more remote): – father, parent. (S)

A couple previously married to other spouses found a conflict in the home because a daughter from the wife's former marriage didn't feel like a daughter to the new husband—even though she had no relationship with her biological father. The parents decided to adopt the girl and give her the stability of identification in name with her mother and new father.

A judge instructed both parents and child about what adoption really means. The girl would no longer be less than a full-fledged, flesh-and-blood daughter. She would have all the legal rights of a biological daughter and would be coheir with any other children that might come to the family.

Interviewing the girl alone, the judge asked if this was what she truly desired. He wanted to make sure she was not being coerced in any way. He interviewed the parents alone to make sure each understood every legal and moral obligation implied by the decision.

The adoption was decreed, and legal forms spelled out the full implications and results of their decision. When we were adopted into the family of God, we were not coerced or made to become a child of His. We each made our own decision; nobody could decide for us.

The glorious result is a binding relationship with the Father—one that is every bit as binding as His relationship with His transcendant Son, Jesus Christ. We have the same inheritance in the kingdom of God that Jesus has. Praise the Lord! (*See #68, #71.*)

70. Lord of Heaven and Earth – *Kurios Ouranos Ge*

"At that time Jesus answered and said, 'I thank You, Father, *Lord of heaven and earth*, that You have hidden these things from the wise and prudent and have revealed them to babes'" (Matthew 11:25, *NKJV*).

"In that hour Jesus rejoiced in the Spirit and said, 'I thank You, Father, *Lord of heaven and earth*, that You have hidden these things from the wise and prudent and revealed them to babes. Even so, Father, for so it seemed good in Your sight'" (Luke 10:21, *NKJV*).

"God, who made the world and everything in it, since He is *Lord of heaven and earth*, does not dwell in temples made with hands" (Acts 17:24 *NKJV*).

Definition: *Kurios* (koo'-ree-os) [2962]; from *kuros* (supremacy); supreme in authority, i.e. (as noun) controller; by implication, Mr. (as a respectful title): – God, Lord, master, Sir. (S)

Ouranos (oo-ran-os) [3772]; perhaps from the same as *oros* (through the idea of elevation); the sky; by extension, heaven (as the abode of God); by implication, happiness, power, eternity; specifically, the Gospel (Christianity): – air, heaven ([-ly]), sky. (S)

Ge (ghay) [1093]; contracted from a primary word; soil; by extension a region, or the solid part or the whole of the terrene globe (including the occupants in each application): – country, earth (-ly), ground, land, world. (S)

Jesus gave this saying immediately after He rebuked the cities where miracles had been done and the people did not repent (Matthew 11:20-24). When Jesus addressed His Father as "Lord of Heaven and Earth," He was thanking God for hiding His wisdom from the world and revealing it to those who were spiritual babes. He concluded His teaching with the familiar verses,

> Come to Me, all you who labor and are heavy laden, and I will give you rest. Take My yoke upon you and learn from Me, for I am gentle and lowly in heart, and you will find rest for your souls. For My yoke is easy and My burden is light (Matthew 11:28-30, *NKJV*).

When a believer truly grasps the rest that is offered in Jesus Christ, it makes a difference in the way everything else in Scripture is interpreted for him or her. We need to know our God as Lord of the heavens and the earth, the One in whom all things live and breathe and have their being. (*See #3, #4, #5, #8, #57, #61.*)

71. Daddy – *Abba*

"For you have not received a spirit of slavery leading to fear again, but you have received a spirit of adoption as sons by which we cry out, '*Abba*! Father!' The Spirit Himself bears witness with our spirit that we are children of God, and if children, heirs also, heirs of God and fellow heirs with Christ, if indeed we suffer with Him in order that we may also be glorified with Him" (Romans 8:15-17, *NASB*).

Definition: *Abba* (ab-bah') [5]; of Aramaic origin [2]; father (as a vocative case): – Abba. (S)

The New Testament Greek word *Abba* has the same intimate meaning as the word *Daddy* has to an American child.

We have a personal and intimate relationship with "Daddy" God. To refer to your dad as "father" is often too formal for most of us. In fact, it makes the fathers I know feel uncomfortable. *Daddy* is an informal and comfortable title that most children use with their fathers.

I derived a certain pleasure when my young son or daughter looked up to me and called me *Daddy*. It would melt my heart and inspire me to do everything I could to confirm the trust shown.

Our Father in heaven wants us to demonstrate the same kind of total trust in Him that our children have in us.

> For you are all sons of God through faith in Christ Jesus. For all of you who were baptized into Christ have clothed yourselves with Christ. There is neither Jew nor Greek, there is neither slave nor free man, there is neither male nor female; for you are all one in Christ Jesus. And if you belong to Christ, then you are Abraham's offspring, heirs according to promise.

> Now I say, as long as the heir is a child, he does not differ at all from a slave although he is owner of everything, but he is under guardians and managers until the date set by the father. So also we, while we were children, were held in bondage under the elemental things of the world. But when the fulness of the time came, God sent forth His Son, born of a woman, born under the Law, in order that He might redeem those who were under the Law, that we might receive the adoption as sons.

> And because you are sons, God has sent forth the Spirit of His Son into our hearts, crying, "*Abba*! Father!" Therefore you are no longer a slave, but a son; and if a son, then an heir through God (Galatians 3:26—4:7, *NASB*).

(See #67, #68, #69.)

PART 3

THE SON OF GOD

PART 3
The Son of God

Hebrew Names From

GENESIS – JOB

72. Seed (of the Woman) – *Zera'*

"And I will put enmity between thee and the woman, and between thy seed and *her seed*; it shall bruise thy head, and thou shalt bruise his heel" (Genesis 3:15).

> **Definition:** *Zera'* (zeh'-rah; from *zara'*) [2233]; seed; figurative fruit, plant, sowing-time, posterity: – X carnally, child, fruitful, seed (-time), sowing-time. (S)

All the potential for life, growth, production and harvest is in the seed. The saying is true that any intelligent person can count the seeds in an apple, but only God can count the apples in a seed. God referred to His Son Jesus as the seed of Eve in this passage. It is the first messianic prophecy in the Bible, and it prophesies the coming of Messiah through the seed of Eve who would crush Satan's head. This scripture was fulfilled when Jesus was born a direct offspring of Eve.

His heels were bruised at the Crucifixion, at which time He defeated Satan, because Jesus was without sin and Satan had no legal right to hold Him.

A main purpose of the Bible is to trace the genealogy of Adam and Eve to the coming of the Christ child. Many chapters are full of the "begets" and "begots" that historically document the legal line of God's Son through the family tree. Too often we rush through these verses, forgetting that according to 2 Timothy 3:16, all Scripture is God-inspired. (*See #189.*)

73. Angel – *Mal'ak*

"And he blessed Joseph, and said: 'God, before whom my fathers Abraham and Isaac walked, the God who has fed me all my life long to this day, *the Angel* who has redeemed me from all evil, bless the lads; let my name be named upon them, and the name of my fathers Abraham and Isaac; and let them grow into a multitude in the midst of the earth'" (Genesis 48:15, 16, *NKJV*).

> **Definition:** *Mal'ak* (mal-awk') [4397]; from an unused root meaning to dispatch as a deputy; a messenger; specifically of God, i.e. an angel (also a prophet, priest or teacher): – ambassador, angel, king, messenger. (S)

The Bible records many instances where angels came to humans. Some occurrences are pre-incarnate visitations of Jesus. Many Christians believe that Jesus appeared to men and women of old at certain times as an angel sent by God to bring a message or to establish a man of God.

For example, Jacob wrestled with the angel of the Lord at Bethel (see Genesis 32), and in the morning the angel touched his hip socket and Jacob never walked the same again. The Lord had come to Jacob, the "twister," the "one who grabs the heel." He left him as Israel, a prince with God.

Genesis 48:15, 16 tells of Jacob blessing Ephraim, the youngest son of Joseph. In these verses Jacob gives honor and glory to the angel of the Lord who appeared to him at Bethel. Jacob knew that the Lord had removed the reproach of his sins and iniquities from him when he met the angel at Bethel; now he prayed for Ephraim, his son, to experience the same thing.

Not every angelic visitation can be attributed to Jesus, however, "For Satan himself transforms himself into an angel of light" (2 Corinthians 11:14, *NKJV*).

74. Shiloh – *Shiyloh*

"The sceptre shall not depart from Judah, nor a lawgiver from between his feet, until *Shiloh* come; and unto him shall the gathering of the people be" (Genesis 49:10).

> **Definition:** *Shiyloh* (shee-lo') [7886]; from *shalah*; tranquil; Shiloh, an epithet of the Messiah: – Shiloh. (S)

This prophecy said that the messianic seed would bring forth a Savior, only this time the seed is seen coming from the tribe of Judah. The Bible story unfolds progressive revelation that leads to the very family God uses to bring the Christ child into the world.

In Matthew 1, the lineage of Christ is traced from Abraham through David, and eventually to Joseph, the carpenter from Nazareth. This genealogy provides proof that Jesus was related to all Jews, because it shows Him to be a son of Abraham.

In Luke 4, Jesus' genealogy begins with the reference to Heli as Joseph's father-in-law (at least that is what is believed the relationship was). This record goes backward from the living Christ all the way to Adam. This is believed to contain the bloodline of Jesus through His mother, Mary, and it shows Jesus to be related to all humanity, not just the Jews.

Strong's Concordance uses the word *tranquil* to define the name *Shiloh*. Jesus is to be our peace, or tranquility. This prophecy, spoken over Jacob's son, prophesies that the peace of God will come out the tribe of Judah. It also says that the scepter shall not depart from Judah's family. The scepter, a symbol of kingship, shows Jesus as the Prince of Peace.

The eldest son always received the largest inheritance and was left as the leader of the family, but Jacob blessed Judah and not Reuben, his eldest son. Obviously God was still speaking through Jacob in his older years as he prophesied over his sons. (*See #38, #224, #225, #263*.)

75. Mighty One of Jacob – *'Abiyr*

"But his bow remained steady, his strong arms stayed limber, because of the hand of the *Mighty One of Jacob*, because of the Shepherd, the Rock of Israel" (Genesis 49:24, *NIV*).

> **Definition:** *'Abiyr* (aw-beer') [46]; from ('abar); mighty (spoken of God): – mighty (one). (S)

This name referred to the Father previously, but it is also a good description of Jesus. When human imagination pictures ultimate strength and power, it conjures up something like Superman ("Faster than a speeding bullet, more powerful than a mighty locomotive, able to leap a tall building in a single bound").

This word Jacob used when he prophesied over Joseph means one who could fly or soar, such as today's dreamers created with the character of Superman. The difference is that the mighty One of Jacob truly does possess those wonderful attributes that are only imagined in Superman. (*See #14*.)

76. Shepherd – *Ra'ah*

"But his bow remained steady, his strong arms stayed limber, because of the hand of the Mighty One of Jacob, because of the *Shepherd*, the Rock of Israel" (Genesis 49:24, *NIV*).

> **Definition:** *Ra'ah* (raw-aw) [7462]; a primitive root; to tend a flock, i.e. pasture it; intransitive to graze (literal or figurative); generally to rule; by extensive to *associate* with (as a friend) : – break, companion, keep company with, devour, eat up, evil entreat, feed, use as a friend, make friendship with, herdman, keep [sheep] (-er), pastor, + shearing house, shepherd, wander, waste. (S)

Israel saw that the Mighty One would also be a Shepherd to Joseph. What an enviable position! Joseph finds himself one of the personal flock of the Mighty One of Jacob. His power was unlimited, His knowledge knew no bounds and He could be in all places at the same time. This God was the shepherd and keeper of Joseph. We share this same relationship because Jesus is our Shepherd and our keeper. (*See #31, #187, #249.*)

77. Rock of Israel – *'Eben Yisra'el*

"But his bow remained steady, his strong arms stayed limber, because of the hand of the Mighty One of Jacob, because of the Shepherd, the *Rock of Israel*" (Genesis 49:24, *NIV*).

> **Definition:** *'Eben* (eh'-ben) [68]; from the root of *banah* through the meaning to build; a stone : – + carbuncle, + mason, + plummet, [chalk-, hail-, head-, sling-] stone (-ny), (divers) weight (-s). (S)
>
> *Yisra'el* (yis-raw-ale') [3478]; from *sarah* and *'el*; he will rule as God; *Jisraël*, a symbolical name of Jacob; also (typically) of his posterity : – Israel. (S)

The name *'Eben*, translated "rock or stone," conveys the idea of a rock that has been formed; a formation of bricks and mortar made by a mason for a specific purpose. God does not sit back and let creation go haphazardly on its way. He has been purposeful and intentional from the beginning. God worked in creation for His own purposes. That Joseph was sold into slavery and ended up in Pharaoh's court was part of the master plan to keep His people separate from the world.

Later, Joseph assured his brothers that they were not in danger of revenge from him because God had put him where he was so that when the famine came, his family would have a place to go for help (see Genesis 50). Events in our lives do not happen by accident; there is a plan and purpose. God is still building His rocks today. (*See #48, #51, #81, #113, #114, #208, #214, #245.*)

78. Righteous One – *Tsaddiyq*

"And Pharaoh sent, and called for Moses and Aaron, and said unto them, I have sinned this time: the *Lord is righteous*, and I and my people are wicked" (Exodus 9:27).

> **Definition:** *Tsaddiyq* (tsad-deek') [6662]; from *tsadaq*; just: – just, lawful, righteous (man). (S)

Pharaoh proclaims the God of the Israelites as righteous. He had experienced the seventh plague, a plague of hail. This plague did not affect the Israelites in Goshen—only the Egyptians had to deal with the last six. This demonstrated God's sovereignty and dominion over the gods of Pharaoh. Every plague Egypt experienced came against a false deity that they worshiped.

Although Pharaoh would not release the Israelites until the plague of the firstborn had brought him to his knees, he proclaimed with his own lips that the God of the Israelites, not any of the gods he served, was the righteous One. Still, Pharaoh did not worship Jehovah. Only those who truly believe that God is the righteous One worship and serve Him.

"The *Lord is righteous*: he hath cut asunder the cords of the wicked" (Psalm 129:4).

"The *Lord is righteous* in all his ways, and holy in all his works" (Psalm 145:17). (*See #28, #42.*)

79. Star Out of Jacob – *Kowkab*

"I shall see him, but not now: I shall behold him, but not nigh: there shall come a *Star out of Jacob*, and a Sceptre shall rise out of Israel" (Numbers 24:17).

> **Definition:** *Kowkab* (ko-kawb') [3556]; probably from the same as *kabbown* (in the sense of rolling) or *kavah* (in the sense of blazing); a star (as round or as shining); figuratively, a prince. (S)

Jesus, a star of blinding light, has come, displacing darkness. Where His light shines, no darkness is found, no sins go unseen. The light of a wondrous star led wise men to the manger where baby Jesus lay. And it is the light of His presence that leads us to Jesus today. (*See #228, #271.*)

80. Scepter Out of Israel – *Shebet*

"I see Him, but not now; I behold Him, but not near; a Star shall come out of Jacob; a *Scepter* shall rise out of Israel, and batter the brow of Moab, and destroy all the sons of tumult" (Numbers 24:17, *NKJV*).

> **Definition:** *Shebet*, (shay'-bet) [7626]; from an unused root probably meaning to branch off; a scion, i.e. (literal) a stick (for punishing, writing, fighting, ruling, walking, etc.) or (figurative) a clan : – X correction, dart, rod, scepter, staff, tribe. (S)

Jesus *is* the scepter; He does not just hold it! *Strong's Concordance* says a scepter is a stick for punishing, fighting and ruling. Jesus is such a stick or rod. Jesus has taken upon Himself the sins of all humanity, but He will actually destroy sin and its power when He returns at His Second Coming.

Since a scepter is the mark of a king or ruler, Jesus is the scepter of God to establish His rule on earth, as well as in heaven and hell. (*See #89.*)

81. Rock – *Tsuwr*

"He is the *Rock*, his work is perfect: for all his ways are judgment: a God of truth and without iniquity, just and right is he" (Deuteronomy 32:4).

> **Definition:** *Tsuwr* (tsoor); or *tsur* (tsoor); from *tsuwr*, properly, a cliff (or sharp rock, as compressed); generally, a rock or boulder; figuratively, a refuge; also an edge (as precipitous): KJV – edge, X (mighty) God (one), rock, X sharp, stone, X strength, X strong. See also 1049. (S)

This quote from the song of Moses was written as a praise to God. Moses knew that the One to come would be a rock. Jesus is His name; He is a hiding place. Jesus is perfect and His judgment is without error. He is always correct and perfect in His decisions. He is the truth. Our Lord is without sin or iniquity. There is no image of softness and weakness in this revelation. He is our strong tower, our rock of refuge. In Him we shall trust. (*See #48, #51, #77, #113, #114, #208, #214, #245, #246, #247.*)

82. Captain of the Host of the Lord – *Sar Tsaba' Yehovah*

"And he said, Nay; but as *captain of the host of the Lord* am I now come. And Joshua fell on his face to the earth, and did worship, and said unto him, What saith my lord unto his servant?" (Joshua 5:14).

> **Definition:** *Sar* (sar) [8269]; from *sarar*, a head person (of any rank or class): – captain (that had rule), chief (captain), general, governor, keeper, lord, ([-taskmaster, prince (-ipal), ruler, steward. (S)

> *Tsaba'* (tsaw-baw') [6633]; or (feminine) *tseba'ah* (tseb-aw-aw'); a mass of persons (or figuratively, things), especially reg. organized for war (an army); by implication, a campaign, literally or figuratively (specifically, hardship, worship): – appointed time, (+)army, (+)battle, company, host, service, soldiers, waiting upon, war (-fare). (S)

Yehovah (yeh-ho-vaw') [1961]; (the) self-Existent or Eternal; Jehovah, Jewish national name of God: – Jehovah, the Lord. (S)

Years of wilderness wandering finally over, Joshua is ready to go into battle against Jericho. The angel of the Lord appears with a sword drawn for battle, standing in the way. Joshua asked the angel, "'Are you for us or for our adversaries?' So [the angel] said, 'No, but as Commander of the army of the Lord I have now come'" (Joshua 5:13, 14, *NKJV*).

The angel was neither for nor against him, but his purpose was to serve the Lord. When Joshua heard the reply, "He fell on his face to the earth and worshiped, and said to Him, 'What does my Lord say to His servant?'" (Joshua 5:14, *NKJV*).

In conflicts between what God says in His Word or by His Spirit, and what others teach, God is always right. It is proper to support your church fellowship and denomination, but the greater priority is serving the Lord. Our first allegiance is first to the Lord Jesus Christ. He is the Captain of the Host of the Lord. (*See #24.*)

83. Friend – *'Ahab*

"O our God, did you not drive out the inhabitants of this land before your people Israel and give it forever to the descendants of Abraham your *friend*?" (2 Chronicles 20:7, *NIV*).

Definition: '*Ahab* (aw-hab') [157]; or '*aheb* (aw-habe') a primitive root; to have affection for (sexually or otherwise): – (be-) love (-d, -ly, -r), like, friend. (S)

Jehoshaphat spoke these words when the armies of Ammon, Moab and Mount Seir came against Judah. Those warring nations had been spared destruction in Moses' day (see Deuteronomy 2, Numbers 20:21). Greatly outnumbered, there seemed to be nothing Jehoshaphat could do . . . until he remembered that Jehovah was a friend to Abraham.

To be a friend meant more in those days than it does today. It was a covenant term of endearment that bound those involved together as one. If the Israelites were facing a foe, then God was bound by His friendship to intervene.

The Lord told Jehoshaphat to gather his army against the enemy and wait on the Lord. They were told they would not even have to fight, "for the battle is not yours, but God's" (2 Chronicles 20:15, *NKJV*). They sent praisers to praise and singers to sing, "Praise the Lord, for His mercy endures forever" (v. 21, *NKJV*).

Do you know God as your friend? Are you as certain of His love and care as Jehoshaphat was? He was victorious because he knew that nothing could come against him unless it first came through his Friend.

> Since, then, you have been raised with Christ, set your hearts on things above, where Christ is seated at the right hand of God. Set your minds on things above, not on earthly things. For you died, and your life is now hidden with Christ in God (Colossians 3:1-3, *NIV*). (*See #149.*)

84. Voice of God – *Qowl*

"God thunders marvelously with *His voice*; He does great things which we cannot comprehend" (Job 37:5, *NKJV*).

> **Definition:** *Qowl*, (kole) [6963]; or *qol* (kole); from an unused root meaning to call aloud; a voice or sound: – + aloud, bleating, crackling, cry (+ out), fame, lightness, lowing, noise, + hold peace, [pro-] claim, proclamation, + sing, sound, + spark, thunder (-ing), voice, + yell." (S)

Jesus is the Voice of God, the speaking part of the Godhead. He spoke worlds into being (John 1:1-3) and light into existence (Genesis 1:3). He has been speaking to creation on behalf of His Father since before the beginning of time and He is still speaking today.

The Son of God

His Hebrew Names In

THE PSALMS – SONG
OF SOLOMON

---

85. Anointed – *Mashiyach*

"The kings of the earth set themselves, and the rulers take counsel together, against the Lord and against His *Anointed*, saying" (Psalm 2:2, *NKJV*).

> **Definition:** *Mashiyach* (maw-shee'-akh) [4899]; from *mashach*; anointed; usually a consecrated person (as a king, priest, or saint); specifically, the Messiah: – anointed, Messiah. (S)

Jesus walked in the fullness of God's three-fold anointing: He was an anointed prophet, priest and king. Since He was the Son of God, Jesus was not limited to these three functions, but He flowed comfortably in each of them. Jesus is known to all believers as King of kings (1 Timothy 6:15). He is our Great High Priest

(Hebrews 4:14). The Lord Jesus Christ has been, and will always be, the Great Prophet (Luke 7:16).

"The Spirit of the Lord is upon Me, because He has anointed Me to preach the gospel to the poor; He has sent Me to heal the brokenhearted, to proclaim liberty to the captives and recovery of sight to the blind, to set at liberty those who are oppressed; to proclaim the acceptable year of the Lord" (Luke 4:18, 19, *NKJV*). (*See #152, #164.*)

86. Shield – *Magen*

"But thou, O Lord, art *a shield* for me; my glory, and the lifter up of mine head" (Psalm 3:3).

> **Definition:** *Magen* (maw-gane') [4043]; also (in plural) feminine *meginnah* (meg-in-naw'); from *ganan*; a shield (i.e. the small one or buckler); figuratively, a protector; also the scaly hide of the crocodile: – X armed, buckler, defence, ruler, + scale, shield. (s)

On the cross, Jesus took Satan's best blows. He did it so that you and I might be protected from the punishment we deserved. Jesus came to earth to deliver us from the law of sin and death. He was our shield then, and He is our shield today.

When we hide behind Jesus and His work on the cross, we take refuge in the only hope we will ever have against such foes. Other scriptures speak of Jesus as our shield.

> After these things the word of the Lord came unto Abram in a vision, saying, Fear not, Abram: *I am thy shield*, and thy exceeding great reward (Genesis 15:1).

> Thou hast also given me the *shield of thy salvation*: and thy gentleness hath made me great (2 Samuel 22:36).

> Thou hast also given me *the shield of thy salvation*: and thy right hand hath holden me up, and thy gentleness hath made me great (Psalm 18:35).

> Our soul waiteth for the Lord: *he is our help and our shield* (Psalm 33:20).

> Behold, O *God our shield*, and look upon the face of thine anointed (Psalm 84:9).
>
> For the *Lord God is a sun and shield*: the Lord will give grace and glory: no good thing will he withhold from them that walk uprightly (Psalm 84:11).
>
> Every word of God is pure: *he is a shield* unto them that put their trust in him (Proverbs 30:5). (*See #52.*)

87. My Glory – *Kabowd*

"But thou, O Lord, art a shield for me; *my glory*, and the lifter up of mine head" (Psalm 3:3).

> **Definition:** *Kabowd* (kaw-bode') [3519]; rarely *kabod* (kaw-bode'); from *kabad*; properly, weight, but only figuratively in a good sense, splendor or copiousness: -glorious (-ly), glory, honor (-able). (S)

David wrote Psalm 3 while fleeing from his son, Absalom, who was trying to take the kingdom. We learned already that God was David's *shield*, now we see that God was also his *glory*.

The Hebrew word *kabod*, translated "glory," implies weight. The weight of God, His manifest presence, is what David claimed for his own. It was God's glory; but when it was imparted, David said it was his. This understanding made him an effective king and ruler over God's people.

"The Word became flesh and dwelt among us, and we beheld His glory, the glory as of the only begotten of the Father, full of grace and truth" (John 1:14, *NKJV*).

When we know Jesus with the same intimacy that David did, we understand that He imparts His weight of glory to everything we do in the name of Jesus!

"Jesus said to her, 'Did I not say to you that if you would believe you would see the glory of God?'" (John 11:40, *NKJV*). (*See #32, #91.*)

88. Lifter of My Head – *Ruwm Ro'sh*

"Thou, O Lord, art a shield for me; my glory, and the *lifter up of mine head*" (Psalm 3:3).

> **Definition:** *Ruwm* (room) [7311]; a primitive root; to be high actively, to rise or raise (in various applications, literally or figuratively): – bring up, exalt (self), extol, give, go up, haughty, heave (up), (be, lift up on, make on, set up on, too) high (-er, one), hold up, levy, lift (-er) up, (be) lofty, (X a-) loud, mount up, offer (up), + presumptuously, (be) promote (-ion), proud, set up, tall (-er), take (away, off, up), breed worms. (S)
>
> *Ro'sh* (roshe) [7218]; from an unused root apparently meaning to shake; the head (as most easily shaken), whether literal or figurative (in many applications, of place, time, rank, etc.): – band, beginning, captain, chapiter, chief (-est place, man, things), company, end, X every [man], excellent, first, forefront, ([be-]) head, height, (on) high (-est part, [priest]), X lead, X poor, principal, ruler, sum, top. (S)

While fleeing from his rogue son who was trying to take over the kingdom, David writes about Jesus, the "lifter of my head." I can imagine David wanting to hang his head in shame because this rebellious son, once his favorite, had orchestrated the murder of his own half-brother, Amnon, who had raped Tamar, his sister.

The palace intrigue and the continual battle for the king's favor in David's household are fascinating. His wives were jealous of each other, and his sons never knew the attention of a man who had neither the time nor the inclination to be an effective father and mentor.

Yet, David had an unusual relationship with God. He blew it as a father and a king, but he knew God in a way few have ever known Him. He was called a man after God's own heart, and in that respect we try to emulate him today.

89. Governor – *Mashal*

"For the kingdom is the Lord's: and he is the *governor* among the nations" (Psalm 22:28).

> **Definition:** *Mashal* (maw-shal') [4910]; a primitive root; to rule: – (have, make to have) dominion, governor, X indeed, reign, (bear, cause to, have) rule (-ing, -r), have power. (S)

The word *governor* denotes political and territorial rule. David had enough understanding of spiritual things to know that while he was king of Israel, Jesus was the true governor of all nations. David had a title of authority and responsibility, but Jesus was still in ultimate control. David was not truly sovereign in Israel, because he always submitted to the rule and authority of the Lord. (*See #80.*)

90. Lord Mighty in Battle – *Jehovah Gibbowr Milchamah*

"Who is this King of glory? The Lord strong and mighty, the *Lord mighty in battle*" (Psalm 24:8).

> **Definition:** *Gibbowr* (ghib-bore') [1368]; or (shortened) *gibbor* (ghib-bore'); intensive from the same as *geber*, powerful; by implication, warrior, tyrant: – champion, chief, X excel, giant, man, mighty (man, one), strong (man), valiant man. (S)
>
> *Milchamah* (mil-khaw-maw') [4421]; from *lacham* (in the sense of fighting); a battle (i.e. the engagement); generally, war (i.e. warfare): – battle, fight (-ing), war ([-rior]). (S)

David and Israel sang this psalm when the ark of the covenant was returned to Jerusalem and they danced before the Lord. Although God is omnipresent, He made His presence known in a special way in the ark, and the people considered it sacred and holy. For all practical purposes, the ark was the very presence of God to them. New Testament Christians are the ark of the covenant in the world today. Jesus lives in the hearts of all believers and where we go, His presence goes too.

Read the entire psalm once again. Remember that your heart must be lifted up for the King of Glory to come in. The Lord who is mighty in battle wants to take up His residence in your heart. Through you, He will make His presence known wherever you go. (*See #10, #11, #257, #291.*)

91. King of Glory – *Melek Kabowd*

"Lift up your heads, O you gates! And be lifted up, you everlasting doors! And the *King of glory* shall come in. Who is this *King of glory?* The Lord strong and mighty, The Lord mighty in battle. Lift up your heads, O you gates! Lift up, you everlasting doors! And the *King of glory* shall come in. Who is this *King of glory?* The Lord of hosts, He is the *King of glory.* Selah" (Psalm 24:7-10, *NKJV*).

> **Definition:** *Melek* (meh'-lek) [4428]; from *malak*; a king: – king, royal. (S)
>
> *Kabowd* (kaw-bode') [3519]; rarely *kabod* (kaw-bode'); from *kabad*; properly, weight, but only figuratively in a good sense, splendor or copiousness: -glorious (-ly), glory, honour (-able). (S)

Before, we saw this name related to the "triune God of the heavens and the earth," but in this passage it refers to the Son of God. Jesus, the Prince of Peace, is at the same time King of Glory.

The word *king* denotes royalty and sovereignty; the word *glory* implies weight or glorious presence. There is in God a presence, a weight, that can make a grown man fall on his face under His influence. Jesus does more than radiate glory, *He is the King of Glory.* His glory knocked Saul from his horse when he was riding to Damascus (see Acts 9:1-4). It was so strong when Solomon's temple was dedicated, the priests could not stand in the house of the Lord (see 1 Kings 8:10, 11).

The glory of our King was often manifested as a light or a cloud. A light drew Moses to the bush on the mountain (Exodus 3:2). Moses had to hide the visible reflection of this glory from the people by putting a veil on his face

(Exodus 34:29-35). A glorious cloud of glory filled the Tabernacle in the wilderness (Exodus 40:34, 35). A pillar of cloud by day and a pillar of fire (or glowing light) by night led the Israelites in the wilderness (Numbers 9:15-23). Over and over again the shimmering light of God's presence was clearly visible when God showed up. He truly is *the King of Glory.* (*See #32, #87, #206.*)

92. Guide Even to Death – *Nahag Muwth*

"For this is God, Our God forever and ever; He will be our *guide Even to death*" (Psalm 48:14, *NKJV*).

> **Definition:** *Nahag* (naw-hag') [5090]; a primitive root; to drive forth (a person, an animal or chariot), i.e. lead, carry away; reflexively, to proceed (i.e. impel or guide oneself); also (from the panting induced by effort), to sigh: – acquaint, bring (away), carry away, drive (away), lead (away, forth), (be) guide, lead (away, forth). (S)
>
> *Muwth* (mooth) [4192]; or *Muwth lab-ben* (mooth lab-bane'); from *muwth* and *ben* with the preposition and article interposed; "To die for the son", probably the title of a popular song: – death, *Muthlabben.* (S)

Psalm 48 was written by the sons of Korah, who rebelled against Moses in the wilderness. The families that joined with him in this rebellion were destroyed when the earth opened up (Numbers 16:31-35). Those who wrote this psalm stood with God and refused to let peer pressure and pride lead them astray.

> Jesus, our faithful guide, knows what death is. Because of the Resurrection, we face death without fear of the unknown.He who did not spare his own Son, but gave him up for us all . . . will he not also . . . graciously give us all things? Who will bring any charge against those whom God has chosen? It is God who justifies. Who is he that condemns? Christ Jesus, who died—more than that, who was raised to life—is at the right hand of God and is also interceding for us (Romans 8:32-34, *NIV*).

"O death, where is thy sting? O grave, where is thy victory? The sting of death is sin; and the strength of sin is the law. But thanks be to God, which giveth us the victory through our Lord Jesus Christ" (1 Corinthians 15:55-57).

> The death of Christ is the procuring cause of all the blessings men enjoy on earth. But specially it is the procuring cause of the actual salvation of all his people, together with all the means that lead thereto. It does not make their salvation merely possible, but certain (Matthew 18:11; Romans 5:10; 2 Corinthians 5:21; Galatians 1:4; 3:13; Ephesians 1:7; 2:16; Romans 8:32-35).

(*See #190, #10.*)

93. Strong Tower – *'Oz Migdal*

"Thou hast been a shelter for me, and *a strong tower* from the enemy" (Psalm 61:3).

> **Definition:** '*Oz* (oze) [5797]; or (fully) '*owz* (oze); from '*azaz*; strength in various applications (force, security, majesty, praise): – boldness, loud, might, power, strength, strong. (S)
>
> *Migdal* (mig-dawl') [4026]; also (in plural) feminine *migdalah* (mig-daw- law'); from *gadal*; a tower (from its size or height); by analogy, a rostrum; figuratively, a (pyramidal) bed of flowers: – castle, flower, tower. (S)

Jesus, our "strong, forceful, secure, majestic and praiseworthy–tower, rostrum or castle," is a shelter for the believer. The word "shelter" is from the Hebrew *machaceh* or *machceh* meaning "hope, a place of refuge, a shelter or a trust." Paul referred to this protection in 2 Corinthians 4:7-9,

> We have this treasure in earthen vessels, that the excellence of the power may be of God and not of us. We are hard pressed on every side, yet not crushed; we are perplexed, but not in despair; persecuted, but not forsaken; struck down, but not destroyed (*NKJV*).

The refuge God offers in His Son, Jesus Christ, is impenetrable. He is well able to keep His own. (*See #54, #97.*)

94. God's Firstborn – *Bekowr*

"Also I will make him *my firstborn*, higher than the kings of the earth" (Psalm 89:27).

> **Definition:** *Bekowr* (bek-ore') [1060]; from *bakar*, first-born; hence, chief: – eldest (son), firstborn (-ling). (S)

To the Hebrews, the word *firstborn* was more than "the eldest sibling." To call someone "firstborn" always spoke of legal rights, inheritance and patriarchal authority. Jesus was, and is, the firstborn Son of Almighty God. As such, He holds a special relationship with the Father.

The most significant result is that we become joint heirs with Christ when we allow Him to become our Lord. The firstborn received a larger inheritance than other members of the family and when he died, his inheritance went to his offspring.

All things in heaven and earth have been placed under Jesus' rule and dominion. When we put our faith in Him, we become heirs to this inheritance, and coheirs with Him in all the Father gives. (*See #201.*)

95. Head Stone of the Corner – *Ro'sh Pinnah*

"The stone which the builders refused is become the *head stone of the corner*" (Psalm 118:22).

> **Definition:** *Ro'sh* (roshe) [7218]; from an unused root apparently meaning to shake; the head (as most easily shaken), whether literal or figurative (in many applications, of place, time, rank, itc.): – band, beginning, captain, chapter, chief (-est place, man, things), company, end, X every [man], excellent, first, forefront, ([be-]) head, height, (on) high (-est part, [priest]), X lead, X poor, principal, ruler, sum, top. (S)

Pinnah (pin-naw') [6438]; feminine of *pen*; an angle; by implication, a pinnacle; figuratively, a chieftain: – bulwark, chief, corner, stay, tower. (S)

Look at the masonry work around arched doorways and windows and you will notice a "keystone" in the center of the arch. This is the stone that holds everything else together. All of the other stones in an arch lean on the keystone, and the relative position of each stone is determined by the mason to achieve maximum strength and a pleasant appearance.

Jesus is our headstone of the corner (or keystone). He is the One for whom all things have been made; in Him we live and move and have our being. This verse tells us that the keystone we must look for is the One whom the world has rejected.

Jesus is the glue that holds everything together. Everything on earth has value and function by its proximity to and purpose in Jesus Christ. (*See #114.*)

96. Keeper – *Shamar*

"The Lord is your *keeper*; the Lord is your shade at your right hand" (Psalm 121:5, *NKJV*).

Definition: *Shamar* (shaw-mar') [8104]; a primitive root; properly, to hedge about (as with thorns), i.e. guard; generally, to protect, attend to, etc.: – beware, be circumspect, take heed (toself), keep (-erself,), mark, look narrowly, observe, preserve, regard, reserve, save (self), sure, (that lay) wait (for), watch (-man). (S)

In Old English, a *keep* was a specific place within the walls of a castle where the guards stayed who had charge over the gates. No one could go in or out of a castle without going past the *keep.* The Lord is our "Keep." No one has access to the inside of the Tabernacle of God (the hearts of His people) without first getting past the Keep. David did not look to the hilltops, the high places or the temples for his help. Instead, he went to the One who made the hilltops and high places, Jehovah.

97. Shade at Thy Right Hand – *Tsel Yamiyn Yad*

"The Lord is thy keeper: the Lord is *thy shade upon thy right hand*" (Psalm 121:5).

> **Definition:** *Tsel* (tsale) [6738]; from *tsalal*; shade, whether literal or figurative: – defence, shade (-ow).
>
> *Yamiyn* (yaw-meen') [3225]; from *yaman*; the right hand or side (leg, eye) of a person or other object (as the stronger and more dexterous); locally, the south: – + left-handed, right (hand, side), south. (S)
>
> *Yad* (yawd) [3027]; a primitive word; a hand (the open one [indicating power, means, direction, etc.], in distinction from *kapf*, the closed one); used (as noun, adverb, etc.) in a great variety of applications, both literally and figuratively, both proximate and remote [as follows]: – (+be) able, X about, + armholes, at, axletree, because of, beside, border, X bounty, + broad, [broken-] handed, X by, charge, coast, + consecrate, + creditor, custody, debt, dominion, X enough, + fellowship, force, X from, hand [-staves, -y work], X he, himself, X in, labor, + large, ledge, [left-] handed, means, X mine, ministry, near, X of, X order, ordinance, X our, parts, pain, power, X presumptuously, service, side, sore, state, stay, draw with strength, stroke, + swear, terror, X thee, X by them, X themselves, X thine own, X thou, through, X throwing, + thumb, times, X to, X under, X us, X wait on, [way-] side, where, + wide, X with (him, me, you), work, + yield, X yourselves. (S)

Jehovah is the shade, protection and hiding place to which the believer can run. In His presence a believer can avoid destructive exposure to the harmful influence of the evil one. God is the shade at "our" right hand, not "His" right hand. He is near and always there for us.

Psalm 121:5 *[5-6] The image of shade, a symbol of protection, is apt: God as shade protects from the harmful effects that ancients believed were caused by the sun and moon. (Psalm 16:8; Psalm 73:23), (*NAB Commentary*).

(*See #54, #93, #119.*)

98. Lovingkindness – *Checed*

"My *lovingkindness* and my fortress, my high tower and my deliverer, my shield and the One in whom I take refuge, who subdues my people under me" (Psalm 144:2, *NKJV*).

Definition: *Checed* (kheh'-sed) [2617]; from *chacad*; kind-ness; by implication (towards God) piety: rarely (by opposition) reproof, or (subject.) beauty: – favor, good deed (-liness, -ness), kindly, (loving-) kindness, merci-ful (kindness), mercy, pity, reproach, wicked thing. (S)

Lovingkindness speaks of God binding Himself to human-kind by a choice of His will. It means His intentions are only to do good toward us and to fulfill the promises of His cov-enant. In some versions this word is translated *mercies*.

It represents a legal contract with the Christian and is the binding force that David held to. Because of God's lovingkindness, he knew that God would always fulfill His promises and would forgive his trespasses and failures.

Jeremiah mentioned this character trait of God in Lamen-tations 3:22, 23, "The Lord's *lovingkindnesses* indeed never cease, For His compassions never fail. They are new every morning; Great is Thy faithfulness" (*NASB*). (*See #64.*)

99. Understanding – *Biynah*

"Counsel is mine, and sound wisdom: I am *understanding*; I have strength" (Proverbs 8:14).

Definition: *Biynah* (bee-naw') [998]; from *biyn*; understanding: – knowledge, meaning, X perfectly, understanding, wisdom. (S)

This verse clearly states that Jesus *is* understanding. Because of His incarnation, Jesus is familiar with all of our testings and temptations. This is comforting and reassuring to as we go through the trials of life.

Saying Jesus *is* understanding is different from saying He *has* understanding. When we receive Christ into our hearts, He dwells within us. Therefore if He is understanding, understanding dwells in us. All we need to understand about this life is found in the One who indwells us and empowers us.

In times of doubt and confusion, He is all the understanding we will ever need! (*See #276.*)

100. Rose of Sharon – *Chabatstseleth*

"I am the *rose of Sharon*, and the lily of the valleys" (Song of Solomon 2:1).

Definition: *Chabatstseleth* (khab-ats-tseh'-leth) [2261]; of uncertain derivation; probably meadow-saffron: – rose. (S)

Jesus is likened to the rose of Sharon in this passage. A tenacious flowering plant native to an area of Palestine, the rose of Sharon grows on rocks and in desolate areas of the desert. This is not a domesticated rose as we know them; it is a wild and small rose, yet the blossoms are delicate and beautiful to behold.

In many ways Jesus is like this flower. He is native to this area of Palestine and tenacious. He makes His presence known even in the most desolate places and does not know a heart in which He cannot grow. He cannot be domesticated or controlled by man. For all His strength and tenacity, He is still delicate in many ways and beautiful to behold. (*See #101.*)

101. Lily of the Valleys – *Shuwshan*

"I am the rose of Sharon, the *lily of the valleys*" (Song of Solomon 2:1).

> **Definition:** *Shuwshan* (shoo-shan') [7799]; or *showshan* (sho-shawn'); or *shoshan* (shoshawn'); and (feminine) *showshannah* (sho-shan-naw'); from *suws*; a lily (from its whiteness), as a flower of arch. ornament; also a (straight) trumpet (from the tubular shape): lily, *Shoshannim*.

This lily produces a white flower that blooms in the spring of the year. It grows from a bulb and returns annually if it is cared for properly. It is a symbol of purity and newness of life. Jesus embodies the very essence of purity and newness of life. We are reminded each spring, about the time this flower blooms, that Jesus offers a fresh new beginning to those who believe in Him.

As an ugly bulb is placed in the ground in anticipation of the coming of this flower, so Jesus was buried in a disfigured state and was said to have been uncomely in appearance. This is how Isaiah described Him in 53:2-5.

Although He was buried in humility and not pleasant to the eyes, He was raised in glory and magnificence. He was, and is, beautiful for all to look upon. (*See #100.*)

PART 3
The Son of God

His Hebrew Names In

ISAIAH

---

102. Branch – *Tsemach*

"In that day the *Branch* of the Lord will be beautiful and glorious, and the fruit of the earth will be the pride and the adornment of the survivors of Israel" (Isaiah 4:2, *NASB*).

"Thus says the Lord of hosts, 'Behold, a man whose name is *Branch*, for *He will branch* out from where He is; and He will build the temple of the Lord'" (Zechariah 6:12, *NASB*).

> **Definition:** *Tsemach* (tseh'-makh) [6780]; from *tsamach*; a sprout (usually concrete), literal or figurative: – branch, bud, that which (where) grew (upon), spring (-ing). (S)

A branch contains the life of the tree from which it projects; Jesus is the "branch of the Lord." There are many Old Testament prophesies of Jesus as a branch:

"And the vineyard which Your right hand has planted, and the *branch* that You made strong for Yourself" (Psalm 80:15, *NKJV*).

"There shall come forth a Rod from the stem of Jesse, and a *Branch* shall grow out of his roots" (Isaiah 11:1, *NKJV*).

"Behold, the days are coming," says the Lord, "That I will raise to David a *Branch of righteousness*; a King shall reign and prosper, and execute judgment and righteousness in the earth" (Jeremiah 23:5, *NKJV*).

"Hear, O Joshua, the high priest, you and your companions who sit before you, for they are a wondrous sign; for behold, I am bringing forth My Servant the *Branch*" (Zechariah 3:8, *NKJV*).

Jesus is the branch foretold by such prophesies. But if you take the concept a step further, we are also branches that have been grafted into the main branch—Jesus. The Lord said in John 15:5, "I am the vine, you are the branches. He who abides in Me, and I in him, bears much fruit; for without Me you can do nothing" (*NKJV*). As branches grafted into the true Vine, we need the life of Christ to flow in our veins.

God chose the people of Israel to bear the seed of Eve through the generations, fulfilling the prophecy of Genesis 3:15. But the very nation that carried the promise, rejected Jesus, so the Gentiles were grafted into the Tree of Life. Yet, Paul warns us in Romans 11:17-24 that we should avoid pride and arrogance concerning our place with the Lord. (*See #111, #129.*)

103. Immanuel – *'Immanuw'el*

"Therefore the Lord himself shall give you a sign; Behold, a virgin shall conceive, and bear a son, and shall call his name *Immanuel*" (Isaiah 7:14).

> **Definition:** '*Immanuw'el* (im-maw-noo-ale') [6005]; from '*im* and '*el* with a pronominal suffix inserted; with us (is) God; Immanuel, a type name of Isaiah's son: – Immanuel. (S)

Jesus is a sign to us now as He was at the time of His birth. Matthew proclaimed this prophecy to be fulfilled when he wrote, "Behold, the virgin shall be with child, and bear a Son, and they shall call His name Emmanuel, which is translated, God with us" (Matthew 1:23, *NKJV*). Matthew saw the significance of the Incarnation and presence of God with man. (*See #144.*)

104. Child – *Na'ar*

"For before the *child* shall know to refuse the evil, and choose the good, the land that thou abhorrest shall be forsaken of both her kings" (Isaiah 7:16).

> **Definition:** *Na'ar* (nah'-ar) [5288]; from *na'ar* (naw-ar'); (concretely) a boy (as active), from the age of infancy to adolescence; by implication, a servant; also (by inter-change of sex), a girl (of similar latitude in age): – babe, boy, child, damsel [from the margin], lad, servant, young (man). (S)

Luke 2:41-50 tells of Jesus traveling, at age 12, to Jerusalem with His parents to observe the Feast of Passover. These verses make it clear that even as a child Jesus was aware that He was the Son of God. Jesus was left behind in Jerusalem after His parents departed for their home town.

When his parents asked why He disappeared, Jesus answered, "'Why did you seek Me? Did you not know that I must be about My Father's business?'" (Luke 2:49, *NKJV*).

In light of this account, His childhood and young manhood are even more of a miracle. Knowing that He was the Son of God and Creator of all that is, Jesus submitted to the authority of an earthly father and mother who were as fallible as any earthly parents. He was a faithful Son to His earthly father and mother just as He was to His heavenly Father. "Jesus increased in wisdom and stature, and in favor with God and men" (Luke 2:52, *NKJV*). (*See #165, #167.*)

105. Wonderful – *Pele'*

"For unto us a child is born, unto us a son is given: and the government shall be upon his shoulder: and his name shall be called *Wonderful*, Counselor, The mighty God, The everlasting Father, The Prince of Peace" (Isaiah 9:6).

> **Definition:** *Pele'* (peh'-leh) [6382]; from *pala'*; a miracle: – marvellous thing, wonder (-ful, -fully). (S)
>
> *Pele'*- a wonder, a marvel (a) a wonder (extraordinary, hard to understand thing) (b) a wonder (used of God's acts of judgment and redemption) – (*Briggs Hebrew and English Lexicon*).

His name is full of wonder. Jesus is as wonderful today as He was on the first day of Creation. Jesus' wonderful power and omnipotence were displayed in creation. Today those same characteristics are manifest, but we also see His wonderful grace and mercy for us, His church.

Not only does Jesus do wonderful things for us, but His very essence is Wonderful. He is bigger than we ever thought Him to be. He is altogether more wonderful than we could ever imagine Him to be.

106. Counselor – *Ya'ats*

"For unto us a child is born, unto us a son is given: and the government shall be upon his shoulder: and his name shall be called Wonderful, *Counsellor*, The mighty God, The everlasting Father, The Prince of Peace" (Isaiah 9:6).

> **Definition:** *Ya'ats* (yaw-ats') [3289]; a primitive root; to advise; reflexively, to deliberate or resolve: – advertise, take advise, advise (well), consult, (give, take) counsel (-lor), determine, devise, guide, purpose. (S)

Jesus is our counselor. He is perfect in knowledge, in counsel and in guidance. When in need of advice, there is no better place to go than to Jesus in prayer. He can speak directly to our hearts and let us know His will for our lives.

David wrote in Psalm 37:4, "Delight yourself also in the Lord, and He shall give you the desires of your heart" (*NKJV*).

Isaiah wrote, "The Spirit of the Lord shall rest upon Him, the Spirit of wisdom and understanding, the Spirit of counsel and might, the Spirit of knowledge and of the fear of the Lord" (11:2, *NKJV*).

The same Spirit that raised Jesus from the dead dwells with believers today (see Ephesians 1:15-21). This means that the Spirit-filled believer today has access to the infinite wisdom and counsel of God through the indwelling Spirit of Christ. Jesus can speak to us through other members of His body. When you need a counselor, find a godly person, not just a wise or well-educated one.

When I have needed wise counsel, I have sought out the advice of my pastor and elders in the church. A woman in our church has a master's degree in counseling, which adds a whole new dimension to the help she gives people who seek her assistance. We prefer to hear from God for ourselves, but He will use others to reveal His will for our lives if we will let Him. (*See #286.*)

107. Mighty God – *El Gibbowr*

"For unto us a child is born, unto us a son is given: and the government shall be upon his shoulder: and his name shall be called Wonderful, Counsellor, the *mighty God*, the everlasting Father, the Prince of Peace" (Isaiah 9:6).

Definition: *Gibbowr* (ghib-bore') [1368]; or (shortened) *gibbor* (ghib-bore'); intensive from the same as *geber*, powerful; by implication, warrior, tyrant: champion, chief, X excel, giant, man, mighty (man, one), strong (man), valiant man. (S)

129

The Son of God, Jesus Christ, is the "mighty God" or the God who is a powerful warrior or champion. It is not the picture of a meek and mild child lying in a manger, but of One who is a mighty and victorious warrior. Many scriptures show that Jesus came to humans in power and might.

"[Israel] drank the same spiritual drink; for they drank from the spiritual rock that accompanied them, and that rock was Christ" (1 Corinthians 10:4, *NIV*).

"Though you already know all this, I want to remind you that the Lord delivered his people out of Egypt, but later destroyed those who did not believe" (Jude 1:5, *NIV*).

Jesus' life did not begin in Bethlehem, nor did His involvement with humanity. He has always been with God and is an active part of the Godhead. "Jesus Christ is the same yesterday, today, and forever" (Hebrews 13:8, *NKJV*).

According to Revelation, He will also return as a warrior (Revelation 19:11-21, *NIV*). (*See #10, #11, #90, #257, #291.*)

108. Everlasting Father – *'Ad 'Ab*

"For unto us a child is born, unto us a son is given: and the government shall be upon his shoulder: and his name shall be called Wonderful, Counsellor, the mighty God, the *everlasting Father*, the Prince of Peace" (Isaiah 9:6).

> **Definition:** *'Ad* (ad) [5703]; from 'adah; properly, a (peremptory) terminus, i.e. (by implication) duration, in the sense of advance or perpetuity (substantially as a noun, either with or without a preposition): – eternity, ever (-lasting, -more), old, perpetually, + world without end. (S)
>
> *'Ab* (awb) [1]; a primitive word; father, in a literal and immediate, or figurative and remote application): – chief, (fore-) father ([-less]), X patrimony, principal. Compare names in "Abi-". (S)

Although we normally think of this name in connection with Father God, there is a sense in which Jesus is also the everlasting Father. Jesus was instrumental in the creation of the heavens and the earth (John 1:1-4).

He was the One who brought reconciliation to humankind by His death and resurrection (2 Corinthians 5:18-21). Jesus is the One in whom we find salvation and newness of life (Acts 4:12). In Jesus' name a man or woman can be born again (John 3:1-21). Jesus is the author and perfecter of our faith (Hebrews 12:2). Jesus is the everlasting Father. (*See #68, #289.*)

109. Prince of Peace – *Sar Shalowm*

"For unto us a child is born, unto us a son is given: and the government shall be upon his shoulder: and his name shall be called Wonderful, Counsellor, the mighty God, the everlasting Father, the *Prince of Peace*" (Isaiah 9:6).

> **Definition:** *Sar* (sar) [8269]; from *sarar*; a head person (of any rank or class): – captain (that had rule), chief (captain), general, governor, keeper, lord, ([-taskmaster, prince (-ipal), ruler, steward. (S)
>
> *Shalowm* (shaw-lome') [7965]; or shalom (shaw-lome'); from *shalam*; safe, i.e. (figuratively) well, happy, friendly; also (abstractly) welfare, i.e. health, prosperity, peace: – X do, familiar, X fare, favour, + friend, X great, (good) health, (X perfect, such as be at) peace (-able, -ably), prosper (-ity, -ous), rest, safe (-ty), salute, welfare, (X all is, be) well, X wholly. (S)

Earlier, we studied *Jehovah-Shalom*, the Lord our peace. Now we see Jesus as Prince of peace. Only in His name can we find true peace. His peace is offered to all who come to Him and place their trust in Him.

Some trust in jobs for peace and security. Others invest in their children, believing their hopes for peace lie in them.

People have placed hope in temporal things throughout history. Unfortunately, jobs are eliminated by modernizing and downsizing. Children grow up and move away, sometimes without fulfilling our dreams for their future. Savings accounts fall short because of inflation, poor health or misguided investments.

But in all ages and circumstances, you can place your trust in Jesus. The Prince of Peace will never let you down. (*See #23, #213.*)

110. Rod Out of the Stem of Jesse – *Choter Geza' Yishay*

"And there shall come forth a *rod out of the stem of Jesse*, and a Branch shall grow out of his roots" (Isaiah 11:1).

> **Definition:** *Choter* (kho'-ter) [2415]; from an unused root of uncertain signification; a twig: – rod. (S)
>
> *Geza'* (geh'-zah) [1503]; from an unused root meaning to cut down (trees); the trunk or stump of a tree (as felled or as planted): – stem, stock. (S)
>
> *Yishay* (yee-shah'-ee) [3448]; by Aramaic '*Iyshay* (ee-shah'-ee); from the same as *yesh*; extant; *Jishai*, David's father: – Jesse. (S)

During the Exodus from Egypt, the people rebelled against Moses and Aaron by challenging their authority (see Numbers 16, 17). God confirmed Aaron as high priest by having the tribal leaders place their rods in the tabernacle and leave them overnight. By the next morning Aaron's rod had sprouted buds, produced blossoms and yielded ripe almonds (17:18). The rod of Aaron became a sign of God's authority and favor, representing the life and anointing of God.

Jesus is the Rod of the stem of Jesse. Nathan prophesied that the kings of Israel would come through David's family, thus the seed of God's promise was in his family and off-spring (2 Samuel 7:15-16). Jesus was the direct descendant of Jesse, David's father, making Jesse the stem on which God hinged history. But Jesus is the Rod that budded, flowered and bore fruit. (*See #193.*)

111. Root of Jesse – *Sheresh Yishay*

"And in that day there shall be a *root of Jesse*, which shall stand for an ensign of the people; to it shall the Gentiles seek: and his rest shall be glorious" (Isaiah 11:10).

> **Definition:** *Sheresh* (sheh'-resh) [8328]; from *sharash*; a root (literally or figuratively): – bottom, deep, heel, root. (S)
>
> *Yishay* (yee-shah'-ee) [3448]; by Aramaic *'Iyshay* (ee-shah'-ee); from the same as *Yesh*; extant; Jishai, David's father: – Jesse. (S)

This verse tells us that there shall be a *root of Jesse*. This root will stand as an *ensign* of the people. Ensign, in this instance, means a flag, a banner or a sign. Jesus will be with us in the new heavens and earth as a banner or standard, representing Jews and Gentiles, and we all shall find rest in Him.

The world experienced the first coming of Christ, and believers now await His Second Coming and the end of sin and death.

> The wolf will live with the lamb, the leopard will lie down with the goat, the calf and the lion and the yearling together; and a little child will lead them. The cow will feed with the bear, their young will lie down together, and the lion will eat straw like the ox. The infant will play near the hole of the cobra, and the young child put his hand into the viper's nest. They will neither harm nor destroy on all my holy mountain. . . . (Isaiah 11:6-9, *NIV*).

(*See #102, #129.*)

112. Banner to His People – *Nec*

"And in that day there shall be a Root of Jesse, who shall stand as a *banner to the people*; for the Gentiles shall seek Him, and His resting place shall be glorious" (Isaiah 11:10, *NKJV*).

> **Definition:** *Nec* (nace) [5251]; from *nacac*; a flag; also a sail; by implication, a flagstaff; generally a signal; figuratively, a token: – banner, pole, sail, (en-) sign, standard. (S)

> *Nec* – a standard, ensign, signal, sign:- banner, Banner, distinguishing mark, sail, signal, standard and warning. (*NASB Dictionary*)

Exodus 17:15 reveals God as *Jehovah-Nissi*, the Lord our banner. We studied this name in relation to the triune God. Isaiah prophesied that Jesus would also be a *banner* to His people. He is also a *warning* to the people of God. He is a *distinguishing mark* on His people. He is a *sign* to the world and a *standard* (or flag) under which His people live. (*See #18.*)

113. Tried Stone – *Bochan 'Eben*

"Therefore thus saith the Lord God, Behold, I lay in Zion for a foundation a stone, a *tried stone*, a precious corner stone, a sure foundation: he that believeth shall not make haste" (Isaiah 28:16).

> **Definition:** *Bochan* (bo'-khan) [976]; from *bachan*; trial: – tried. (S)

> *'Eben* (eh'-ben) [68]; from the root of *banah* through the meaning to build; a stone: – + carbuncle, + mason, + plummet, [chalk-, hail-, head-, sling-] stone (-ny), (divers) weight (-s). (S)

Jesus is likened to a rock that has been made, just as we would make a stone by forming concrete. Jesus was formed by the Master Builder. He has withstood the test of time, conquered death, and evercome everything Satan could throw against Him. To test metal, heat is applied to remove all the impurities. When Jesus stood the test, not even a hint of dross came to the surface. (*See #48, #51, #77, #81, #114, #208, #245, #246, #247.*)

114. Precious Corner Stone – *Yaqar Pinnah*

"Therefore thus saith the Lord God, Behold, I lay in Zion for a foundation a stone, a tried stone, *a precious corner stone*, a sure foundation: he that believeth shall not make haste" (Isaiah 28:16).

> **Definition:** *Yaqar* (yaw-kawr') [3368]; from *yaqar* (yaw-kar'); valuable (objective or subjective): - brightness, clear, costly, excellent, fat, honourable women, precious, reputation. (S)
>
> *Pinnah* (pin-naw') [6438]; feminine of *pen*; an angle; by implication, a pinnacle; figuratively, a chieftain: – bulwark, chief, corner, stay, tower. (S)

Jesus is not just any stone to be placed in God's tabernacle; He is precious, costly and excellent. His position is not incidental; Jesus is placed in such a location within the structure that were He removed, God's church would crumble and fall apart, just as removing the cornerstone would weaken the structure of a material building.

Jesus is the Cornerstone of God's whole Creation; it all rests on Him. By Christ all things were made and in Him everything is held together. (*See #48, #51, #77, #81, #95, #113, #208, #245, #246, #247.*)

115. Sure Foundation – *Yacad 'Eben*

"Therefore thus saith the Lord God, Behold, I lay in Zion for a foundation a stone, a tried stone, a precious corner stone, a *sure foundation*: he that believeth shall not make haste" (Isaiah 28:16).

Definition: *Yacad* (yaw-sad') [3245]; a primitive root; to set (literally or figuratively); intensively, to found; reflexively, to sit down together, i.e. settle, consult: – appoint, take counsel, establish, (lay the, lay for a) found (-ation), instruct, lay, ordain, set, X sure. (S)

God has built His Kingdom on the foundation of Jesus Christ, a sure foundation and immovable structure. Builders of skyscrapers begin by driving pilings into the ground until they reach the bedrock. When building a skyscraper, construction workers often spend more time on the foundation where the work cannot be seen than they do on the visible structure aboveground.

The Lord prepared Jesus as "the Lamb slain from the foundation of the world" (Revelation 13:8). He is the foundation upon which all of Christianity rests. Jesus said of Himself, "I am Alpha and Omega, the beginning and the ending, saith the Lord, which is, and which was, and which is to come, the Almighty" (Revelation 1:8).

116. Hiding Place From the Wind – *Machabe'*

"And a man shall be as an *hiding place from the wind*, and a covert from the tempest; as rivers of water in a dry place, as the shadow of a great rock in a weary land" (Isaiah 32:2).

Definition: *Machabe'* (makh-ab-ay') [4224]; or *machabo'* (makh-ab-o'); from *chaba'*; a refuge: – hiding (lurking) place. (S)

When seasonal winds batter the desert areas of Israel, I am told, the sand gets into everything. It is so fine and is driven by the wind so hard that little can be done to protect your belongings.

Panic can set in quickly, and some have been driven to do foolish things in their frenzied attempts to get away from the wind and sand.

Even in areas of the countryside where sand is not a problem, the combination of intense heat, blaring sunshine and a hot wind can be stifling and deadly. One must be able to get out of such conditions—find a place of shelter—in order to survive.

Jesus is such a shelter for the soul and spirit. He is always there for the believer to run to and hide in. In one of Satan's sandstorms of testing, when there is no place to get away from the penetrating irritation, Jesus is there. When the heat of trials seem unbearable, Jesus will be your refuge and shelter. (*See #97, #117.*)

117. Cover From the Tempest – *Cether*

"A man will be as a hiding place from the wind, and a *cover from the tempest,* as rivers of water in a dry place, as the shadow of a great rock in a weary land" (Isaiah 32:2, *NKJV*).

> **Definition:** *Cether* (say'-ther) [5643]; or (feminine) *cithrah* (Deuteronomy 32:38), (sith-raw'); from *cathar*; a cover (in a good or a bad, a literal or a figurative sense): – backbiting, covering, covert, X disguise [-th], hiding place, privily, protection, secret (-ly, place). (S)

I lived in monsoon rains in Vietnam. At times they would set in for weeks on end without letting up. We were not stationed in fine hotels or army barracks, we were in the mountains with no cover from the tempest.

The effects of long exposure to such elements were staggering. Many men actually lost the skin and callouses from their feet because of constant exposure to moisture and the inevitable fungi and infections. We prayed for a cover, but there was none. Jesus offers believers cover in the storms of life. When it seems we are caught in a monsoon season of conflicts and trials, He offers protection. When there is nowhere to go, Jesus is a shelter. He wants us to come to Him in times of need.

"*You are my hiding place*; You shall preserve me from trouble; You shall surround me with songs of deliverance. Selah" (Psalm 32:7, *NKJV*).

"*You are my hiding place* and my shield; I hope in Your word" (Psalm 119:114, *NKJV*). (*See #116.*)

118. Rivers of Water in a Dry Place – *Peleg Mayim Tsiyown*

"And a man shall be as an hiding place from the wind, and a covert from the tempest; as *rivers of water in a dry place*, as the shadow of a great rock in a weary land" (Isaiah 32:2).

> **Definition:** *Peleg* (peh'-leg) [6388]; from *palag*; a rill (i.e. small channel of water, as in irrigation): – river, stream. (S)
>
> *Mayim* [565b]; a primitive root; *waters, water*:- flood(1), loins(m)(1), pool(1), water(373), Water(5), watering(1), waterless*(1), waters(191) (*NASB Dictionary*).
>
> *Tsiyown* (tsee-yone') [6724]; from the same as *tsyiah*; a desert: – dry place. (S)

Jesus is not just a pool or puddle of stagnant water. He is likened to a river, supplying cool, moving water for the thirsty. Jesus can satisfy our thirst as no other fountain can.

In Vietnam I served as platoon leader of the 1st Platoon, Charley Company, 1st Battalion in the 506th Infantry Brigade, 101st Airborne Division. We were located in the mountainous regions of the north, near the demilitarized zone on one extremely hot and humid day. I took my platoon on a reconnaissance mission where we literally chopped our way through the jungle, as in old Tarzan movies.

A serious mistake almost cost me my life that day. I hadn't taken salt tablets for a week, and didn't understand the implications of this error in judgment. As platoon leader I stayed at the front of the unit at all times, while rotating the point man and the point squad. We worked through the jungle as the day wore on, and I began to feel lightheaded. I noticed I had stopped perspiring, and my condition got progressively worse. Eventually, even drinking water made no difference. I began to hallucinate as someone on drugs or a strange liqueur.

My radio telephone operator saw what was going on and had the medic to check me out, but there was nothing they could do in the jungle to bring relief. I was sure to suffer permanent brain damage or possible death if my body temperature was not brought down and the natural functions restored.

About that time we passed a small stream and found a pool of cool, moving water. They literally forced me into the water as soon as they could get me there. I stayed in the cool water for about 30 minutes, and the rest of the story is predictable. I was given a saline solution to drink and allowed to rest a while. Soon I returned to the mission at hand, my mind and body once again functioning as they should.

Jesus is like a stream of cool water for relief from the fiery trials of life. When it seems that there is no place to run or hide from the heat, Jesus is a pool of clear, cool water that brings relief and newness of life. (*See #180.*)

119. Shadow of a Great Rock – *Tsel Kabed Cela'*

"A man will be as a hiding place from the wind, and a cover from the tempest, as rivers of water in a dry place, as the *shadow of a great rock* in a weary land" (Isaiah 32:2, *NKJV*).

Definition: *Tsel* (tsale) [6738]; from *tsalal*; shade, whether literal or figurative: – defence, shade (-ow). (S)

Kabed (kaw-bade') [3515]; from *kabad*; heavy; figuratively in a good sense (numerous) or in a bad sense (severe, difficult, stupid): – (so) great, grievous, hard (-ened), (too) heavy (-ier), laden, much, slow, sore, thick. (S)

Cela' (seh'-lah) [5553]; from an unused root meaning to be lofty; a craggy rock, literally or figuratively (a fortress): – (ragged) rock, stone (-ny), strong hold. (S)

How can the Lord be light and shadow at the same time? Isaiah prophesied in Judah during the reigns of Uzziah, Jotham, Ahaz, and Hezekiah (Isaiah 1:1). From about 760 B.C. to 698 B.C., he was called to condemn the sins of Judah.

This was immediately following the Assyrian captivity of the northern kingdom and the prophet saw, by the Spirit, the inevitable fall of the southern kingdom. He tried to fend it off by warning the people, but the kings and people saw him as a troublemaker.

During these times Isaiah knew only one place to go for rest and refuge from the storms of life and from man's disapproval—that place was Jesus. Jesus was the shadow of a great rock in the life of this prophet, offering comfort and protection. (*See #97.*)

120. God's Elect – *Bachiyr*

"Behold my servant, whom I uphold; *mine elect*, in whom my soul delighteth; I have put my spirit upon him: he shall bring forth judgment to the Gentiles" (Isaiah 42:1).

Definition: *Bachiyr* [972] - chosen, a choice one, a chosen one, elect (of God) (*Briggs Hebrew and English Lexicon*).

Jesus is God's chosen One; He is God's elect. He was chosen before the foundation of the world (Revelation 13:8). Years before the events occurred, the prophets spoke of the works of God, including the prophecy of Jesus. No human could ever pass the test of purity and completeness that redemption required, so God *elected* to send His only Son, Jesus, to restore fellowship with His creation once again. (*See #171.*)

121. Light of the Gentiles – *'Owr Gowy*

"I the Lord have called thee in righteousness, and will hold thine hand, and will keep thee, and give thee for a covenant of the people, for a *light of the Gentiles*" (Isaiah 42:6).

> **Definition:** *'Owr* (ore) [216]; illumination or (concrete) luminary (in every sense, including lightning, happiness, etc.): – bright, clear, + day, light (-ning), morning, sun. (S)
>
> *Gowy* (go'ee) [1471]; rarely (shortened) goy (go'-ee); apparently from the same root as *gevah* (in the sense of massing); a foreign nation; hence, a Gentile; also (figuratively) a troop of animals, or a flight of locusts: – Gentile, heathen, nation, people. (S)

Non-Jewish people have hope for salvation and unity with the Father. Most Old Testament promises concerning the Messiah were made to the Jewish nation. Most messianic prophesies concerned the first coming of Christ and were fulfilled during His birth and life. Other prophecies, like this one, foresaw the time when His life would affect Gentiles as well.

All promises made to the nation of Israel are available to the church of Jesus Christ, which consists of Christians of all ethnic and national backgrounds. As a physical light draws moths and other insects, the light of Christ draws men and women from all nations to the Father. He truly is *a light of the Gentiles. (See #2, #63, #173, #184, #271.)*

122. Savior – *Yasha'*

"For I am the Lord thy God, the Holy One of Israel, thy Savior" (Isaiah 43:3).

> **Definition:** *Yasha'* (yaw-shah') [3467]; a primitive root; properly, to be open, wide or free, i.e. (by implication) to be safe; causatively, to free or succor: – X at all, avenging, defend, deliver (-er), help, preserve, rescue, be safe, bring (having) salvation, save (-iour), get victory. (S)

Salvation really began before Calvary, although that is where Christ made a way for you and me to have renewed fellowship with the Father. In all truth, Jesus has been the Savior since the beginning of time.

An example is Joshua 5:13-15, where God sent the commander of the army of the Lord to lead Israel into the Promised Land. (*See #56, #161, #181.*)

123. Redeemer of Israel – *Ga'al Yisra'el*

"Thus says the Lord, the *Redeemer of Israel*, and its Holy One, to the despised One, to the One abhorred by the nation, to the Servant of rulers, 'Kings shall see and arise, princes shall also bow down; because of the Lord who is faithful, the Holy One of Israel who has chosen You'" (Isaiah 49:7, *NASB*).

> **Definition:** *Ga'al* (gaw-al') [1350]; a primitive root, to redeem (according to the Oriental law of kinship), i.e. to be the next of kin (and as such to buy back a relative's property, marry his widow, etc.): – X in any wise, X at all, avenger, deliver, (do, perform the part of near, next) kinsfolk (-man), purchase, ransom, redeem (-er), revenger. (S)

The Redeemer of Israel was sent to all humankind, not just to the "pretty people" of this world.

He comes to the despised, abhorred servants, as well as to the socially acceptable. His redemption seeks to buy back those who have been taken captive by this world's system, both Jews and Gentiles alike. He welcomes all who will return to Him, just as the father welcomed the prodigal who returned in Luke 15:11-32.

Jesus is *Kinsman Redeemer* and *the Redeemer of Israel* for every person who will receive Him. The grace of God, in offering salvation as a free gift to all, has been misunderstood by those who have not thought through what it cost God. Although it is a free gift, salvation was not purchased cheaply. It cost God the blood of His only Son. (*See #26.*)

124. Holy One of Israel – *Qadowsh Yisra'el*

"Thus says the Lord, the Redeemer of Israel, and its Holy One, to the despised One, to the One abhorred by the nation, to the Servant of rulers, 'Kings shall see and arise, princes shall also bow down; because of the Lord who is faithful, the *Holy One of Israel* who has chosen You'" (Isaiah 49:7, *NASB*).

> **Definition:** *Qadowsh* (kaw-doshe') [6918]; or *qadosh* (kaw-doshe'); from *kadash*; sacred (ceremonially or morally); (as noun) God (by eminence), an angel, a saint, a sanctuary: – holy (One), saint. (S)

To be holy is to be set apart by God and for God. Implements used in Moses' Tabernacle and David's Temple were set apart at the time of their creation for use by God. Priests and Levites were set apart for God's service.

In the same way, Jesus was set apart for the purpose of redeeming humankind. He was set apart before the Creation, and He was also set apart while He was in the flesh. He was without sin and above reproach in every area of His life.

Our Lord faced crucifixion and death, and did not fear Satan because Satan had no legal right to hold Him or punish Him. Jesus Christ was and is the Holy One of Israel. (*See #156, #295.*)

125. Arm of the Lord – *Zerowa' Yehovih*

"Awake, awake, put on strength, O *arm of the Lord*; awake as in the days of old, the generations of long ago. Was it not Thou who cut Rahab in pieces, who pierced the dragon?" (Isaiah 51:9, *NASB*).

> **Definition:** *Zerowa'* (zer-o'-ah) [2220]; or (shortened) *zeroa'* (zer-o'-ah); and (feminine) *zerow' ah* (zer-o-aw'); or *zero' ah* (zer-o-aw'); from *zara'*; the arm (as stretched out), or (of animals) the foreleg; figuratively, force: – arm, + help, mighty, power, shoulder, strength. (S)

Yehovih (yeh-ho-vee') [3069]; a variation of *Yehovah* [used after '*Adonay*, and pronounced by Jews as '*Elohiym*, in order to prevent the repetition of the same sound, since they elsewhere pronounce *Yehovah* as 'Adonay]: – God. (S)

The *arm of the Lord* could have several allegorical meanings. We hold weapons with our arm when we go to war. With it we embrace loved ones. We extend the arm in greeting. We use it in the workplace to earn a living and to determine our value to others. We vote by lifting an arm. We raise a hand if we know the answer to questions at school.

Arms extended toward the heavens denotes praise and adoration of God during times of worship. Isaiah saw Jesus, the coming Messiah, as the arm of the Lord.

Isaiah described Jesus as an "arm of the Lord." This is called an *anthropomorphism*. The *Life Application Study Bible* defines anthropomorphisms as "figures of speech, which attribute human forms, acts and affections to God."

God is a spirit (John 4:24), but to help us understand the Eternal One and His ways, the Bible often depicts His characteristics and activities in human terms.

Thus we read of God's ear (Psalm 31:2), His breath (33:6), His voice (Ezekiel 1:24), His tongue/speech (Habakkuk 1:13), His eyes/ears (1 Peter 3:12) and His chariot (Psalm 68:17). In Exodus 2:24, He hears and remembers; in Psalm 94:9, He sees and hears; and in Ezekiel 1:28, He speaks.

God is pictured as laughing (Psalm 2:4), sleeping (Psalm 78:65), grieving (Hebrews 3:10), wondering in amazement (Isaiah 59:16), and confirming His promises with oaths (Hebrews 6:17). He even walks in space (Job 22:14).

God not only remembers (Isaiah 63:11), but He deliberately forgets (Isaiah 43:25). He memorializes His promises

(Genesis 9:16), reasons (Isaiah 1:18), understands (Psalm 147:5) and wills (Romans 9:19). He rests (Hebrews 4:4), although He never faints or gets tired (Isaiah 40:28).

126. Man of Sorrows – *'Iysh Mak'ob*

"He is despised and rejected of men; a *man of sorrows*, and acquainted with grief: and we hid as it were our faces from him; he was despised, and we esteemed him not" (Isaiah 53:3).

> **Definition:** *'Iysh* (eesh) [376]; contracted for *'enowsh* [or perhaps rather from an unused root meaning to be extant]; a man as an individual or a male person; often used as an adjunct to a more definite term (and in such cases frequently not expressed in translation): – also, another, any (man), a certain, + champion, consent, each, every (one), fellow, [foot-, husband-] man, [good-, great, mighty) man, he, high (degree), him (that is), husband, man [-kind], + none, one, people, person, + steward, what (man) soever, whoso (-ever), worthy. Compare *'ishshah*. (S)
>
> *Mak'ob* (mak-obe') [4341]; sometimes mak'owb (mak-obe'); also (feminine Isaiah 53:3) mak'obah (mak-o-baw'); from *ka'ab*; anguish or (figuratively) affliction: – grief, pain, sorrow. (S)

Our Lord left the joys of heaven to become the Man of Sorrows. Jesus suffered rejection when his own friends and neighbors failed to believe in Him. He watched John and Peter work their way around the courtyard of Caiaphas to see His trial, then refuse to make their presence known when given the opportunity to defend Him (Matthew 26:57-75). Whipped, punched and beaten, Jesus bore the excruciating pain, suffered terrible thirst and watched those who hanged Him, gamble for His clothing.

Crucified prisoners usually suffocated after many hours of torture. Jesus spent six hours on the cross, awaiting the scriptural fulfillment of references about His death, then He gave up His Spirit. Consider this: "Looking unto Jesus the author and finisher of our faith; who *for the joy that was set before him endured the cross*, despising the shame, and is set down at the right hand of the throne of God" (Hebrews 12:2).

127. Righteous Servant – *Tsaddiyq 'Ebed*

"He shall see of the travail of his soul, and shall be satisfied: by his knowledge shall my *righteous servant* justify many; for he shall bear their iniquities" (Isaiah 53:11).

> **Definition:** *Tsaddiyq* (tsad-deek') [6662]; from *tsadaq*; just: – just, lawful, righteous (man). (S)
>
> *'Ebed* (eh'-bed) [5650]; from '*abad*; a servant: – X bondage, bondman, [bond-] servant, (man-) servant. (S)

The Hebrew word, *Ebed*, translated "servant," means that He was a "bond" servant. In those times if a servant decided he did not wish to be released from the household of his master, he could ask to become a bond slave.

This required a public statement of chosen servitude, made while away from the influence of the master. No duress or force could be applied which might influence such a decision. When the authorities determined that the servant's desires were valid, they would drive an awl through the man's ear, pinning him to the door post of his master's house. This identified him as a bond slave—one who voluntarily gave himself to be a servant.

Bond slave convincingly describes our Lord and Savior, Jesus Christ. He came voluntarily, choosing a positiong of service to humankind, willingly giving Himself to all who would receive Him. He was pinned to a tree. When He would convince Thomas who He was, He showed the doubting disciple His scars—the nails in His hands and feet. (See *#150*.)

PART 3
The Son of God

Hebrew Names In

JEREMIAH – MALACHI

---

128. Balm in Gilead – *Tseriy*

"Is there no *balm in Gilead*; is there no physician there? why then is not the health of the daughter of my people recovered?" (Jeremiah 8:22).

> **Definition:** *Tseriy* (tser-ee') [6875]; or *tsoriy* (tsor-ee');
> from an unused root meaning to crack [as by pressure],
> hence, to leak; distillation, i.e. balsam: – balm. (S)

Gilead was on the east side of the Jordan where Reuben, Gad and the half-tribe of Manasseh received their inheritance. Jeremiah was prophesying the fall of Judah and mourning for the people of Israel and Judah. He saw a time when the people would be hurting and suffering, yet resisting the very balm that offered them hope of healing and relief.

A balm is an ointment made by a crushing action. Often this type of ointment was contained in a jar that had to be broken to get to its contents. These hard-to-open vessels kept ointments from contamination or evaporation in the hostile climate of Israel's desert. A woman anointed Jesus' feet with perfume from an alabaster jar that was normally used for anointing the dead.

Jesus is such a balm. "Surely He has borne our griefs and carried our sorrows; yet we esteemed Him stricken, smitten by God, and afflicted. But He was wounded for our transgressions, He was bruised for our iniquities; the chastisement for our peace was upon Him, and by His stripes we are healed" (Isaiah 53:4, 5, *NKJV*).

Jesus' body was broken and His blood was shed, but His spirit was never destroyed. He said: "The thief does not come except to steal, and to kill, and to destroy. I have come that they may have life, and that they may have it more abundantly" (John 10:10, *NKJV*). Through the centuries the balm of Jesus' blood has been a source of life and healing to all who apply it to their lives. An Aftican-American spiritual we sang frequently a few years ago is based on this passage.

There Is a Balm in Gilead

Sometimes I feel discouraged, And think my work's in vain,
But then the Holy Spirit Revives my soul again.

If you can't preach like Peter, If you can't pray like Paul,
Just tell the love of Jesus, And say He died for all.

There is a balm in Gilead To make the wounded whole;
There is a balm in Gilead To heal the sin-sick soul.

(*See #17, #68.*)

129. Righteous Branch – *Tsaddiyq Tsemach*

"Behold, the days come, saith the Lord, that I will raise unto David a *righteous Branch*, and a King shall reign and prosper, and shall execute judgment and justice in the earth" (Jeremiah 23:5).

Definition: *Tsaddiyq* (tsad-deek') [6662]; from *tsadaq*; just: – just, lawful, righteous (man). (S)

Tsemach (tseh'-makh) [6780]; from *tsamach*; a sprout (usually concrete), literal or figurative: – branch, bud, that which (where) grew (upon), spring (-ing). (S)

Jesus, the righteous branch, is the tree of life in Eden's garden. His roots go deep and His life is available to all. The word *branch* speaks of newness of life, budding and springing forth. Eat the fruit of the Tree of Life today for everlasting life forever. Jesus offers and gives a quality to life that is to be desired. (*See #102, #111.*)

130. Resting Place – *Rebets*

"My people hath been lost sheep: their shepherds have caused them to go astray, they have turned them away on the mountains: they have gone from mountain to hill, they have forgotten their *restingplace*" (Jeremiah 50:6).

Definition: *Rebets* (reh'-bets) [7258]; from *rabats*; a couch or place of repose: – where each lay, lie down in, resting place. (S)

Jesus is a resting place to those who come to Him. He is a place of repose where the weary can find true rest and protection. Jesus makes an offer no Christian should ever refuse:

Come to Me, all you who labor and are heavy laden, and I will give you rest. Take My yoke upon you and learn from Me, for I am gentle and lowly in heart, and you will find rest for your souls. For My yoke *is* easy and My burden is light (Matthew 11:28-30, *NKJV*).

Why not accept Jesus' offer? The Lord has not changed, nor will He in the future. He wants us to find rest in Him and be released from the guilt and shame the world heaps on us. Paul saw Jesus as a resting place from the law. He said we were saved by grace, not by works (see Ephesians 2:8, 9). If works couldn't save us, then works can't keep us. (See Galatians 3:1-9).

Both Jeremiah 31:31-34 and Ezekiel 36:24-27 tell us that God is able to place His law in the hearts of His people, and the desire for obedience in the minds of believers. He truly is our resting place. (*See #39.*)

131. Prince of Princes – *Sar Sar*

"Through his cunning He shall cause deceit to prosper under his rule; and he shall exalt himself in his heart. He shall destroy many in their prosperity. He shall even rise against the *Prince of princes*; but he shall be broken without human means" (Daniel 8:25, *NKJV*).

> **Definition:** *Sar* (sar) [8269]; from *sarar*; a head person (of any rank or class): – captain (that had rule), chief (captain), general, governor, keeper, lord, ([-taskmaster], prince (-ipal), ruler, steward. (S)

Daniel became a captive of Nebuchadnezzar, king of Babylon, around 606 B.C. In Babylon, he was instructed in all the wisdom of the Chaldeans, along with Shadrach, Meshach and Abednego. Much has been written about Daniel's prophetic visions and dreams, many of which were fulfilled during his lifetime. The remainder will be fulfilled in the last days of this world system.

During Daniel's lifetime, Babylon fell to the Persian Empire. The Medes and Persians set up princes and satraps around the empire. Daniel was one of three governors in authority over them, showing that he understood government and its chains of command.

Chapter 10 records the story of Daniel's fasting and praying for three weeks. Afterwards, an angel visited him and told him that his prayers had been heard from the first day, "But the prince of the kingdom of Persia withstood me twenty-one days" (Daniel 10:13, *NKJV*). Michael, one of the "chief princes," came to help the lesser angel fight off the prince of Persia.

This helps us to understand Daniel's meaning when he refers to Jesus as the "Prince of princes." The prophet saw a chain of command including worldly kings, princes, satraps and governors. He also saw the spiritual equivalents of each. When he called Jesus the Prince of princes, he was affirming the omnipotence and total sovereignty of God. Daniel saw the Lord as the absolute ruler over heaven and earth. (*See #255.*)

132. Messiah the Prince – *Mashiyach Nagiyd*

"Know therefore and understand, that from the going forth of the commandment to restore and to build Jerusalem unto the *Messiah the Prince* shall be seven weeks, and threescore and two weeks: the street shall be built again, and the wall, even in troublous times" (Daniel 9:25).

> **Definition:** *Mashiyach* (maw-shee'-akh) [4899]; from *mashach*; anointed; usually a consecrated person (as a king, priest, or saint); specifically, the Messiah: – anointed, Messiah. (S)
>
> *Nagiyd* (naw-gheed') [5057]; or *nagid* (naw-gheed'); from *nagad*, a commander (as occupying the front), civil, military or religious; generally (abstractly, plural), honorable themes: – captain, chief, excellent thing, (chief) governor, leader, noble, prince, (chief) ruler. (S)

Throughout the Old Testament, men of God were anointed for priestly, prophetic and kingly duties. It was common for a ram's horn full of olive oil to be poured over the head of the person so called by God. Some classic examples are . . .

Priestly Anointing: "And the holy garments of Aaron shall be his sons' after him, to be anointed in them and to be consecrated in them" (Exodus 29:29, *NKJV*).

Kingly Anointing: "So Samuel took the horn of oil and anointed him in the presence of his brothers, and from that day on the Spirit of the Lord came upon David in power" (1 Samuel 16:13, *NIV*).

151

Prophetic Anointing: "Also, anoint Jehu son of Nimshi king over Israel, and anoint Elisha son of Shaphat from Abel Meholah to succeed you as prophet" (1 Kings 19:16, *NIV*).

The Greek word *Christos* (or Christ) has the same meaning as the Hebrew word *Messiah*. Jesus was anointed as prophet, priest and king. He is the Great High Priest, ever interceding to the Father on behalf of His church. He is the greatest prophet who ever walked the face of the earth, and He spoke with authority on behalf of His Father. Jesus also holds the kingly anointing, as He is King of kings and Lord of lords.

We see the meaning of Jesus as the Anointed Prince in this scripture. As Prince, He holds the same anointings held by His Father, who is portrayed here as the King. There was a time in Jesus' life, just as it was for any other young prince, when He was in the charge of caretakers (Joseph and Mary). Jesus' mother and stepfather were given charge over Messiah the Prince as He was growing into His role as Sovereign Lord. What an awesome responsibility! (*See #122, #176.*)

133. Dew of Israel – *Tal Yisra'el*

"I will be as the *dew unto Israel*: he shall grow as the lily, and cast forth his roots as Lebanon" (Hosea 14:5).

> **Definition:** *Tal* [378b]; from an unused word; night mist, dew:- dew (31) (S).
>
> *Yisra'el* (yis-raw-ale') [3478]; from *sarah* and '*el*; he will rule as God; Jisrael, a symbolical name of Jacob; also (typically) of his posterity: - Israel. (S)

In desert areas few streams water the land. Only seasonal rains bring relief from the summer drought. At night, however, dew forms on the surface of the earth to bring a small ration of water to all the plants and soil. "A mist went up from the earth and watered the whole face of the ground"

(Genesis 2:6, *NKJV*). The animals received this moisture by grazing the grasses and plants. Dew was all that stood between life and death during the frequent dry seasons encountered in this climate. Today, deep wells and irrigation systems bring life where it would not be possible otherwise, but in Bible days this was not the case.

See the obvious analogy? Jesus was as important and necessary to Israel as the dew was to the plants in the desert.

Hosea said that Israel would grow and flourish as the lily of the valley common to the area. This lily has a large bulb to hold and store the moisture it receives from the dew that waters it. The heat and the brightness of the sun would wither the lily anc cause it to die, without the daily ration of water the dew provided.

In John 4:10, Jesus refers to Himself as living water; and in John 14:6, He calls Himself the way, the truth and the life. Without the life of Christ flowing in us, we too would wither and die. We must appropriate our daily ration of the *Dew of Israel* to survive and thrive in His kingdom on earth.

134. Breaker – *Parats*

"*The breaker* is come up before them: they have broken up, and have passed through the gate, and are gone out by it: and their king shall pass before them, and the Lord on the head of them" (Micah 2:13).

> **Definition:** *Parats* (paw-rats') [6555]; a primitive root; to break out (in many applications, direct and indirect, literal and figurative): – X abroad, (make a) breach, break (away, down, -er, forth, in, up), burst out, come (spread) abroad, compel, disperse, grow, increase, open, press, scatter, urge. (S)

Micah is speaking of the restoration of Israel as a nation after a season of testing and suffering due to the people's sin and hardness of heart. Micah calls the Lord the "breaker," or "the One who breaks open" (*NIV*). The Lord allowed the fall of Israel and the dispersion of its people, but the Lord would also break open the doors that held them captive. The latter part of this story is contained in the pages of Nehemiah, Ezra and Daniel.

So it is in our lives. The Lord who allows trials and sufferings to come against Christians will also break down the walls and doors that hold us in bondage as we submit to Him. Jesus is the breaker, we are not. No matter how good we are, no matter how strong we think ourselves to be, no matter how much we memorize and study the Word of God, it is the Lord who frees us from the bondage we find ourselves in. Jesus is the God of breakthroughs, and He desires to break through all the areas of bondage in the lives of believers.

135. Ruler in Israel – *Mashal Yisra'el*

"But thou, Bethlehem Ephratah, though thou be little among the thousands of Judah, yet out of thee shall he come forth unto me that is to be *ruler in Israel*; whose goings forth have been from of old, from everlasting" (Micah 5:2).

> **Definition:** *Mashal* (maw-shal') [4910]; a primitive root; to rule: – (have, make to have) dominion, governor, X indeed, reign, (bear, cause to, have) rule (-ing, -r), have power. (S)

Many people today are waiting for the future when Jesus will truly become Lord of His creation. I believe that when Jesus comes back to gather up His church, there will be a move of God unlike anything we have ever seen. Heaven is a physical place somewhere that God has prepared for His church. The church will reign and rule with Him and His Son, Jesus. Jesus is already the ruler in Israel. I am not talking about some "pie in the sky, by and by" promise. We, the church, are the New Jerusalem come to earth (Revelation 21:2), and Jesus rules in our hearts even now.

Yes, there will be a second coming of the Christ, which all of us should look forward to; but our hopes are not limited to the future. Jesus is Lord of lords and King of kings now. (*See #74.*)

136. Desire of All Nations – *Chemdah Kol Gowy*

"And I will shake all nations, and the *desire of all nations* shall come: and I will fill this house with glory, saith the Lord of hosts" (Haggai 2:7).

> **Definition:** *Chemdah* (khem-daw') [2532]; feminine of *chemed*; delight: – desire, goodly, pleasant, precious. *Hemdan.* (S)
>
> *Kol* (kole) [3605]; or (Jeremiah 33:8) *kowl* (kole); from *kalal*; properly, the whole; hence, all, any or every (in the singular only, but often in a plural sense): – (in) all (manner, [ye]), altogether, any (manner), enough, every (one, place, thing), howsoever, as many as, [no-] thing, ought, whatsoever, (the) whole, whoso (-ever). (S)
>
> *Gowy* (go'-ee) [1471]; rarely (shortened) *goy* (go'-ee); apparently from the same root as *geveh* (in the sense of massing); a foreign nation; hence, a Gentile; also (figuratively) a troop of animals, or a flight of locusts: – Gentile, heathen, nation, people. (S)

Many Christians have the common misconception that the world does not want to hear about Jesus. A vocal minority tells us we have no right to impose our religion on them, and too many of us have bought into the lie that Christianity is something for which we must apologize.

If the truth were known, most everyone you meet would like to believe that there is a God who really cares about him. The problem is that most have never been introduced to Jesus personally. Consequently, they have assumed that Christianity is just another religion, with its own set of rules and guidelines for membership, rejection or punishment.

The punishment we deserved was put on Jesus, and this is our hope for acceptance with the Father. At the moment of conversion, Jesus comes to dwell within the newborn believer. We become His body on earth.

Understand that Jesus is not a philosophy or teaching—He is a person. He saves us so that we can live His life through the members of His body. The good news is that "God so loved the world that He gave His only begotten Son, that whosoever believes in Him should not perish but have everlasting life" (John 3:16, *NKJV*). Jesus truly is the *desire of all nations.*

137. Wall of Fire – *Chowmah 'Esh*

"For I, saith the Lord, will be unto her a *wall of fire* round about, and will be the glory in the midst of her" (Zechariah 2:5).

> **Definition:** *Chowmah* (kho-maw') [2346]; feminine active participle of an unused root apparently meaning to join; a wall of protection: – wall, walled. (S)

> *'Esh* (aysh) [784]; a primitive word; fire (literally or figuratively): – burning, fiery, fire, flaming, hot. (S)

Major cities in Zechariah's day were built with large walls to protect the inhabitants. In Zechariah's vision, a measuring line was used to measure Jerusalem.

> Then I raised my eyes and looked, and behold, a man with a measuring line in his hand. So I said, "Where are you going?" And he said to me, "To measure Jerusalem, to see what is its width and what is its length." And there was the angel who talked with me, going out; and another angel was coming out to meet him, who said to him, "Run, speak to this young man, saying: 'Jerusalem shall be inhabited as towns without walls, because of the multitude of men and livestock in it. For I,' says the Lord, 'will be a *wall of fire* all around her, and I will be the glory in her midst'" (Zechariah 2:1-5, *NKJV*).

Through Zechariah, the Lord assured His people that they could rest within the walls of His presence without fear of an attacking enemy breaching His protection. We trust in what we can see with our eyes and build with our own hands; God tells us that we need to trust in Jesus, His wall of fire. God told Zechariah that He would be a wall of fire around them and allow His glory to be a testimony to all who would come in.

Everyone who comes to visit the New Jerusalem should know God's peace, protection, and presence in a special way. When visitors come into our meetings, they should sense His love and protection, and see His glory in our midst.

138. Builder of the Temple – *Banah Heykal*

"Thus says the Lord of hosts, saying: 'Behold, the Man whose name is the Branch! From His place He shall branch out, and *He shall build the temple of the Lord*'" (Zechariah 6:12, *NKJV*).

> **Definition:** *Banah* (baw-naw') [1129]; a primitive root; to build (literally and figuratively): – (begin to) build (-er), obtain children, make, repair, set (up), X surely. (S)
>
> *Heykal* (hay-kawl') [1964]; probably from *yakol* (in the sense of capacity); a large public building, such as a palace or temple: – palace, temple. (S)

The temple in Jerusalem was a type and shadow of the reality God desired for His people, Israel. When Adam fell in the Garden, a great separation occurred between God and man. God told Adam that in the day he ate of the tree of the knowledge of good and evil, he must die (see Genesis 2:17). The only atonement for sin was death.

For 4,000 years, God allowed animals' blood applied to His altar at certain seasons and times to atone for humans' sins. The blood of Jesus was the only sacrifice that could restore a divine relationship permanently between God and humanity.

Since man sinned, a man had to make it right. But no mortal could restore that relationship with the Father. So God became man through the incarnation of Jesus, and the way was secured once again for fellowship and relationship with the Father. This is how God built His true temple.

When the true temple was completed, the veil in the natural Temple that separated man from God was torn from top to bottom by God. He no longer allows anything to separate us from His presence except our own free wills. He does not interfere with the free will, and we decide whether to receive Him as Lord and Savior. God persists in calling us, but in the end we alone have the choice to receive or reject Him.

> Having been built on the foundation of the apostles and prophets, Jesus Christ Himself being the chief cornerstone, in whom the whole building, being joined together, grows into a holy temple in the Lord, in whom you also are being built together for a dwelling place of God in the Spirit (Ephesians 2:20-22, *NKJV*). (*See #233*.)

139. Messenger of the Covenant – *Mal'ak Beriyth*

"Behold, I will send my messenger, and he shall prepare the way before me: and the Lord, whom ye seek, shall suddenly come to his temple, even the *messenger of the covenant*, whom ye delight in: behold, he shall come, saith the Lord of hosts" (Malachi 3:1).

Definition: *Mal'ak* (mal-awk') [4397]; from an unused root meaning to dispatch as a deputy; a messenger; specifically, of God, i.e. an angel (also a prophet, priest or teacher): – ambassador, angel, king, messenger. (S)

Beriyth (ber-eeth') [1285]; from *barah* (in the sense of cutting [like *bara'*]); a compact (because made by passing between pieces of flesh): -confederacy, [con-] feder [-ate], covenant, league. (S)

The Bible records the covenants made between God and man. One can see within this context the progressive revelation of who God is. He initiates the covenants with His chosen ones, and Jesus is the messenger of the covenant. Jeremiah saw this.

> But this shall be the covenant that I will make with the house of Israel; After those days, saith the Lord, I will put my law in their inward parts, and write it in their hearts; and will be their God, and they shall be my people. And they shall teach no more every man his neighbour, and every man his brother, saying, Know the Lord: for they shall all know me, from the least of them unto the greatest of them, saith the Lord; for I will forgive their iniquity, and I will remember their sin no more (Jeremiah 31:33, 34).

When we believe on Jesus, He comes to live His life within us. Jesus is the *messenger of the covenant* that God makes with each believer. (*See #8.*)

140. Refiner – *Tsaraph*

"He will sit as a *refiner* and a purifier of silver; He will purify the sons of Levi, and purge them as gold and silver, that they may offer to the Lord an offering in righteousness" (Malachi 3:3, *NKJV*).

"The crucible for silver and the furnace for gold, but the Lord tests the heart" (Proverbs 17:3, *NIV*).

"The crucible for silver and the furnace for gold, but man is tested by the praise he receives" (Proverbs 27:21, *NIV*).

"Consider it pure joy, my brothers, whenever you face trials of many kinds, because you know that the testing of your faith develops perseverance" (James 1:2, 3, *NIV*).

Definition: *Tsaraph* (tsaw-raf') [6884]; a primitive root; to fuse (metal), i.e. refine (literally or figuratively): – cast, (re-) fine (-er), founder, goldsmith, melt, pure, purge away, try. (S)

159

Refine means "to reduce to a pure state, often used figuratively of moral cleansing" (*Holman's Bible Dictionary*). To refine a natural ore, you remove the soil and apply a combination of heat, chemicals and pressure to take away what you consider valuable from the rock around it. Different metals or minerals require different tests to separate them from the rock or dirt that contains them.

So it is with us. We are formed by God and placed in the world amid many types of spiritual soils and rocks. People in the Bible Belt are encrusted with a certain type of spiritual soil. Others are raised with another type of world surrounding them. But we all have been placed somewhere, and we must be spiritually cleansed from our environment before we can be pure. In His time and by His grace, we can be made new in Christ and be born again. When this happens, we are placed within His spiritual kingdom. (*See #141.*)

141. Purifier – *Taher*

"He will sit as a refiner and a *purifier* of silver; He will purify the sons of Levi, and purge them as gold and silver, that they may offer to the Lord an offering in righteousness" (Malachi 3:3, *NKJV*).

> **Definition:** *Taher* (taw-hare') [2891]; a primitive root; properly, to be bright; i.e. (by implication) to be pure (physical sound, clear, unadulterated; Levitically, uncontaminated; morally, innocent or holy): – be (make, makeself, pronounce) clean, cleanse (self), purge, purify (-ierself). (S)

Jesus refines us, making us pure and shiny with the glow of His glory. When Smith Wigglesworth he walked through a room or railroad car, it was said, people who had no clue who he was often fell on their faces, repenting of their sins. The purity and power of God in his life affected them.

Oh, that more of us would only allow God to purify us. Heat and pressure in the lives of believers purify and uncover impurities and imperfections. Silver is placed in the crucible for purification. Heat is applied to melt it down, and the impurities rise to the surface. The refiner then scoops off the dross or impurities and lets the metal cool. If the silver needs to be especially precious, this process may be repeated to further cleanse and purify it.

As fiery trials come to us, human nature discloses flaws and imperfections in our character. Once they are visible, we must allow God to draw off the dross. When I came to know Jesus as personal Lord and Savior, I knew my lifestyle was not pleasing to Him. Immediately He began to clean up my life. He sent the Holy Spirit to help me overcome evil habits and turn me from sin. As I walked with Him I found myself being transformed almost daily into His likeness.

Time and circumstances uncovered sins that were less obvious but more insidious—sins I would rather have left alone. Pride, bitterness, unforgiveness and arrogance surfaced. Wrongly, I thought it was my right to feel angry or bitter. But God would not let me hold to them. Like many people, I fought His dealings in certain areas of my life in the beginning. I "kept going around the mountain" instead of tunneling through it.

The Lord refines and purifies. He never gave up on me or relented in His dealings with me. He is still uncovering areas of my life that He wants to purify. As I allow God to deal with me and turn from my sinful ways, He forgives and purifies. "If we confess our sins, he is faithful and just and will forgive us our sins and purify us from all unrighteousness" (1 John 1:9, *NIV*).

The process of refining and purifying removes precious metal from the dirt and the dirt from the precious metal. It takes gold from the soil, then the dross from the gold. In the same way, God refined us by removing us from the world when we were born again. He purifies us by removing the world from us.

"For You, O God, have tested us; You have refined us as silver is refined. You brought us into the net; You laid affliction on our backs. You have caused men to ride over our heads; we went through fire and through water; but You brought us to rich fulfillment" (Psalm 66:10-12, *NKJV*). (*See #140.*)

142. Sun of Righteousness – *Shemesh Tsedaqah*

"But unto you that fear my name shall the *Sun of righteousness* arise with healing in his wings; and ye shall go forth, and grow up as calves of the stall" (Malachi 4:2).

> **Definition:** *Shemesh* (sheh'-mesh) [8121]; from an unused root meaning to be brilliant; the sun; by implication, the east; figuratively, a ray, i.e. (arch.) a notched battlement: – + east side (-ward), sun ([rising]), + west (-ward), window. See also *Beyth Shemesh.* (S)
>
> *Tsedaqah* (tsed-aw-kaw') [6666]; from *tsadaq*; rightness (abstractly), subjectively (rectitude), objectively (justice), morally (virtue) or figuratively (prosperity): – justice, moderately, right (-eous) (act, -ly, -ness). (S)

The light of the sun brings life and the movement of the sun marks the passage of time. Without heat and light from the sun, there would be no life on earth. The purity of the sun's rays can make a garden grow, or they can burn up a dry forest.

The last Old Testament name for our Lord Jesus is likened to the sun. This passage refers to the intents and desires of our hearts for His righteousness. The righteousness of our Lord can bring the light of understanding and conviction of sin to the holiest of saints and to the most wicked of sinners.

The intense righteousness of our Lord exposes sin within the believer, but He also sends the healing balm of Gilead to forgive and heal a sinsick soul. While His burning heat discloses our sins, He also comes with healing in His wings.

PART 3
The Son of God

His Greek Names in

MATTHEW

---

143. Jesus – *Iesous*

"And she shall bring forth a son, and thou shalt call his name *Jesus*: for he shall save his people from their sins" (Matthew 1:21).

> **Definition:** *Iesous* (ee-ay-sooce') [2424]; of Hebrew origin [*Iof*]; Jesus (i.e. *Jehoshua*), the name of our Lord and two (three) other Israelites: – Jesus. (S)

Some say that "Jesus" is the name of God in humility, "our Lord in blue jeans." I do not mean to sound sacrilegious, I am just saying that this name was used for our Lord while He was on earth as a carpenter's son. It was a common name in His time, and you still see it frequently used as a name in Spanish-speaking countries. Unbelievers use it as a common curse word. I marvel at how the name of Jesus is taken in vain so lightly by the media.

> And being found in appearance as a man, He humbled Himself and became obedient to the point of death, even the death of the cross. Therefore God also has highly exalted Him and given Him the name which is above every name, that at the name of Jesus every knee should bow, of those in heaven, and of those on earth, and of those under the earth, and that every tongue should confess that Jesus Christ is Lord, to the glory of God the Father (Philippians 2:8-11, *NKJV*).

Many people believe that Jesus was a real man, a mighty prophet, an anointed teacher and a leader of men. The Mormons, Jehovah's Witnesses and Muslims all agree with this, but only those who have received Him as their personal Savior know Him as Lord. You need to know Him as Lord if you expect to have live a fulfilled life on earth or enjoy eternal life in eternity. (*See #198.*)

144. Emmanuel – *Emmanouel*

"Behold, a virgin shall be with child, and shall bring forth a son, and they shall call his name *Emmanuel*, which being interpreted is, God with us" (Matthew 1:23).

> **Definition:** Emmanouel [1694]- *Emmanuel* = "God with us" the title applied to the Messiah, born of the virgin, Matthew 1:23, Isaiah 7:14, because Jesus was God united with man, and showed that God was dwelling with man." (S)

God with us! This is a title applied to Jesus, our Messiah. Since the fall of man in the Garden of Eden, God has been working out His plans to reunite Himself with His creation. When the Lord came to us as a man, this plan saw its fulfillment in Him. Jesus was, and still is, God's only provision for our fellowship with the eternal God. Jesus wants to come into our hearts and dwell with us. He wants to live His life through us in the world.

" 'For this reason a man shall leave his father and mother and be joined to his wife, and the two shall become one flesh.' This is a great mystery, but I speak concerning Christ and the church" (Ephesians 5:31, 32, *NKJV*). As a husband and wife are united in marriage, so God wants to unite with us now. Do not reject Him or turn away. Receive Jesus and you will know great peace and fulfillment.

When you allow Jesus to live His life in you, a new power is released in and upon your life that goes beyond your wildest dreams. Paul referred to this truth in Galatians 2:20: "I have been crucified with Christ; it is no longer I who live, but Christ lives in me; and the life which I now live in the flesh I live by faith in the Son of God, who loved me and gave Himself for me" (*NKJV*). (*See #103.*)

145. King of the Jews – *Basileus Ioudaios*

"Where is He who has been born *King of the Jews?* For we saw His star in the east, and have come to worship Him" (Matthew 2:2, *NASB*).

> **Definition:** *Basileus* - a leader of the people, a prince, a commander, a lord of the land, a king" (NTGEL).
>
> *Ioudaios* (ee-oo-dah'-yos) [2453]; from *Iouda* (in the sense of *Ioudas* as a country); Judaean, i.e. belonging to Jehudah: – Jew (-ess), of Judaea. (S)

The Bible is a record of God's establishing a king of His own lineage to rule over His chosen people. From the time He called Abram from Ur (see Genesis 11:31–12:5), He was establishing a people for Himself.

The Jews were God's chosen people (Deuteronomy 7:7, 8; Psalm 105:43), meaning that they had been chosen by God to bear the seed through whom the Savior of the world would come. They looked for a Savior who would make them a great nation and humble the nations around them. Instead, Jesus was a humble servant who desired a people from all the nations to be gathered to Him.

Jesus is King of the Jews, but the Jewish nation is no longer limited to those with the blood of Abraham flowing in their veins. Jesus rules over a nation of people from all backgrounds and lineages. The unifying factor among the people of God's kingdom is faith in the Lord Jesus Christ. (*See #223.*)

146. Nazarene – *Nazoraios*

"And he came and dwelt in a city called Nazareth: that it might be fulfilled which was spoken by the prophets, He shall be called a *Nazarene*" (Matthew 2:23).

> **Definition:** *Nazoraios* (nad-zo-rah'-yos) [3480]; from *Nazareth*; a *Nazoraean*, i.e. inhabitant of Nazareth; by extension, a Christian: – Nazarene, of Nazareth. (S)

This name seems insignificant when compared to some of the more popular revelations of God's names. Nazareth was a small, insignificant village west of the Sea of Galilee. Jesus' life was marked by small beginnings by all earthly standards. Joseph, His earthly father, raised Him as a carpenter's son.

The Lord grew up unnoticed by religious leaders or government rulers. Nobody even knew Jesus was there, until God called Him out to be baptized by John. Then God spoke audibly to those who were gathered at the Jordan River, acknowledging Jesus as His Son, in whom He was well pleased (Matthew 3:17).

The most significant thing about Nazareth, in this context, was its insignificance. It was not by accident that God chose to come to an unknown girl, Mary, and her betrothed spouse, Joseph. God's plan was for Jesus to come to earth through people who had no significance of their own.

Our Lord is a jealous God who will not share His glory with anyone. Neither man, woman, family, nation, city or town was going to get any credit for what God was would do through this unassuming Nazarene.

147. Son of Man – *Huios Anthropos*

"And Jesus saith unto him, The foxes have holes, and the birds of the air have nests; but the *Son of Man* hath not where to lay his head" (Matthew 8:20).

> **Definition:** *Huios* (hwee-os') [5207]; apparently a primary word; a "son" (sometimes of animals), used very widely of immediate, remote or figuratively, kinship: – child, foal, son. (S)
>
> *Anthropos* (anth'-ro-pos) [444]; from *aner* and *ops* (the countenance; from *optamonai*); man-faced, i.e. a human being: – certain, man. (S)

Sometimes I think it is easier to accept Jesus as the Son of God than as the Son of Man. Many Christians do not know why God had to send His Son to us as a man.

In the Garden of Eden, Adam sinned by disobeying God's command not to eat of the fruit from the tree. God had promised that, in the day Adam ate of the fruit, he would surely die (Genesis 2:17). When Adam ate the fruit, he knew he was disobeying God, but I do not think he knew what death meant.

Adam could not understand the concept of death, because there had been no death in the garden. Some have wondered about this passage, questioning whether God lied to Adam because Adam did not physically die then.

The death that occurred that day was in the relationship between Adam and God. Adam must have felt an awful sense of loss at no longer having close fellowship with his Father. The Garden story gives the first case of substitutionary atonement.

After partaking of the forbidden fruit, Adam and Eve found themselves naked. Nothing had changed in their appearances, but for the first time, shame and guilt compelled them to cover their nakedness. They chose to sew fig leaves together to make a covering for their bodies.

When God found them, however, He clothed them in tunics of skin (Genesis 3:20). Instead of Adam and Eve's dying for their sin, God took the life of an animal and covered human sin with its blood and human nakedness with its skin. In the Old Testament, this incident recurred again and again. God commanded animal sacrifice to atone for human sins. But the best that they could hope for was only a covering.

It would take an extraordinary Man to suffer the final punishment for not just one person, but all of humanity's sin. God made provision for a sacrifice in Jesus long before Adam fell, however. He had required all sacrifices made by the sons of Abraham to be animals without blemish.

When it came to finding a perfect man for the final sacrifice, none could be found, for "all have sinned and fall short of the glory of God" (Romans 3:23, *NKJV*). The only hope was for God himself to take the form of a man and become the perfect sacrifice for the sins of humankind.

Jesus came as the Son of Man, so that He could legally atone for the sins of humanity. At the cross, the justice of God and the mercy of God met, making a way once again for men and women to experience close fellowship with the Father. (*See #194.*)

148. Lord of the Harvest – *Kurios Therismos*

"Therefore pray the *Lord of the harvest* to send out laborers into His harvest" (Matthew 9:38, *NKJV*).

Definition: *Kurios* (koo'-ree-os) [2962]; from kuros (supremacy); supreme in authority, i.e. (as noun) controller;

by implication, Mr. (as a respectful title): – God, Lord, master, Sir. (S)

Therismos (ther-is-mos') [2326]; from *therizo*; reaping, i.e. the crop: – harvest. (S)

Jesus is master of the harvest. He sits in authority over the details of the harvest and the workers. We are not commanded to pray for the harvest; we are told to pray to the Lord *of* the harvest to send out workers *into* the harvest.

Jesus said, "No one can come to Me unless the Father who sent Me draws him; and I will raise him up at the last day" (John 6:44, *NKJV*). We are to witness to the lost, because God has said that redeemed humanity will participate in ruling the universe.

But nobody can come into His kingdom unless the Father draws him. "A man can receive nothing unless it has been given to him from heaven" (John 3:27, *NKJV*). Whether salvation or a ministry to the lost, unless God does the work it will not be done correctly and will lack His anointing.

149. Friend of Sinners – *Philos Hamartolos*

"The Son of man came eating and drinking, and they say, Behold a man gluttonous, and a winebibber, a *friend of publicans and sinners*. But wisdom is justified of her children" (Matthew 11:19).

Definition: *Philos* (fee'-los) [5384]; properly, dear, i.e. a friend; actively, fond, i.e. friendly (still as a noun, an associate, neighbor, etc.): – friend. (S)

Hamartolos [268] - devoted to sin, a sinner: a) not free from sin b) preeminently sinful, especially wicked 1) all wicked men 2) specifically used of men stained with certain definite vices or crimes: tax collectors, the heathen, pagans. (S)

Jesus was criticized for His involvement with the outcasts. The Lord ministered to more than the rich or influential who were considered acceptable to the religious people of the day, and the Pharisees had difficulty with Jesus' choice of companions. He was always a friend to those who were outcasts and of little value to the world. He knew that they were more likely to receive Him and His message of repentance, because they were in a place of need.

In reality the drug addict or alcoholic is more likely to see his need for salvation than one who carefully follows the law as the Pharisees did. At Matthew's house, the Pharisees asked Jesus why He ate with tax collectors and sinners. He answered, "Those who are well have no need of a physician, but those who are sick" (Matthew 9:12, *NKJV*). I pray that we may acquire the heart of God for the lost and needy. (*See #83.*)

150. God's Servant – *Pais*

"Behold *my servant*, whom I have chosen; my beloved, in whom my soul is well pleased: I will put my spirit upon him, and he shall shew judgment to the Gentiles" (Matthew 12:18).

> **Definition:** *Pais* (paheece) [3816]; perhaps from *paio*; a boy (as often beaten with impunity), or (by analogy,) a girl, and (genitive case) a child; specifically, a slave or servant (especially a minister to a king; and by eminence to God): – child, maid (-en), (man) servant, son, young man. (S)

Jesus was (is) God, but He was (is) God's servant as well. Jesus came to serve both God and humankind. He served God by obedience and loving service in submission to His Father. He served humankind by offering His life on Calvary as an atonement for sin.

The Lord could have called a legion of angels to fight for Him, but chose instead to go silently as a lamb to the slaughter. Jesus fulfilled every prophesy spoken concerning Him, including this one from Isaiah:

"Here is my servant, whom I have chosen, the one I love, in whom I delight; I will put my Spirit on him and he will proclaim justice to the nations. He will not quarrel or cry out; no one will hear his voice in the streets. A bruised reed he will not break, and a smoldering wick he will not snuff out, till he leads justice to victory. In his name the nations will put their hope" (Matthew 12:18-21, *NIV*).

A servant doesn't have the option of serving his own interests instead of his master's. A servant has to do the wishes of his master always, before he is allowed to even think about what he wants personally. Jesus spoke of this when He said,

Suppose one of you had a servant plowing or looking after the sheep. Would he say to the servant when he comes in from the field, "Come along now and sit down to eat"? Would he not rather say, "Prepare my supper, get yourself ready and wait on me while I eat and drink; after that you may eat and drink"? (Luke 17:7, 8, *NIV*).

Jesus was a willing and humble servant to His Father in everything He did in life. (*See #127.*)

151. God's Beloved – *Agapetos*

"Behold my servant, whom I have chosen; *my beloved*, in whom my soul is well pleased: I will put my spirit upon him, and he shall shew judgment to the Gentiles" (Matthew 12:18).

Definition: *Agapetos* - beloved, esteemed, dear, worthy of love. (S)

There are not enough words in the English language to effectively describe the love that God has for His Son, Jesus. God's love, *agape* in the Greek, is unmerited, undeserved, without repentance, unchangeable and greater than anything we have ever known of love or affection. This is the best humans can do in describing God's love for us. But it does nothing to explain His love for His Only Begotten Son.

"The Love Chapter," a favorite in the Bible, describes in human language the love that God is, and that He gives to those who receive Him.

> If I speak in the tongues of men and of angels, but have not love, I am only a resounding gong or a clanging cymbal. If I have the gift of prophecy and can fathom all mysteries and all knowledge, and if I have a faith that can move mountains, but have not love, I am nothing. If I give all I possess to the poor and surrender my body to the flames, but have not love, I gain nothing.
>
> Love is patient, love is kind. It does not envy, it does not boast, it is not proud. It is not rude, it is not self-seeking, it is not easily angered, it keeps no record of wrongs. Love does not delight in evil but rejoices with the truth. It always protects, always trusts, always hopes, always perseveres.
>
> Love never fails. But where there are prophecies, they will cease; where there are tongues, they will be stilled; where there is knowledge, it will pass away. For we know in part and we prophesy in part, but when perfection comes, the imperfect disappears. When I was a child, I talked like a child, I thought like a child, I reasoned like a child. When I became a man, I put childish ways behind me. Now we see but a poor reflection as in a mirror; then we shall see face to face. Now I know in part; then I shall know fully, even as I am fully known.
>
> And now these three remain: faith, hope and love. But the greatest of these is love" (1 Corinthians 13:1-13, *NIV*).

To say that Jesus is God's beloved means that He is the object of God's love in a special way. The Song of Songs (Songs of Solomon) can give us more understanding of what it means to be the object of this love. The wonder of it all is that Jesus dwells within each believer. This means that the overwhelming love God the Father has for His "Only Begotten" is now focused directly upon each believer. (*See #153, #155, #159, #160, #174.*)

152. Christ – *Christos*

"And Simon Peter answered and said, 'Thou art the *Christ*, the Son of the living God'" (Matthew 16:16, *NASB*).

"And they said unto the woman, Now we believe, not because of thy saying: for we have heard him ourselves, and know that this is indeed the *Christ*, the Saviour of the world" (John 4:42).

> **Definition:** *Christos* (khris-tos'); from *chrio*; anointed, i.e. the Messiah, an epithet of Jesus: – Christ. (S)

Jesus is "the Christ" (or the Anointed One). Jesus was (and is) a prophet without equal, a priest in the order of Melchizedek, and the King of kings. We studied before that these three anointings were common in the Hebrew world. When God anoints an individual for service, He always proves Himself to be no "respecter of persons"—that is, He "shows no partiality" (Acts 10:34, *NKJV*).

The Lord instructed Samuel to anoint a young boy named David, the smallest and most insignificant son of Jesse, to be king (see 1 Samuel 16:7). When no man would accept the call to judge Israel, God called and used a woman, Deborah, to rule over His people and deliver them from their enemies (Judges 4).

When the people complained to God about not having a king like all the other nations, He sent Samuel to Saul, the son of Kish, to anoint him to be king over the nation of Israel. "Then Samuel took a flask of oil and poured it on his head, and kissed him and said: 'Is it not because the Lord has anointed you commander over His inheritance?'" (1 Samuel 10:1, *NKJV*).

God often picked the least of people to demonstrate His greatness. "For you see your calling, brethren, that not many wise according to the flesh, not many mighty, not many noble, are called. But God has chosen the foolish things of the world to put to shame the wise, and God has chosen the weak things of the world to put to shame the things which are mighty" (1 Corinthians 1:26, 27, *NKJV*).

With the anointing always comes the power and ability to do whatever is required of the vessel being used.

Jesus received another anointing during the week before the Crucifixion. He was anointed for burial in Bethany by Mary, the sister of Lazarus and Martha, in an unusual and unorthodox way.

> Then, six days before the Passover, Jesus came to Bethany, where Lazarus was who had been dead, whom He had raised from the dead. There they made Him a supper; and Martha served, but Lazarus was one of those who sat at the table with Him. Then Mary took a pound of very costly oil of spikenard, anointed the feet of Jesus, and wiped His feet with her hair. And the house was filled with the fragrance of the oil. Then one of His disciples, Judas Iscariot, Simon's son, who would betray Him, said, "Why was this fragrant oil not sold for three hundred denarii and given to the poor?" This he said, not that he cared for the poor, but because he was a thief, and had the money box; and he used to take what was put in it. But Jesus said, "Let her alone; she has kept this for the day of My burial" (John 12:1-7, *NKJV*).

When Jesus was anointed for burial, none but Mary seemed to understand His words of prophecy concerning the events that were soon to follow. She was there when her brother was raised from the dead and had heard Jesus state that He was "the resurrection, and the life" (John 11:25).

She took Jesus at His word and began to anoint Him for His burial. This act was usually done after a person died, not while they were alive and apparently healthy. This bold act caused resentment among those who did not understand the things of God. (*See #85, #164.*)

174

153. Beloved Son – *Agapetos Huios*

"While he yet spake, behold, a bright cloud overshadowed them: and behold a voice out of the cloud, which said, This is my *beloved Son*, in whom I am well pleased; hear ye him" (Matthew 17:5).

"For he received from God the Father honour and glory, when there came such a voice to him from the excellent glory, This is my *beloved Son*, in whom I am well pleased" (2 Peter 1:17).

> **Definition:** *Agapetos* (ag-ap-ay-tos') [27]; from *agapao*; beloved: – (dearly, well) beloved, dear. (S)
>
> *Huios* (hwee-os') [5207]; apparently a primary word; a "son" (sometimes of animals), used very widely of immediate, remote or figuratively, kinship: – child, foal, son. (S)

Jesus was, and is, the Son of God. Begotten of the Father before the foundations of the world, Jesus was and is God's beloved Son. This name supports the image of the Father/Son relationship as one of favor and intimacy, and shows that Jesus was one with the Father and Spirit.

This verse from Matthew 17 is from the first recorded account of the Transfiguration. God came to His Son in the presence of three disciples—Peter, James and John—and openly blessed His Son. He also admonished the disciples to listen to what Jesus had to say. God honored His Son by acknowledging and reenforcing His authority and the intimacy of Jesus' relationship with the Father. (*See #151, #155, #159, #160, #174.*)

154. Bridegroom – *Numphios*

"And while they went to buy, the *bridegroom* came; and they that were ready went in with him to the marriage: and the door was shut" (Matthew 25:10).

Definition: *Numphios* (noom-fee'-os) [3566]; from *numphe*; a bride-groom (literally or figuratively): – bridegroom. (S)

Christ is the bridegroom and we are called to be His bride. This gives a new understanding to a passage of Scripture that is often quoted to women in instructions on what God requires of them as wives.

Consider yourself to be the bride of Christ and apply these requirements to your Christian walk. Just as a woman in Christ becomes a son of God, the men in Christ must understand that they are to be a part of the bride to Christ. No one can live up to the high ideals of this passage without the direct intervention of a good and holy God.

In the parable of the ten virgins (Matthew 25:1-13), Jesus said that the kingdom of heaven shall be likened to ten virgins (v. 1). Five were wise and five were foolish. The only obvious difference between them, according to the story, is what they did with their lamps and how much oil they took with them. The oil represents the Holy Spirit, and they needed oil to keep a light in their lamps that would guide the bridegroom to the bride.

Jesus is our Bridegroom! He is coming for His bride, the church, at an hour no one knows except the Father who sent Him (Matthew 24:36). We, the chosen bride, have two requirements in this parable: to keep the wick trimmed and to keep a supply of oil.

Trimming a wick is necessary for the oil to burn clean. To trim a wick, you cut off the black, charred portions of it so that the lamp will give off a pure fire and a clean light. We trim our wicks when we cut from our lives the things that bring impurities and cause His light to appear dingy and smoky. God will tell us what we need to cut out of our lives.

The wise virgins did not allow themselves to be without the oil necessary for their lamps. When asked by the foolish ones for a portion of oil, they refused and kept it for themselves. Some would criticize them for selfishness, but Jesus gave no rebuke or correction in this parable. You see, if the five wise virgins had shared their oil with the foolish ones, there would not have been enough for any of them.

There will always be people who want what you have in the Lord, but who are not willing to pay the price. Although you can share with others the glories of Christ and the good news of the gospel, you cannot give them the portion of the Holy Spirit that God has given you. They must come to the altar themselves and become His bride, thereby entering into a relationship with Jesus for themselves and receiving the portion He has set apart for them.

155. Son of the Living God – *Huios Zao Theos*

"And Simon Peter answered and said, Thou art the Christ, the *Son of the living God*" (Matthew 16:16).

> **Definition:** *Huios* (hwee-os') [5207]; apparently a primary word; a "son" (sometimes of animals), used very widely of immediate, remote or figuratively, kinship: – child, foal, son. (S)
>
> *Zao* (dzah'-o) [2198]; a primary verb; to live (literally or figuratively): – life (-time), (a-) live (-ly), quick. (S)
>
> *Theos* (theh'-os) [2316]; of uncertain affinity; a deity, especially (with *Ho*) the supreme Divinity; figuratively, a magistrate; by Hebraism, very: – X exceeding, God, god [-ly, -ward]. (S)

Peter was not the first one to recognize Jesus as the Son of God when He was on the earth.

Satan acknowledged the Lord to be the Son of God during the temptation in the wilderness (Matthew 4:3).

Two demon-possessed men in Gadara recognized Jesus as the Son of God (Matthew 8:29).

177

After being saved from a near drowning in the Sea of Galilee, the disciples realized that Jesus was the Son of God (Matthew 14:33).

At the foot of the cross, the centurion saw the way Jesus died and called Him the Son of God (Matthew 27:54).

But Peter is the only person in Scripture who is reported to have called Jesus the Son of the *living* God (Matthew 16:16; John 6:69).

Zao describes living that goes beyond just existing. It is living that regenerates, that makes others come alive, that is spontaneous and contagious to all who come in contact with it. Jesus is the Son of the living (regenerating, contagious, spontaneous, life-giving) God.

It is interesting that Satan and his demons recognized Jesus as the Son of God before the disciples did. They knew that Jesus existed, and that He was related to God by blood. They knew Jesus to be the Son of God. However, this does not make them "born again."

Paul wrote in Romans 10:9, "If you confess with your mouth, 'Jesus is Lord,' and believe in your heart that God raised him from the dead, you will be saved" (*NIV*).

The key to salvation is acknowledging Jesus as Lord, not recognizing Him to be the Son of God. You must place your faith in Jesus as Savior and Lord if you wish to walk with Him as a brother. (*See #153, #159, #160, #174.*)

PART 3
The Son of God

His Greek Names in
MARK – LUKE

---

156. Holy One of God – *Hagios Theos*

"What do we have to do with You, Jesus of Nazareth? Have You come to destroy us? I know who You are— the *Holy One of God*!" (Mark 1:24, *NASB*).

> **Definition:** *Hagios* (hag'-ee-os) [40]; from *hagos* (an awful thing) [compare *hagnos*, *thalpo*]; sacred (physically, pure, morally blameless or religious, ceremonially, consecrated): – (most) holy (one, thing), saint. (S)

To be *holy* means to be "set apart" or consecrated, sacred, pure and morally blameless. Jesus was set apart *by God* before the foundations of the earth were set. He was set apart *to God* from the time of His baptism by John. In this passage the demons recognize that He was set apart *of God* (Mark 1:24). I still find it amazing that the demons and Satan first recognized Jesus for the spirit-man He was. They knew that Jesus was *of God* (one with God in authority and Spirit), yet they refused to humble themselves before Him. It takes more than knowing about God or having head knowledge. Jesus requires us to know God by having a relationship with Him. (*See #124, #295.*)

157. Carpenter – *Tekton*

"Is not this the *carpenter*, the son of Mary, the brother of James, and Joses, and of Juda, and Simon? And are not his sisters here with us? And they were offended at him" (Mark 6:3).

> **Definition:** *Tekton* (tek'-tone) [5045]; from the base of *timoria*; an artificer (as producer of fabrics), i.e. (specifically) a craftsman in wood: – carpenter. (S)

Jesus' earthly father, Joseph, was a carpenter; so naturally, Jesus was a carpenter too. It was typical in those days for the father to train his son the trade in which he (the father) was proficient. Consider what could have been, but wasn't.

Jesus could have been trained as a lawyer—this would have helped Him argue the law with Satan in the wilderness. He could have been a scribe or Pharisee—this would have prepared Him for His teaching ministry. The King of kings could have been raised a prince or nobleman to prepare Him to take the throne of the universe and to assure proper respect for Him on earth.

When Yahweh became flesh, however, He was a man of no earthly position or nobility. A common man, He chose to come as a carpenter. The Lord of lords came to serve, not to be served, and worked with His hands in His father's shop while learning a trade like other Jewish boys. He submitted to His earthly father just as He did to His Father in heaven.

Jesus did not come to argue law, but to fulfill it and to release us from its bondage. Jesus did not come to honor a single class of people or a nation on earth. The Lord did not come to be worshiped as a great Hebrew leader. He came to live humbly among us, then be worshiped as Lord of all after His ascension.

158. Good Master – *Agathos Didaskalos*

"And when he was gone forth into the way, there came one running, and kneeled to him, and asked him, *Good Master,* what shall I do that I may inherit eternal life?" (Mark 10:17).

> **Definition:** *Agathos* (ag-ath-os') [18]; a primary word; "good" (in any sense, often as noun): – benefit, good (-s, things), well. Compare *kalos.* (S)
>
> *Didaskalos* (did-as'-kal-os) [1320]; from *didasko*; an instructor (genitive case or specially): – doctor, master, teacher. (S)

Jesus came as the "good master," not the taskmaster. To say that He is good seems trite, but it is important to our faith to know Him as the good master. Many religions center around a character or personage who is demanding and hard. Religion is bondage to a set of rules that somebody has come up with. They believe that it will make us "OK" with God. But Christianity is not a religion. It is not a set of rules or list of things that must be done to earn the Father's love.

Instead, Christianity is a relationship with the Good Master, Jesus Christ. Jesus desires only good for us and demands little in return. He wants us to receive Him and the Holy Spirit; He wants us to be born again (John 3:16; 1 Timothy 2:4). He wants us to allow Him to live His life through us (Galatians 2:20).

He wants us to be transformed by renewing our minds (Romans 12:1-3), and to become new creations in Christ (2 Corinthians 5:17). Little else is required, when you get down to it. Jesus wants us to be holy as He is holy (1 Peter 1:15), but that happens only if He is in us. The Lord never asks anything of us that He does not equip us to do.

"And when she had so said, she went her way, and called Mary her sister secretly, saying, The *Master* is come, and calleth for thee" (John 11:28).

"Ye call me *Master* and Lord: and ye say well; for so I am" (John 13:13).

159. Son of the Highest – *Huios Hupsistos*

"He shall be great, and shall be called the *Son of the Highest*: and the Lord God shall give unto him the throne of his father David" (Luke 1:32).

> **Definition:** *Huios* (hwee-os') [5207]; apparently a primary word; a "son" (sometimes of animals), used very widely of immediate, remote or figuratively, kinship: – child, foal, son. (S)
>
> *Hupsistos* (hoop'-sis-tos) [5310]; superlative from the base of *hupsos*; highest, i.e. (masculine singular) the Supreme (God), or (neuter plural) the heavens: – most high, highest. (S)

As Son of the Highest, Jesus is the legal heir-apparent to the throne of the Almighty as the King of kings and Lord of lords. A beautiful revelation occurs when a believer realizes that the Son of God dwells within the heart of each Christian, making us coheirs with Christ and able to walk in the fulfillment of His promises.

We should not live as spiritual paupers while the Son of the Highest is dwelling within. We do not have to beg for the Father's attention or love. God loves us because He made us; He answers our prayers because His Son dwells with us. (*See #153, #155, #160, #174.*)

160. Son of God – *Huios Theos*

"And the angel answered and said unto her, The Holy Ghost shall come upon thee, and the power of the Highest shall overshadow thee: therefore also that holy thing which shall be born of thee shall be called the *Son of God*" (Luke 1:35).

"And I saw, and bare record that this is the *Son of God*" (John 1:34).

> **Definition:** *Theos* (theh'-os) [2316]; of uncertain affinity; a deity, especially (with *Ho*) the supreme Divinity; figuratively, a magistrate; by Hebraism, very: – X exceeding, God, god [-ly, -ward]. (S)

Jesus was the Son of God by divine appointment. The angel of the Lord delivered this promise to Mary and she was made pregnant by supernatural means. Jesus was, and still is the Son of God. Even more amazing, as Christians we have become the sons of God by legal adoption.

"Those who are led by the Spirit of God are sons of God" (Romans 8:14, *NIV*).

"I will be a Father to you, and you will be my sons and daughters, says the Lord Almighty" (2 Corinthians 6:18, *NIV*).

> But when the time had fully come, God sent his Son, born of a woman, born under law, to redeem those under law, that we might receive the full rights of sons. Because you are sons, God sent the Spirit of his Son into our hearts, the Spirit who calls out, "Abba, Father" (Galatians 4:4-6, *NIV*).

"So that you may become blameless and pure, children of God without fault in a crooked and depraved generation, in which you shine like stars in the universe" (Philippians 2:15, *NIV*).

> How great is the love the Father has lavished on us, that we should be called children of God! And that is what we are! The reason the world does not know us is that it did not know him. Dear friends, now we are children of God, and what we will be has not yet been made known. But we know that when he appears, we shall be like him, for we shall see him as he is (1 John 3:1, 2, *NIV*). (*See #153, #155, #159.*)

161. Savior – *Soter*

"And my spirit hath rejoiced in God my *Saviour*" (Luke 1:47).

Definition: *Soter* (so-tare') [4990]; from *sozo*; a deliverer, i.e. God or Christ: – savior. (S)

This is one of several references to Jesus as Savior. Mary was rejoicing in God her Savior who was still in her womb. Early in the pregnancy Mary knew that the One within her was her Savior as well as her child.

Holman's Bible Dictionary points out that salvation in Jesus is more than security or spiritual fire insurance. The salvation God offers through His Son provides believers with a deliverer, a healer and a benefactor. Our Savior wants to affect every part of our lives, as His salvation is an ongoing process. (*See #56, #122, #181.*)

162. Horn of Salvation – *Keras Soteria*

"And hath raised up an *horn of salvation* for us in the house of his servant David" (Luke 1:69).

Definition: *Keras* - a horn (a) of animals (b) since animals (especially bulls) defend themselves with their horns, the horn with the Hebrews (and other nations) is a symbol of strength and courage, and used as such in a variety of phrases; a mighty and valiant helper, the author of deliverance, used of the Messiah (c) a projecting extremity in a shape like a horn, a point, an apex: as of an altar. (*Thayer's Greek-English Lexicon*)

Soteria - (1) deliverance, preservation, safety, salvation (a) deliverance from the molestation of enemies (b) in an ethical sense, what concludes to the souls safety or salvation; used of Messianic salvation (2) salvation as the present possession of all true Christians (3) future salvation, the sum of benefits and blessings which the Christians, redeemed from all earthly ills, will enjoy after the visible return of Christ from

heaven in the consummated and eternal kingdom of God.
(*Thayer's Greek-English Lexicon*)

The horn here is a horn of masculine strength and virility; it is not a musical instrument. It depicts our Lord as capable of protecting His "turf," so to speak. Nature shows on television feature stories about life in the herd.

No matter what species is pictured, there always seems to be a kind of struggle or test the male must pass to demonstrate his ability to rule the herd. In the deer family the horn symbolizes male strength, the ability to defend and lead the rest of the herd. Jesus is the power of God and the horn of salvation. He is God's expression of power and ability to both save and keep His church. (*See #53.*)

163. Dayspring – *Anatole*

"Through the tender mercy of our God; whereby the *dayspring* from on high hath visited us" (Luke 1:78).

Definition: *Anatole* (an-at-ol-ay') [395]; from *anatello*; a rising of light, i.e. dawn (figuratively); by implication, the east (also in plural): – dayspring, east, rising. (S)

Zachariah was a priest and the father of John the Baptist. An angel appeared to him as he offered incense in the temple. He was informed that he and his wife, Elizabeth, were going to have a baby boy and they were to name him John.

The angel told the priest of the wonderful plans God had for his son, but because he and his wife were old, Zachariah doubted. Consequently, he was mute for months as a sign or confirmation of the word he had received.

On the eighth day of the child's life, Zachariah took him to the temple to be circumcised and named. After Zachariah confirmed the name would be John by writing it out for all to see, his lips were opened and he spoke again. The Holy Spirit came on him and he prophesied what is written in Luke 1:68-79.

Zachariah proclaimed Jesus to be the dayspring. *Dayspring* has been translated as a rising of light, the dawn, the dawn of the morning, eastern light and a rising of the sun or stars. *Jesus is our dayspring.* He is the point of light sent from the Father to drive out the darkness as to attract the lost to Him.

As a moth is drawn to a porch light during summer evenings, so God wants us to be drawn to the light of Christ. The moth usually dies in the process and so must the believer who is drawn to Jesus. We must die to the flesh in order to truly come alive in Christ. (*See #2, #63, #79, #121, #142.*)

164. Christ the Lord – *Christos Kurios*

"For there is born to you this day in the city of David a Savior, who is *Christ the Lord*" (Luke 2:11, *NKJV*).

> **Definition:** *Christos* - Christ = "anointed"; (1) Christ was the Messiah, the Son of God (2) anointed (*Thayer's Greek English Lexicon*).
>
> *Kurios* (koo'-ree-os) [2962]; from *kuros* (supremacy); supreme in authority, i.e. (as noun) controller; by implication, Mr. (as a respectful title): – God, Lord, master, Sir. (S)

Luke 2:8-14 tells of angels appearing to shepherds and announcing the birth of the Savior. To the wise men, Jesus was revealed as "King of the Jews," an earthly title (Matthew 2:1-12). But to the shepherds, Jesus was revealed as the Anointed One (the Christ) who was Lord and sovereign Savior.

God shows Himself over and over again as One who is no respecter of persons. Talking with Nicodemus, our Lord told him, a religious leader, he had to be born again (see John 3). Talking with the woman at the well, Jesus discussed theological issues with immense implications, completely ignoring her roles of "insignificance"—the double burden of being a woman and a Samaritan.

We learned earlier that Jesus' title "Lord" placed Him in authority over everything in heaven and on earth. Both names were combined here to show the shepherds that His anointing as priest, prophet and king surpassed every other anointing. It shows that Jesus' Lordship did not depend on earthly performance or social status.

God came to an ordinary couple in an extraordinary way, bringing forth a Son who depended only on His relationship with the Father in heaven and the power of God for His ministry. (*See #85, #152.*)

165. Babe – *Brephos*

"And this shall be a sign unto you; Ye shall find the *babe* wrapped in swaddling clothes, lying in a manger" (Luke 2:12).

> **Definition:** *Brephos* (bref'-os) [1025]; of uncertain affinity.; an infant (properly, unborn) literally or figuratively: – babe, (young) child, infant. (S)

I am struck by the stunning reality that God came in the form of a baby. Nothing is so vulnerable as a newborn babe. It is beyond my comprehension what the angels must have thought when they beheld this mysterious sight. The very God who spoke the planets into being, the One who separated the dry land from the seas by His Word came as a human baby in weakness and in need.

What was it like to nurse the Lord of lords? How did it feel to change the diapers of the Prince of Peace? What must it have been like to teach the Word of God how to read and write? These things are too profound for me to understand or figure out, but they remind me of a gospel song I heard several years ago. It is a Christmas carol in the truest sense of the word.

The Wonder of Wonders

The wonder of wonders as she looked on His face,
That this little boy spoke the worlds in their place;
The stars and the moon, shining brightly on them,
The earth and the sun were created by Him.

The wonder of wonders as she heard His small cry,
That this voice had thundered on Mount Sinai;
The hand that she held so tenderly,
Had made a dry path thru the mighty Red Sea.

The wonder of wonders as she looked down and smiled,
That He was her maker as well as her Child;
He created the womb that had given Him birth,
He was God incarnate, come down to the earth.

The wonder of wonders as the Father looked on,
In eternity past, this was His Son;
He had sent Him to die on Calvary's tree
And that is the wonder of wonders to me.

The wonder of wonders, oh, how could it be
That God became flesh and was given for me?
The Almighty came down and walked among men
And died on the cross for every man's sin.

I can barely write those words without weeping. Just the thought of my God taking on the form of a baby and developing in a womb that He himself had created is more than I can comprehend.

Jesus is infinitely grand; yet He came to earth as tiny and weak as a babe. (*See #104, #167, #196.*)

166. Consolation of Israel – *Paraklesis Israel*

"And, behold, there was a man in Jerusalem, whose name was Simeon; and the same man was just and devout, waiting for the *consolation of Israel*: and the Holy Ghost was upon him" (Luke 2:25).

Definition: *Paraklesis* - (1) a calling near, summons, (especially for help) (2) importation, supplication, entreaty (3) exhortation, admonition, encouragement (4) consolation, comfort, solace; what affords comfort or refreshment, thus of the Messianic salvation (so the rabbis call the Messiah the Consoler, the Comforter) (5) persuasive discourse, stirring address; instructive, admonitory, conciliatory, powerful oratory discourse. (*Thayer's Greek-English Lexicon*)

Israel - Israel = "he shall be a prince of God" (1) the name given to the patriarch Jacob (and borne by him in addition to his former name) (2) the family or descendants of Israel, the race of Israel (3) Christians, the Israel of God (Gal. 6:16), for not all those who draw their bodily descent from Israel are true Israelites, that is, are those whom God pronounces to be Israelites and has chosen to salvation." (*Thayer's Greek-English Lexicon*)

Simeon, an old man, was an example of godly character and behavior. God had promised him that he would not see death before his eyes beheld the Christ (Luke 2:26). Joseph and Mary took baby Jesus to the temple to dedicate Him as their firstborn, and Simeon recognized this baby as the fulfillment of God's promise.

Simeon had seen the failures of God's people, Israel; but now he rightly sees the Christ child as the "consolation of Israel," the One who would plead Israel's case before Jehovah.

The Old Testament records Israel failing God in many ways. Prophets were sent to to the nation to proclaim judgment and punishment for their failures; but the prayers of others, like Simeon, stayed God's hand and protected the people.

Jesus was the Advocate for whom Simeon prayed. He interceded for the Jewish nation, as well as for Gentile nations. He lamented and prayed over Jerusalem (Matthew 23:37). He understood human fears and weaknesses.

167. Child Jesus – *Pais Iesous*

"And when they had fulfilled the days, as they returned, the *child Jesus* tarried behind in Jerusalem; and Joseph and his mother knew not of it" (Luke 2:43).

> **Definition:** *Pais* (paheece) [3816]; perhaps from *paio*; a boy (as often beaten with impunity), or (by analogy,) a girl, and (genitive case) a child; specifically, a slave or servant (especially a minister to a king; and by eminence to God): – child, maid (-en), (man) servant, son, young man. (S)

> *Iesous* - Jesus = Jehovah (Yahweh) is salvation" (1) Joshua was the famous captain of the Israelites, Moses' successor (2) Jesus, son of Eliezer, one of the ancestors of Christ (3) Jesus, the Son of God, the Savior of mankind, God incarnate (4) Jesus Barabbas was the captive robber whom the Jews begged Pilate to release instead of Jesus Christ (5) Jesus, surnamed Justus, a Jewish Christian, an associate with Paul in the preaching of the gospel. (*Thayer's Greek-English Lexicon*)

This Greek word for child implies subservience. Jesus was subservient to His parents. As a young man He studied the history of His people and worked in a carpenter's shop nearly every day. At 12, Jesus showed on the trip to Jerusalem that He was a model child and a blessing to His parents.

Not only was Jesus subservient to His parents, but His life demonstrated over and over again His chosen service to Israel and to the Gentile nations that neither knew Him nor cared about Him. (*See #104, #165, #196.*)

168. Physician – *Iatros*

"No doubt you will quote this proverb to Me, '*Physician*, heal yourself! Whatever we heard was done at Capernaum, do here in your hometown as well'" (Luke 4:23, *NASB*).

> **Definition:** *Iatros* (ee-at-ros') [2395]; from *iaomai*; a physician: – physician. (S)

Jesus was "the Great Physician." There is no disease over which Jesus cannot demonstrate His authority. He healed the lame (Matthew 9:1-8), cleansed the leper (Matthew 8:1-4), gave sight to the blind (Matthew 9:27-31), caused the mute to speak (Matthew 9:32-34), raised the dead to life (Matthew 9:18-26), and cast out tormenting spirits (Matthew17:14-21).

Many references of healing throughout the four Gospels illustrate the ministry that Jesus had to the sick.

> Jesus went throughout Galilee, teaching in their synagogues, preaching the good news of the kingdom, and healing every disease and sickness among the people. News about him spread all over Syria, and people brought to him all who were ill with various diseases, those suffering severe pain, the demon-possessed, those having seizures, and the paralyzed, and he healed them. Large crowds from Galilee, the Decapolis, Jerusalem, Judea and the region across the Jordan followed him (Matthew 4:23-25, *NIV*).

The Book of the Acts shows that these healing virtues were manifested through the ministry of the Holy Spirit in the lives of the early converts to Christianity. Many were healed, and some raised from the dead, as the promised Holy Spirit came to empower believers with the same power that raised Jesus from the dead. In his letter to the Ephesian church, Paul prayed:

> Therefore I also, after I heard of your faith in the Lord Jesus and your love for all the saints, do not cease to give thanks for you, making mention of you in my prayers: that the God of our Lord Jesus Christ, the Father of glory, may give to you the spirit of wisdom and revelation in the knowledge of Him, the eyes of your understanding being enlightened; that you may know what is the hope of His calling, what are the riches of the glory of His inheritance in the saints, and what is the exceeding greatness of His power toward us who believe, according to the working of His mighty power which He worked in Christ when He raised Him from the dead and seated Him at His right

hand in the heavenly places, far above all principality and power and might and dominion, and every name that is named, not only in this age but also in that which is to come (1:15-21, *NKJV*).

Jesus still heals through His people. That is why we are told to pray for the sick in James 5:13-16. We need to release the results to Him and let God do His part in all of this. He does not change (Hebrews 13:8), and this means that He is still in the healing business today.

The Lord uses doctors at times, and the passage of time heals some things. Still, there are times when Jesus sends a miracle of healing to reveal His glory and demonstrate His grace. Jesus is our Physician! (*See #17, #128.*)

169. Lord of the Sabbath – *Kurios Sabbaton*

"And He said to them, 'The Son of Man is also *Lord of the Sabbath*'" (Luke 6:5, *NKJV*).

> **Definition:** *Sabbaton* (sab'-bat-on) [4521]; of Hebrew origin [*shabbath*]; the Sabbath (i.e. Shabbath), or day of weekly repose from secular avocations (also the observance or institution itself); by extension, a *se'nnight*, i.e. the interval between two Sabbaths; likewise the plural in all the above applications: – sabbath (day), week. (S)

Jesus was often rebuked for not celebrating and honoring the Sabbath as the Pharisees thought He should. The Lord healed the sick and gave sight to the blind on the Sabbath, just as He did on other days of the week.

Everything Jesus did was from an attitude of rest and submission to His Father. The fulfillment of God's law concerning the Sabbath is for the believer to have an attitude of peace and rest in God's provision. Jesus was, and is, Lord of all things—even the Sabbath. He wants to rule every part of the believer's life. (*See #123.*)

170. Great Prophet – *Megas Prophetes*

"And there came a fear on all: and they glorified God, saying, That a *great prophet* is risen up among us; and, That God hath visited his people" (Luke 7:16).

"And he said unto them, 'What things?' And they said unto him, 'Concerning Jesus of Nazareth, which was a *prophet mighty in deed* and word before God and all the people'" (Luke 24:19).

> **Definition:** *Megas* (meg'-as) [3173]; [including the prolonged forms, feminine *megale*, plural *megaloi*, etc.; compare also *megistos, meizon*]; big (literally or figuratively, in a very wide application): – (+fear) exceedingly, great (-est), high, large, loud, mighty, + (be) sore (afraid), strong, X to years. (S)
>
> *Prophetes* (prof-ay'-tace) [4396]; from a compound of *pro* and *phemi*; a foreteller ("prophet"); by analogy, an inspired speaker; by extension, a poet: – prophet. (S)

A prophecy may contain words of future events, but it always contains the speaking forth of the glories of God. Ministers who prophesy tell their listeners about the glories of the Lord and Savior. John wrote:

> At this I fell at his feet to worship him. But he said to me, "Do not do it! I am a fellow servant with you and with your brothers who hold to the testimony of Jesus. Worship God! For the testimony of Jesus is the spirit of prophecy" (Revelation 19:10, *NIV*).

Jesus was the *Great Prophet.* None of His words missed the mark. Everything Jesus said would happen, did so perfectly. He glorified God with everything He said and did.

Prophecy is speaking forth in edification, exhortation and comfort as we testify of Jesus (see 1 Corinthians 14:3). When we follow these guidelines, we fulfill God's plan for us. If we are as submitted to God's control and can hear His words clearly, nothing we say will miss the mark either.

Peter displayed this truth when he proclaimed that Jesus was "the Christ, the Son of the living God" (Matthew 16:16); although he rebuked Jesus wrongly in the same chapter and was used as a mouthpiece for Satan (see Matthew 16:21-23). (*See #38.*)

171. Chosen of God – *Eklektos Theos*

"And the people stood beholding. And the rulers also with them derided him, saying, 'He saved others; let him save himself, if he be Christ, the *chosen of God*'" (Luke 23:35).

> **Definition:** *Eklektos* - picked out, chosen, chosen by God, (1) to obtain salvation through Christ; Christians are called "chosen or elect" of God (2) the Messiah is called "elect", as appointed by God to the most exalted office conceivable (3) choice, select, that is, the best of its kind or class, excellence preeminent: applied to certain individual Christians (*Thayer's Greek-English Lexicon*).

This phrase was yelled in sarcasm as Jesus hung on the cross. Even at this point, they did not believe that Jesus was chosen by God. They doubted His deity and denied His Lordship because His life did not fit their doctrinal teachings concerning the Messiah. They had expected God to send a Messiah who would be a mighty king on earth, cast off the reproach of the people of Israel and once again make them a great nation.

Jesus *was* the Chosen of God, but the rulers of Israel did not understand the purpose for which He was chosen. Jesus was chosen by the Father to die for them as the final Passover Lamb. He was chosen to suffer the punishment due them for their sins and transgressions. He was chosen to bear their sicknesses and receive the chastisement due them.

Jesus was chosen by God to live a humble life, demonstrating humility and obedience in everything He did. Jesus was chosen by God to die for you and me as well. (*See #120.*)

The Son of God

His Greek Names in

JOHN

---

172. Word – *Logos*

"In the beginning was the *Word*, and the *Word* was with God, and the *Word* was God" (John 1:1).

> **Definition:** *Logos* (log'-os) [3056]; from *lego*; something said (including the thought); by implication a topic (subject of discourse), also reasoning (the mental faculty) or motive; by extension, a computation; specifically (with the article in John) the Divine Expression (i.e. Christ): – account, cause, communication, X concerning, doctrine, fame, X have to do, intent, matter, mouth, preaching, question, reason, + reckon, remove, say (-ing), shew, X speaker, speech, talk, thing, + none of these things move me, tidings, treatise, utterance, word, work. (S)

"The Word of God" means that He is the language God speaks and He is the content of what God has to say to this generation. "In the past God spoke to our forefathers through the prophets at many times and in various ways, but in these last days he has spoken to us by his Son, whom he appointed heir of all things, and through whom he made the universe" (Hebrews 1:1, 2, *NIV*).

God communicates with His people and with those to whom He is calling through the written Word of God. It has a life o its own and can impart God's life to those who will receive it

At one point in his life, a man I know had dropped out of society and had become consumed with alcohol. He had lost nearly everything he had and was doing time in a county jail when a member of The Gideons, International, came by his cell and gave him a New Testament. As he read the Word of God, he believed on Jesus and his life was completely turned around. Nobody preached to him or explained the Word; he just read it and received Jesus into his heart.

This demonstrates the awesome power of the written Word of God. "The word of God is living, and powerful, and sharper than any two-edged sword, piercing even to the division of soul and spirit, and of joints and marrow, and is a discerner of the thoughts and intents of the heart" (Hebrews 4:12, *NKJV*).

To those who have eyes to see and ears to hear, Jesus also declares His presence through creation. I heard the Reverend Malcom Smith relate a testimony he heard in an African village.

The people worshiped idols and witch doctors when he was a child, an old man testified. But he was convinced there had to be more than a whittled log or painted man to worship as God. He would go to the woods and pray to the unknown Creator that he knew must be there, but he had no idea what His name was or what His character was like. In the midst of a prayer time one day, he saw a vision of a white woman carrying a black book, and was told by an unknown voice that this woman could tell him God's name.

A month later, a female missionary walked into his village, the first white missionary to go to this area. Reverend Smith said the missionary who was still in the village, picked up the story at this point.

> It was startling to a young missionary on her first assignment in Africa to have a naked black man jump on her as she entered the village, shouting in his native tongue, "Tell me His name! Tell me His name!"

This true story demonstrates that Jesus *is* the Word of God. The Lord speaks to us by His Holy Spirit, through His creation and through the written Word.

"For since the creation of the world God's invisible qualities—his eternal power and divine nature—have been clearly seen, being understood from what has been made, so that men are without excuse" (Romans 1:20, *NIV*).

> The heavens declare the glory of God; the skies proclaim the work of his hands. Day after day they pour forth speech; night after night they display knowledge. There is no speech or language where their voice is not heard. Their voice goes out into all the earth, their words to the ends of the world (Psalm 19:1-4, *NIV*).

Just as the written Word can bring someone to faith in Christ, Jesus can reveal Himself to those who are open to Him. Jesus, after all, is the Word of God made flesh. (*See #84, #250, #268.*)

173. True Light – *Alethinos Phos*

"That was the *true Light*, which lighteth every man that cometh into the world" (John 1:9).

Definition: *Alethinos* - (1) what has not only the name and resemblance, but the real nature corresponding to the name, in every respect corresponding to the idea signified by the name, real, true genuine (a) opposite to what is fictitious, counterfeit, imaginary, simulated or pretended (b) it contrasts

> realities with their semblances (c) opposite to what is imperfect defective, frail, uncertain (2) true, veracious, sincere (*Thayer's Greek-English Lexicon*).
>
> *Phos* (foce) [5457]; from an obsolete *phao* (to shine or make manifest, especially by rays; compare *phaino, phemi*); luminousness (in the widest application, nat. or artificial, abstract or concrete, literal or figurative): – fire, light. (S)

Light is as much an attribute of God as it is a name of Jesus. Throughout history, God has frequently appeared as light to those He visited. Note the order of the Creation in Genesis. On the first day God said, "Let there be light," and there was light (Genesis 1:3). On the third day God created the sun, the moon and the stars.

> And God said, "Let there be lights in the expanse of the sky to separate the day from the night, and let them serve as signs to mark seasons and days and years, and let them be lights in the expanse of the sky to give light on the earth." And it was so. God made two great lights—the greater light to govern the day and the lesser light to govern the night. He also made the stars. God set them in the expanse of the sky to give light on the earth, to govern the day and the night, and to separate light from darkness. And God saw that it was good (Genesis 1:14-18, *NIV*).

In the New Jerusalem, it is interesting to note, God again will be all the light we need, "There will be no more night. They will not need the light of a lamp or the light of the sun, for the Lord God will give them light. And they will reign for ever and ever" (Revelation 22:5, *NIV*).

Light is the way God is, and light is the way He often reveals Himself to those who search for Him. He appeared as light to Moses at the burning bush (Exodus 3); in the shining face of Moses (Exodus 34:29); in the cloud by day and the pillar of shimmering light by night, leading the Israelites in the wilderness (Exodus 40, Numbers 9); in the glory that filled

Solomon's temple (2 Chronicles 5, 7); and around Jesus at the Mount of Transfiguration (Matthew 17). (*See #2, #63, #121, #184, #271.*)

174. Only Begotten Son – *Monogenes Theos*

"No man hath seen God at any time; the *only begotten Son*, which is in the bosom of the Father, he hath declared him" (John 1:18).

> **Definition:** *Monogenes* - single of its kind, only (a) used of only sons or only daughters (viewed in relation to their parents) (b) used of Christ, denotes the one and only son of God. (*Thayer's Greek-English Lexicon*)

There is a sense in which every person on earth is a son of God, in that God created Adam and all of us are also of Adam. But Jesus was not just a created being. Jesus was, and is, the Son of God, the "Only Begotten Son." Jesus was not made; He was begotten of the Father. Jesus is equal with the Father and the Holy Spirit, as members together of the Godhead. (*See #153, #155, #159, #160.*)

175. Lamb of God – *Amnos Ho Theos*

"The next day John seeth Jesus coming unto him, and saith, Behold the *Lamb of God*, which taketh away the sin of the world" (John 1:29).

> **Definition:** *Amnos* (am-nos') [286]; apparently a primary word; a lamb: – lamb. (S)

Abraham stood on Mt. Moriah with a knife in his hand, ready to take the life of his only son, Isaac. The Lord had promised Abraham an inheritance through the blood line of Isaac so he trusted God. At the last moment, God revealed a ram in the thicket for a substitute sacrifice. Through Israel's history, lambs were sacrificed at least twice a day. Many of the feasts centered around the sacrifices required during certain times of the year. Other animals used were the bullock the dove and the goat, but lambs were the most used source of sacrificial blood.

Jesus fulfilled all the types and shadows of Old Testament law concerning blood sacrifice. He was the final sacrifice in that He was the perfect Lamb of God. Without spot or blemish in any way, His blood was capable of making final payment for the sins of humankind. Jesus said,

> Do not think that I have come to abolish the Law or the Prophets; I have not come to abolish them but to fulfill them. I tell you the truth, until heaven and earth disappear, not the smallest letter, not the least stroke of a pen, will by any means disappear from the Law until everything is accomplished (Matthew 5:17, 18, *NIV*).

Jesus showed His obedience to God and His love for humankind by going to the cross as the Lamb of God. (*See #207.*)

176. Messiah – *Messias*

"He found first his own brother Simon, and said to him, 'We have found the *Messiah*' (which translated means Christ)" (John 1:41, *NASB*).

> **Definition:** *Messias* - (Messias) = "anointed" (1) the Greek form of the Hebrew word "Messiah" (2) a name of Christ." (*Thayer's Greek-English Lexicon*)

This is another Greek word meaning "the Christ" or "Anointed One." There is much talk in religious circles today about "anointings," and the "anointed" men and women of God. The Bible never tells us to follow "anointings." We are to follow the Lord God who watches over His flock jealously. While God may speak to us through anointed men and women, we are to follow Him and not allow ourselves to give too much honor to the vessels He chooses to use. (*See #122, #132.*)

177. Rabbi – *Rhabbi*

"Nathanael answered and saith unto him, *Rabbi*, thou art the Son of God; thou art the King of Israel" (John 1:49).

> **Definition:** *Rhabbi* (hrab-bee') [4461]; of Hebrew origin [*rab* with pronominal suffix); my master, i.e Rabbi, as an official title of honor: – Master, Rabbi. (S)
>
> *Rhabbi* – (1) my great one, my honorable sir (2) Rabbi, a title used by the Jews to address their teachers (and also honor them when not addressing them) (*Thayer's Greek-English Lexicon*).

The word *rabbi* means "teacher." Jesus truly is the greatest teacher who ever lived. On earth He taught the 12 disciples as well as the multitudes. Jesus spoke in parables, using stories that painted memorable pictures on the minds of all who heard Him. He practiced a lifestyle of teaching and training for all who had eyes to see and ears to hear. He taught truth in an uncompromising way.

Still, they needed the Holy Spirit to translate the meanings. As He teaches us through the Holy Spirit, I pray that we will allow Him to fill and instruct us on how to teach and train His church.

178. Jew – *Ioudaios*

"Then the woman of Samaria said to Him, 'How is it that You, being *a Jew*, ask a drink from me, a Samaritan woman?' For Jews have no dealings with Samaritans" (John 4:9, *NKJV*).

> **Definition:** *Ioudaios* (ee-oo-dah'-yos); from *Iouda* (in the sense of *Ioudas* as a country); Judaean, i.e. belonging to *Jehudah*: – Jew (-ess), of Judaea. (S)

After Solomon died, Rehoboam and Jeroboam had a disagreement and divided the nation. The 10 northern tribes called themselves Israel, while Judah and Benjamin formed the southern kingdom. These southern tribes were commonly called "Jews" because they were mostly from the tribe of Judah. After the exile, all Israelites were called Jews because the tribal identities were intermixed.

Jesus had to be a Jew for His blood to cover the sins of all the nations. If defiled in any way, His sacrifice would have been worthless. God's covenant promises to the patriarchs had to be fulfilled exactly as spoken in order to maintain His perfection and goodness.

179. Gift of God – *Dorea Theos*

"Jesus answered and said to her, 'If you knew the *gift of God*, and who it is who says to you, "Give Me a drink," you would have asked Him, and He would have given you living water'" (John 4:10, *NKJV*).

> **Definition:** *Dorea* (do-reh-ah') [1431]; from *doron*; a gratuity: – gift. (S)

Jesus Christ is the gift of God; He is not a wage we have earned. Nor is Jesus a payment that we can lay claim to or demand. Jesus is a gratuity, something that mankind dreamed of but never fully understood or even partially deserved. "For God so loved the world that He gave His only begotten Son, that whoever believes in Him should not perish but have everlasting life" (John 3:16, *NKJV*).

God cared enough to send the very best, His Son, Jesus. We celebrate the Lord's coming by giving gifts on December 25. His life is an available Gift to all who take the time to know Him. He is special to those who have received healing or renewed life from His Word. The death of Jesus was the grandest gift of all, for through His death we who call on His name have everlasting life and a place at the banquet table of God.

> (a) Jesus Christ is the gift of God, the richest token of God's love to us, and the richest treasure of all good for

us; a gift, not a debt which we could demand from God; not a loan, which he will demand from us again, but a gift, a free gift" John 3:16. (b) It is an unspeakable privilege to have this gift of God proposed and offered to us; to have an opportunity of embracing it: "He who is the gift of God is now set before thee, and addresses himself to thee; it is he that saith, Give me to drink; this gift comes a begging to thee." (c) Though Christ is set before us, and [soothes] us in and by his gospel, yet there are multitudes that know him not. They know not who it is that speaks to them in the gospel, that saith, Give me to drink; they perceive not that it is the Lord that calls them (*Matthew Henry's Commentary*).

180. Living Water – *Zao Hudor*

"Jesus answered and said unto her, If thou knewest the gift of God, and who it is that saith to thee, Give me to drink; thou wouldest have asked of him, and he would have given thee *living water*. The woman saith unto him, Sir, thou hast nothing to draw with, and the well is deep: from whence then hast thou that living water? Art thou greater than our father Jacob, which gave us the well, and drank thereof himself, and his children, and his cattle? Jesus answered and said unto her, Whosoever drinketh of this water shall thirst again: but whosoever drinketh of the water that I shall give him shall never thirst; but the water that I shall give him shall be in him a well of water springing up into everlasting life" (John 4:10-14).

Definition: *Zao* - (1) to live, to breathe, to be among the living (not lifeless, not dead) (2) to enjoy real life: (a) to have true life that is worthy of the name (b) to be active, blessed, and endless in the kingdom of God (3) to live, that is, to pass life, in the manner of the living and acting of mortals or character (4) living water, having vital power in itself and exerting the same upon the soul (5) metaphorically, to be in full vigor (a) to be fresh, strong, efficient, (b) as adjective: active, powerful, efficacious. (*The New Thayer's Greek-English Lexicon*)

203

Hudor (hoo'-dore) [5204]; genitive case, *hudatos* (hoo'-dat-os), etc.; from the base of *huetos*; water (as if rainy) literally or figuratively: – water. (S)

Water is necessary for life as we know it. When scientists study other planets, the criterion for the ability to sustain life is the mean temperature of the surface because of the need for water in a usable state.

During the Creation, God spent day 2 placing the proper amount of water in the heavens and on earth (see Genesis 1:6-9). On the third day, He gathered the waters into seas and lakes, separating them from dry land. In Noah's day, God used water to destroy all life except that in the ark (Genesis 6:17).

The first plague God sent to Egypt affected the water of Egypt and demonstrated God's power over the Nile River, an Egyptian diety (see Exodus 7:14-25). God parted the Red Sea, again demonstrating His power to control water (Exodus 14:21). He performed a similar miracle when the Israelites crossed the Jordan River to enter the Promised Land (Joshua 3:14-17).

Jesus walked on the water (Matthew 14:25), quieted a raging sea (Luke 8:24, 25) and turned water into wine (John 2:1-11). These things demonstrate the role water has played in God's creation and in life. They show how God has used water to demonstrate His sovereignty and control over His creation.

Jesus told the woman at the well that if she asked, He could give her living water. Nobody had ever claimed to have living water; but she knew that if such a thing existed, she wanted some of it. The water Jesus offered was the life-giving water of the Holy Spirit. The Lord was offering her eternal life from a new life-giving source, the very blood of Jesus.

Jesus went a step further when He told the woman that she would have wells of living water coming out of her, also. The water Jesus spoke of contains His life. It will come gushing out of those who will partake of it, giving that same life and flow of the Spirit. He still offers living water today. Bring your cup and drink of Christ. The price has already been paid, and there is no charge. The only requirement is that you realize your thirst and come to Jesus for His abundant supply. (*See #118.*)

181. Savior of the World – *Soter Ho Kosmos*

"And said unto the woman, Now we believe, not because of thy saying: for we have heard him ourselves, and know that this is indeed the Christ, the *Saviour of the world*" (John 4:42).

> **Definition:** *Soter* [4990] - a savior, a deliverer, a preserver; The name was given by the ancients to deities, especially tutelary deities, to princes, kings, and in general to men who had conferred signal benefits upon their country, and in more degenerate days by the way of flattery to personages of influence. (*Thayer's Greek-English Lexicon*)
>
> *Kosmos* (kos'-mos) [2889]; probably from the base of *komizo*; orderly arrangement, i.e. decoration; by implication, the world (in a wide or narrow sense, including its inhabitants, literally or figuratively [morally]): – adorning, world. (S)

Jesus was the Savior of the church, but He was (and is) the Savior of the world. This refers to the fact that Jesus is the only One who can be the Savior of humanity. He is also the only hope for our world system. We try to fix things with the political and legal systems of this country, when in reality the only hope for America or any other nation is Jesus. To see lasting change, we must introduce this world to the One who can make it right again. (*See #56, #122, #161, #235.*)

182. Bread of Life – *Artos Zoe*

"And Jesus said unto them, I am the *bread of life*: he that cometh to me shall never hunger; and he that believeth on me shall never thirst" (John 6:35).

"I am the *bread of life*" (John 6:48, *NKJV*).

> **Definition:** *Artos* (ar'-tos) [740]; from *airo*; bread (as raised) or a loaf: – (shew-) bread, loaf. (S)

Look at how *Thayer's Greek-English Lexicon* defines *Zoe*, the word for "life":

> (1) life (a) the state of one who is possessed of vitality or is animate (b) every living soul (2) life (a) used of the absolute fullness of life, both essential and ethical, which belongs to God, and through him both to the hypostatic "logos" and to Christ in whom the "logos" put on human nature (b) life real and genuine, a life active and vigorous, devoted to God, blessed, in the portion even in this world of those who put their trust in Christ, but after the resurrection to be consummated by new accessions (among them a more perfect body), and to last forever.

(*See #183, #259.*)

183. Living Bread – *Zao Artos*

"I am the *living bread* which came down from heaven. If anyone eats of this bread, he will live forever; and the bread that I shall give is My flesh, which I shall give for the life of the world" (John 6:51, *NKJV*).

> **Definition:** *Zao* (dzah'-o) [2198]; a primary verb; to live (literally or figuratively): – life (-time), (a-) live (-ly), quick. (S)

To fully appreciate this revelation of Jesus, you have to understand how much bread meant to the people of Jesus' day. They had much more than a slice of bread with a meal as we commonly do. Bread was a staple on which the Hebrew family based much of its diet.

See how God provided bread for them to eat while they wandered in the wilderness. They called this bread *manna* (see Exodus 16). *Manna* is actually the Hebrew word for a query.

They couldn't really tell for sure what the bread-like substance was that appeared outside the camp each morning so they called it "What is it?" or manna.

This bread that God provided in the wilderness was the only thing they needed to eat. If Americans tried to live on the wimpy stuff we pass off as bread, we would suffer malnutrition in no time. Even the rich, whole-grain breads of the Holy Land could not sustain the lives of 3 or 4 million people for 40 years while they wandered in the wilderness.

The bread God gave them contained all the vitamins and minerals needed for survival; it was sufficient to provide a quality life with health and vitality.

Jesus is living bread today! We partake of Him when we place our trust and confidence in Him and His work at Calvary. We are born again with His *Zao* life when we ask Jesus into our hearts. He then lives within us the victorious life available through the blood of Christ. The same One who was the "Living Bread" has also become the "Bread of Life." He who was able to keep us alive is also able to use us for sharing His life with others. (*See #182, #259.*)

184. Light of the World – *Phos Kosmos*

"Then spake Jesus again unto them, saying, I am the *light of the world*: he that followeth me shall not walk in darkness, but shall have the light of life" (John 8:12).

Definition: *Phos* (foce) [5457]; from an obsolete *phao* (to shine or make manifest, especially by rays; compare *phaino*, *phemi*); luminousness (in the widest application, nat. or artificial, abstract or concrete, literal or figurative): – fire, light. (S)

Kosmos (kos'-mos) [2889]; probably from the base of *komizo*; orderly arrangement, i.e. decoration; by implication, the world (in a wide or narrow sense, including its inhabitants, literally or figuratively [morally]): – adorning, world. (S)

"If I say, 'Surely the darkness will hide me and the light become night around me,' even the darkness will not be dark to you; the night will shine like the day, for darkness is as light to you" (Psalm 139:11, 12, *NIV*).

"This is the verdict: Light has come into the world, but men loved darkness instead of light because their deeds were evil. Everyone who does evil hates the light, and will not come into the light for fear that his deeds will be exposed. But whoever lives by the truth comes into the light, so that it may be seen plainly that what he has done has been done through God" (John 3:19-21, *NIV*).

"This is the message we have heard from him and declare to you: God is light; in him there is no darkness at all" (1 John 1:5, *NIV*).

"The city does not need the sun or the moon to shine on it, for the glory of God gives it light, and the Lamb is its lamp" (Revelation 21:23, *NIV*).

According to Matthew 5:14, we are also the light of the world. We must be sure that the world sees Christ's light in us. As the moon shines with a reflected glory of the sun to light up the night, so God has chosen us to reflect the manifest glory of His Son, Jesus, to light the way for those trapped in the darkness of this world.

Let the Lord's light shine without blocking the radiance, and others will notice and be affected in a positive way for the kingdom of God. (*See #2, #63, #121, #173, #271.*)

185. I Am – *Ego Eimi*

"Jesus said unto them, Verily, verily, I say unto you, Before Abraham was, *I am*" (John 8:58).

Definition: *Ego* (eg-o') [1473]; a primary pronoun of the first person I (only expressed when emphatic): – I, me. (S)

Eimi (i-mee') [1510]; the first person singular present indicative; a prolonged form of a primary and defective verb; I exist (used only when emphatic): – am, have been, X it is I, was. (S)

The New Testament is filled with proclamations of who Jesus is. The study of the "I Am's" of Jesus will bring an inspiring revelation to the believer who seeks to know God in a more intimate way. We will look at most of these separately throughout this book, but this is a good place to put them all together for collective study.

"Take My yoke upon you and learn from Me, for I am gentle and lowly in heart, and you will find rest for your souls" (Matthew 11:29, *NKJV*).

"I am the God of Abraham, the God of Isaac, and the God of Jacob? God is not the God of the dead, but of the living" (Matthew 22:32, *NKJV*).

"Then they all said, 'Are You then the Son of God?' And He said to them, 'You rightly say that I am'" (Luke 22:70, *NKJV*).

"I am the living bread . . . from heaven. If anyone eats of this bread, he will live forever; and the bread that I shall give is My flesh, which I shall give for the life of the world" (John 6:51, *NKJV*).

Then Jesus spoke to them again, saying, "I am the light of the world. He who follows Me shall not walk in darkness, but have the light of life" (John 8:12, *NKJV*).

"I am One who bears witness of Myself, and the Father who sent Me bears witness of Me" (John 8:18, *NKJV*).

Jesus said to them, "Most assuredly, I say to you, before Abraham was, I AM" (John 8:58, *NKJV*).

Then Jesus said to them again, "Most assuredly, I say to you, I am the door of the sheep" (John 10:7, *NKJV*).

"I am the door. If anyone enters by Me, he will be saved, and will go in and out and find pasture" (John 10:9, *NKJV*).

"I am the good shepherd. The good shepherd gives His life for the sheep" (John 10:11, *NKJV*).

"Do you say of Him whom the Father sanctified and sent into the world, 'You are blaspheming,' because I said, 'I am the Son of God'?" (John 10:36, *NKJV*).

Jesus said to her, "I am the resurrection and the life. He who believes in Me, though he may die, he shall live" (John 11:25, *NKJV*).

Jesus said . . . "I am the way, the truth, and the life. No one comes to the Father except through Me" (John 14:6, *NKJV*).

"I am the vine, you are the branches. He who abides in Me, and I in him, bears much fruit" (John 15:5, *NKJV*).

"They are not of the world, just as I am not of the world" (John 17:16, *NKJV*).

Jesus answered, "You say rightly that I am a king. For this cause I was born, and for this cause I have come into the world" (John 18:37, *NKJV*).

"I am with you, and no one will attack you to hurt you; for I have many people in this city" (Acts 18:10, *NKJV*).

"I am the Alpha and the Omega, the Beginning and the End," says the Lord, "who is and who was and who is to come, the Almighty" (Revelation 1:8, *NKJV*).

And when I saw Him, I fell at His feet as dead. But He laid His right hand on me, saying to me, "Do not be afraid; I am the First and the Last. I am He who lives, and was dead, and behold, I am alive forevermore. Amen. And I have the keys of Hades and of Death" (Revelation 1:17, 18, *NKJV*).

"Behold, I come quickly! Hold fast what you have, that no one may take your crown" (Revelation 3:11, *NKJV*).

"Behold, I am coming as a thief. Blessed is he who watches. . ." (Revelation 16:15, *NKJV*).

"I am the Alpha and the Omega, the Beginning and the End, the First and the Last" (Revelation 22:13, *NKJV*).

"I am the root and the Offspring of David, and the Bright and Morning Star" (Revelation 22:16, *NKJV*).

(See #16.)

186. Door – *Thura*

"Then said Jesus unto them again, Verily, verily, I say unto you, I am the *door* of the sheep" (John 10:7).

> **Definition:** *Thura* - a door (a) the vestibule (b) used of any opening like a door, an entrance, way or passage into (c) in a parable or metaphor (1) the door through which sheep go in and out, the name of him who brings salvation to those who follow his guidance (2) "an open door" is used for the opportunity of doing something (3) the door of the kingdom of heaven (likened to a palace) denotes the conditions which must be complied with in order to be received into the kingdom of God. (*Thayer's Greek-English Lexicon*)

When Jesus proclaimed that He is the door, He was focusing on His protection for the flock of God. Jesus is not one of many entrances, he is the *only* way into the sheepfold. No bear, lion or thief could get a sheep from God's flock without going through the door (Jesus) first. (*See #92, #190.*)

187. Good Shepherd – *Kalos Poimen*

"I am the *good shepherd*: the good shepherd giveth his life for the sheep" (John 10:11).

> **Definition:** *Kalos* (kal-os') [2570]; of uncertain affinity; properly, beautiful, but chiefly (figuratively) good (literally or morally), i.e. valuable or virtuous (for appearance or use, and thus distinguished from *agathos*, which is properly intrinsic): (S) X better, fair, good (-ly), honest, meet, well, worthy. (S)
>
> *Poimen* (poy-mane') [4166]; of uncertain affinity; a shepherd (literally or figuratively): – shepherd, pastor. (S)

We have studied this revelation of God's nature as it relates to the triune Godhead being in Psalm 23 where God is called "the Lord our Shepherd" (*see #31*). We have also looked at the Old Testament Hebrew word *Ra'ah* in Genesis 49:24 as it applies to our Lord and Savior Jesus Christ (*see #76*). Now we look at this New Testament Greek word *Poimen* to see what it meant to the contemporaries of Jesus when He used it of Himself.

Poimen is translated "shepherd" or "shepherds" 17 times in the New Testament. It is also translated "pastor" in Ephesians 4:11. Jesus is not just a shepherd to His flock, He is the "Good Shepherd." The Greek word *Kalos*, translated "good," means beautiful, valuable or virtuous. Jesus is *always* good. He cannot be or act in any other way. The circumstances of life may not always seem good, but Jesus is good all the time.

If Jesus is our Good Shepherd, where does that place our church pastors? They are considered under-shepherds if they are in correct relationship with the Chief Shepherd, Jesus (1 Peter 5:4). But they can never be the head of His body.

Jesus is the head of the church (Ephesians 5:23). He and the Word of God, not the local pastor, must be the highest authorities in the life of the believer. This is a moot point if one is submitted to a godly pastor, but it is important to understand this truth, should any discrepancy arise. (*See #31, #76, #249.*)

188. Resurrection and the Life – *Anastasis Zoe*

"Jesus said unto her, "I am the *resurrection, and the life*: he that believeth in me, though he were dead, yet shall he live" (John 11:25).

> **Definition:** *Anastasis* (an-as'-tas-is) [386]; from *anastemi*; a standing up again, i.e. (literally) a resurrection from death (individual, genitive case or by implication [its author]), or (figuratively) a (moral) recovery (of spiritual truth): – raised to life again, resurrection, rise from the dead, that should rise, rising again. (S)

John 11:25, 26. Jesus has power over life and death as well as power to forgive sins. This is because he is the Creator of life (see John 14:6). He who *is* life can surely restore life. Whoever believes in Christ has a spiritual life that death cannot conquer or diminish in any way. When we realize his power and how wonderful his offer to us really is, how can we help but commit our lives to him! To those of us who believe, what wonderful assurance and certainty we have: "Because I live, you also will live" (John 14:19). (*Life Application Study Bible*)

Jesus referred to Himself the resurrection and the life in a conversation with Martha after Lazarus had died, but before Jesus resurrected him from the tomb. Jesus spoke of His authority over death at that time and at His Second Coming in the future. Without doubt, Jesus exercises His authority over death today.

We are promised in the scriptures that death cannot separate us from the love of God.

Nay, in all these things we are more than conquerors through him that loved us. For I am persuaded, that neither death, nor life, nor angels, nor principalities, nor powers, nor things present, nor things to come, nor height, nor depth, nor any other creature, shall be able to separate us from the love of God, which is in Christ Jesus our Lord (Romans 8:37-39).

The fear of death should no longer hold the believer hostage. All of our hope is not tied up in this life. Jesus is our resurrection now. The Lord is our life now, and He is the promise of life to come. (*See #192, #195, #289.*)

189. Corn of Wheat – *Kokkos Sitos*

"Verily, verily, I say unto you, Except a *corn of wheat* fall into the ground and die, it abideth alone: but if it die, it bringeth forth much fruit" (John 12:24).

Definition: *Kokkos* (kok'-kos) [2848]; apparently a primary word; a kernel of seed: – corn, grain. (S)

Sitos (see'-tos) [4621]; plural irregular neuter *sita* (see'-tah); of uncertain derivation; grain, especially wheat: – corn, wheat. (S)

John 12:23-25. This is a beautiful picture of the necessary sacrifice of Jesus. Unless a kernel of wheat is buried in the ground, it will not become a blade of wheat producing many more seeds. Jesus had to die to pay the penalty for our sin, but also to show his power over death. His resurrection proves he has eternal life. Because Jesus is God, Jesus can give this same eternal life to all who believe in him. (*Life Application Study Bible*)

To know about seeds and planting, talk to a farmer. A farmer knows that all the potential for a crop lies in the seed planted. Other things may contribute to the final outcome of a growing season, but the seed is probably the most important single ingredient in assuring a successful season.

Many of today's crops are hybrid, meaning that the seeds are derived through a careful process of pollinating specific types of plants in a way that cannot be duplicated in the farmer's field. Often you can plant a seed grown in your own field and it will not even germinate.

Also, the seed a farmer buys is more disease-resistant than what he might find in his own field. Interbreeding of seed predisposes the resultant crop to be less resistant to genetic weaknesses and defects. Hence, the farmer may spend more money to acquire a quality seed than what he would expect to get for the same amount of grain when the crop comes in.

A seed must die in order to germinate! A farmer never plants a seed that has not gone through a period of dormancy and apparent death. The seed is usually dried and sprayed with chemicals to repel the common pests that would otherwise consume or ruin it. By the time it is ready for planting, the seed rarely appears appetizing or ready for cooking. In the case of corn, the seed is extremely dry and shriveled up by the time it is ready for planting.

You cannot tell what the crop is going to look like by the appearance of the seed. For example, corn seed is yellow, orange or white, and its shape is somewhat squared or boxy. The plant that grows up out of properly planted corn seed is green and leafy, tall and magnificent in its appearance, nothing like the seed planted.

Christ had to die and be buried before the resurrection life of God could be released to all believers. The body buried was not like the body resurrected. "He shall grow up before him as a tender plant, and as a root out of a dry ground: he hath no form nor comeliness; and when we shall see him, there is no beauty that we should desire him" (Isaiah 53:2). That which was planted was nothing like that which was raised. (*See #72.*)

190. Way – *Hodos*

"Jesus saith unto him, 'I am the *way*, the truth, and the life: no man cometh unto the Father, but by me" (John 14:6).

> **Definition:** *Hodos* - (1) properly: (a) a way, a traveled way, a road (b) a traveler's way, a journey, traveling (2) metaphorically: (a) a course of conduct (b) a way (that is, manner) of thinking, feeling, deciding (*Thayer's Greek-English Lexicon*). (S)

Jesus is not just *one* way, He is the *only* way. There is no channel through which we can have a relationship with the Father except through Jesus, the Son. Humanity was given dominion over the earth at Creation (Genesis 1:26), and the result of that dominion was that when one man (Adam) sinned, all sinned through him. If God's justice was to be served, man must die for his sins. But in the sovereignty of God, He became flesh through Jesus and took the penalty for sin upon Himself.

Mercy and justice met at the cross. Now, through the grace of God, we all have the choice to enter into the fullness of His joy. This resulted from the relationship secured at the cost of the most precious blood ever shed for the remission of sin!

> **14:5, 6.** This is one of the most basic and important passages in Scripture. How can we know the way to God? Only through Jesus. Jesus is the way because he is both God and man. By uniting our lives with his, we are united with God. Trust Jesus to take you to the Father, and all the benefits of being God's child will be yours.

> **14:6.** Jesus says he is the *only* way to God the Father. Some people may argue that this way is too narrow. In reality, it is wide enough for the whole world, if the world chooses to accept it. Instead of worrying about how limited it sounds to have only one way, we should be saying, "Thank you, God, for providing a sure way to get to you!" (*Life Application Study Bible*)

People seek other ways to God. Religions offer laws to obey that are purported to make a way to God. Martin Luther saw this when he received a revelation from God concerning Romans 1:17: "The just shall live by faith." He immediately realized that his religion was keeping him from a true understanding of God's grace. Good works or good intentions will not establish a relationship with the godhead and your failures and shortcomings will not break that relationship. Christ is all, and in all. (*See #39, #92, #186.*)

191. Truth – *Aletheia*

"Jesus saith unto him, 'I am the way, the *truth*, and the life: no man cometh unto the Father, but by me" (John 14:6).

> **Definition:** *Aletheia* - (1) objectively: (a) what is true in any matter under consideration (1) truly, in truth, According to truth (2) of a truth, in reality, in fact, certainly (b) what is true

in things pertaining to God and the duties of man, moral and religious truth (1) in the greatest latitude (2) the true notions of God which are open to human reason without his supernatural intervention (c) the truth as taught in the Christian faith, respecting God and the execution of his purposes through Christ, and respecting the duties of man, opposing alike to the superstitions of the Gentiles (non-Jews) and the inventions of the Jews, and the corrupt opinions and precepts of false teachers even among Christians (2) subjectively: truth as a personal excellence: that candor of mind which is free from affection, pretense, simulation, falsehood, deceit. (*Thayer's Greek-English Lexicon*)

Some say that Jesus is the answer to every question in life. You have to be asking the right questions for Jesus to be the true and perfect answer. The same thing holds true as we consider Jesus as the "truth." There are a lot of things that are true, but Jesus is divine "truth" and God's most perfect answer for all the struggles and trials of this life.

If I told you that the skies were blue on a clear wintry day in South Carolina, that would be a true statement. In your mind's eye, you may even conjure up a vision of the right shade of blue, based on your own experiences and imaginations. But in the overall workings of God in His creation, such a truth is not absolute nor universal. There are many shades of sky blue, depending on the angle of the sun and the time of day as well asatmospheric conditions. These facts may be true, they definitely are not *absolute* truth.

The truths concerning Jesus are not based on experiences or imaginations alone. In no circumstance do these truths vary or are lessened in their impact or application. What we read in the Word of God is true, whether we see it with our own eyes or not. Jesus is truth amid a world of lies and deceit. Jesus is immutable, as are His teachings and revelations. God's truth is unchanging in a fickle world. (*See #287, #31.*)

192. Life – *Zoe*

"Jesus saith unto him, 'I am the way, the truth, and the *life*: no man cometh unto the Father, but by me" (John 14:6).

> **Definition:** *Zoe* - (1) life (a) the state of one who is possessed of vitality or is animate (b) every living soul (2) life (a) used of the absolute fullness of life, both essential and ethical, which belongs to God, and through him both to the hypostatic "logos" and to Christ in whom the "logos" put on human nature (b) life real and genuine, a life active and vigorous, devoted to God, blessed, in the portion even in this world of those who put their trust in Christ, but after the resurrection to be consummated by new accessions (among them a more perfect body), and to last forever. (*Thayer's Greek-English Lexicon*)

The best definition I know for the Greek word *zoe* is: "Life as God *has* it." It is a quality of life that supercedes plain existence.

Two other Greek words translated "life" relate to an understanding of the Biblical meaning of life: *bios* and *psuche*. The study of *psuche* life is called psychology; the study of *bios* life is called biology; the study of what the intellectuals understand *zoe* life to be is called zoology.

Unfortunately many zoology teachers have no grasp of the true *zoe* life that God offers all of His children. (*See #188, #195, #288.*)

193. True Vine – *Alethinos Ampelos*

"I am the *true vine*, and my Father is the husbandman" (John 15:1).

> **Definition:** *Alethinos* (al-ay-thee-nos') [228]; from *alethes*; truthful: – true. (S)
>
> *Ampelos* (am'-pel-os) [288]; probably from the base of *amphoteros* and that of *halon*; a vine (as coiling about a support): – vine. (S)

Jesus is likened to a vine, probably a grapevine. A vine is the stalk or trunk of the plant, responsible for establishing the flow of nutrients from the soil in which it is planted to the branches that are expected to bear the fruit.

In John 15:1, Jesus establishes the fact that He is not just a vine, He is the true vine of God. He has life in Himself, yet He chose to submit to His Father's life and will. When we are in a proper relationship with Jesus, His life and power are manifested in us.

> The grapevine is a prolific plant; a single vine bears many grapes. In the Old Testament, grapes symbolized Israel's fruitfulness in doing God's work on the earth (Psalm 80:8; Isaiah 5:1-7; Ezekiel 19:10-14). In the Passover meal, the fruit of the vine symbolized God's goodness to his people. (*Life Application Study Bible*)

"I am the vine, you are the branches. He who abides in Me, and I in him, bears much fruit; for without Me you can do nothing" (John 15:5, *NKJV*). (*See #110.*)

194. The Man – *Ho Anthropos*

"Then came Jesus forth, wearing the crown of thorns, and the purple robe. And Pilate saith unto them, Behold *the man!*" (John 19:5).

"For *there is* one God and one Mediator between God and men, *the Man* Christ Jesus" (1 Timothy 2:5, *NKJV*).

> **Definition:** *Ho* (including the feminine *he*, and the neuter *to*) - this, that, these, etc. (*The New Thayer's Greek-English Lexicon*).

> *Anthropos* (anth'-ro-pos) [444]; from *aner* and *ops* (the countenance; from *optanomai*); man-faced, i.e. a human being: – certain, man. (S)

Jesus was, and is, God with the face of a man. The incarnation is a mystery at best.

God of gods, Lord of lords!

One hundred percent man and, at the same time, 100 percent God. Jesus never was anything less than God.

Yet, He walked through His life on earth, never allowing His godliness to separate Him from the obvious limitations of His human body. He did it willingly for our sakes.

Because of the incarnation, God, through Jesus Christ, has overcome the world and the world system. Jesus knows our weaknesses and desires. He knows perfectly the pains and trials we face in this lifetime. Jesus did all this without compromising truth or allowing Himself to sin.

This is the Christian's hope in the present life. Because Jesus overcame the world, I know that there is hope for us to do the same as we allow Him to penetrate every nook and cranny of our lives and hearts.

In all truth, Jesus is still the name of God with the face of man. Only now the spirit of Jesus dwells within the hearts of all born again believers and we become the only face of God most of this generation will ever see. We are living epistles and the world must be able to know through us the glory and presence of a holy God. (*See #147.*)

PART 3
The Son of God

His Greek Names in

ACTS – CORINTHIANS

195. Prince of Life – *Archegos Zoe*

"And killed the *Prince of life*, whom God hath raised from the dead; whereof we are witnesses" (Acts 3:15).

> **Definition:** *Archegos* (ar-khay-gos') [747]; from *arche* and *ago*; a chief leader: – author, captain, prince. (S)

> **Acts 3:15.** *The author of life*: Other possible translations of the Greek title are "leader of life" or "pioneer of life." The title clearly points to Jesus as the source and originator of salvation" (*NAB Commentary*).

This explains fairly well the depth of meaning in the Greek word *archegos*. We studied the Greek word for "life" in our study of John 14:6. Now, in the Acts of the Apostles, we see Jesus as the "author, captain, prince or chief leader" of this life. I believe that this *zoe* life was breathed into Adam at Creation. I also believe it was this same breath of life that Ezekiel said was breathed into the dry bones in his vision in Ezekiel 37. Here Jesus is called "prince or author" of that kind of life. *Zoe* is the quality of life that separates one who knows God from those who don't in God's creation. (*See #192, #288.*)

196. Holy Child – *Hagios Pais*

"For of a truth against thy *holy child* Jesus, whom thou hast anointed, both Herod, and Pontius Pilate, with the Gentiles, and the people of Israel, were gathered together" (Acts 4:27).

> **Definition:** *Hagios* (hag'-ee-os) [40]; from *hagos* (an awful thing) [compare *hagnos*, *thalpo*]; sacred (physically, pure, morally blameless or religious, ceremonially, consecrated): – (most) holy (one, thing), saint. (S)

> *Pais* (paheece) [3816]; perhaps from *paio*; a boy (as often beaten with impunity), or (by analogy,) a girl, and (genitive case) a child; specifically, a slave or servant (especially a minister to a king; and by eminence to God): – child, maid (-en), (man) servant, son, young man. (S)

Jesus is the holy child of God. He was set apart, sanctified and ceremonially consecrated for the work before Him. As a child, Jesus fulfilled the call to be submitted to the Father. He was a servant (slave) to the things of God.

Peter faced the Sanhedrin Council after he and John were arrested for preaching in the name of Jesus. With boldness, the apostle spoke of his responsibility to be true to what he knew God wanted him to do. Peter was quick to point out to these spiritual leaders that they had placed the Son of God, Jesus, on a cross.

Leaving the council, both men joined with other believers in praying for more boldness and conviction to preach the gospel. They asked God to confirm their prayers with signs and wonders so that the world would know they had been with the Lord.

> When they had prayed, the place where they were assembled together was shaken; and they were all filled with the Holy Spirit, and they spoke the word of God with boldness" (Acts 4:31, *NKJV*).

(*See #104, #165, #167.*)

197. Just One – *Dikaios*

"Which of the prophets did your fathers not persecute? And they killed those who foretold the coming of the *Just One*, of whom you now have become the betrayers and murderers" (Acts 7:52, *NKJV*).

Definition: *Dikaios* (dik'-ah-yos) [1342]; from *dike*; equitable (in character or act); by implication, innocent, holy (absolutely or relatively): – just, meet, right (-eous). (S)

Stephen's audience represented religious legalists who had persecuted most of the prophets of history. They eventually hung Jesus on the cross. The three synoptic Gospels record Jesus' parable accusing the leaders of Israel of murdering the prophets and foretold the Crucifixion He knew would come (see Mark 12:1-12).

Here, Stephen is accusing the people he spoke to of fulfilling Jesus' prophecy. They immediately took Stephen outside the city and stoned him to death.

These people were vindictive. Jesus was, and is, just. Praise God, the justice I receive from Jesus passes through the mercy of God on its way to me. Jesus took the punishment due to me, and paid the ultimate price for my redemption with His blood.

Foolishly, some wish the people they know will get "what is coming to them." I do not want any of us to get what we are due, for we all deserve death and hell from a just God. (*See #36, #226.*)

198. Lord Jesus – *Kurios Iesous*

"And they stoned Stephen as he was calling on God and saying, '*Lord Jesus*, receive my spirit'" (Acts 7:59, *NKJV*).

> **Definition:** *Kurios* (koo'-ree-os) [2962]; from *kuros* (supremacy); supreme in authority, i.e. (as noun) controller; by implication, Mr. (as a respectful title): – God, Lord, master, Sir. (S)
>
> *Iesous* (ee-ay-sooce') [2424]; of Hebrew origin [*Lot*]; Jesus (i.e. *Jehoshua*), the name of our Lord and two (three) other Israelites: – Jesus. (S)

Stephen's comments placed his life on the line. He knew that the Lord Jesus had the power of eternal life, not these men. He stood on the promises of God and trusted entirely in the Word of God spoken through Jesus.

In John 11:25, Jesus had proclaimed Himself to be "the resurrection and the life." In John 14:6, He claimed to be "the life." Believing these truths to be accurate requires the believer to throw himself into the arms of God. God's Word says, "Trust in the Lord with all your heart, and lean not on your own understanding" (Proverbs 3:5, *NKJV*).

In Luke 23:34, Jesus prayed for those who crucified Him. He asked the Father to forgive them because they did not know what they were doing. Here, Stephen prays for his executioners in the same way Jesus did. Stephen asked the Lord to release his persecutors from the guilt of their crime. His knowing Jesus as Lord assured Stephen his prayer would be answered. (*See #143*.)

199. Lord of All – *Kurios Pas*

"You know the message God sent to the people of Israel, telling the good news of peace through Jesus Christ, who is *Lord of all*" (Acts 10:36, *NIV*).

> **Definition:** *Pas* (pas) [3956]; including all the forms of
> declension; apparently a primary word; all, any, every,
> the whole: – all (manner of, means), alway (-s), any (one),
> X daily, + ever, every (one, way), as many as, + no
> (-thing), X thoroughly, whatsoever, whole, whosoever. (S)

Up to this point in the brief history of the Christian church,
the gospel had gone out only to the Jewish people. The Jews
knew Jehovah to be their personal God, and themselves to be
His personal possession. In Acts 10, the gospel was preached
to Cornelius and his family. It was received, and God's favor
confirmed the Word in the hearts of those who received it.

In this context Peter proclaims Jesus to be *Lord of All.*
Jesus is not only the Jewish Messiah, He is also Lord of all
who receive Him. This should affect the way we pray and think.
No one of any social standing or moral makeup is beyond the
redemption Jesus offers. Nobody is beyond His reach or His
love. (*See #22, #29, #59, #300.*)

200. Mercy Seat (Propitiation) – *Hilasterion*

"Whom God hath set forth to be a *propitiation* through
faith in his blood, to declare his righteousness for the remission of sins that are past, through the forbearance of God"
(Romans 3:25).

> **Definition:** *Hilasterion* (hil-as-tay'-ree-on) [2435]; neuter
> of a derivative of *hilaskomai*; an expiatory (place or thing),
> i.e. (concretely) an atoning victim, or (specially) the lid
> of the Ark (in the Temple): – mercyseat, propitiation. (S)

The mercy seat was the lid on the ark of the covenant where
blood was poured for the remission of sins. Yearly, the high
priest entered into the Holy of Holies and offered a sacrifice
for the atonement of the sins of Israel. He first offered a young
bull, pouring out its blood for his own sins. Then he took two
goats and cast lots for them. One became the "scapegoat," the

other was sacrificed and its blood sprinkled on the mercy seat (see Leviticus 16).

Jesus is the great High Priest (Hebrews 3:1; 4:14, 15). And He is the *mercy seat* on which the sacrificial blood is offered (Romans 3:25).

201. Firstborn Among Many Brethren – *Prototokos Adelphos*

"For whom He foreknew, He also predestined to be conformed to the image of His Son, that He might be the *firstborn among many brethren*" (Romans 8:29, *NKJV*).

> **Definitions:** *Prototokos* - the firstborn a) of man or beast b) of Christ, the first born of all creation" (*The New Thayer's Greek-English Lexicon*).
>
> *Prototokos* (pro-tot-ok'-os) [4416]; from *protos* and the alternate of *tikto*; first-born (usually as noun, literally or figuratively): – firstbegotten (-born). (S)
>
> *Adephos* (ad-el-fos') [80]; from *a* (as a connective particle) and *delphus* (the womb); a brother (literally or figuratively) near or remote [much like a]: – brother. (S)

The human race is different from the rest of creation. God made all that is, but He breathed His life into the clay He had formed, and Adam came alive with God's own life.

Humanity was created with the capacity for a closer and more intimate relationship with the Father than any other created being had. When Adam fell, we all fell from that relationship in him. We were in Adam's loins and are, consequently, his sons and daughters. As such, we are co-heirs of the results of the fall.

When Jesus became flesh and dwelt among us, He was without sin. He became our way to regain the level of relationship with the Father that Adam once knew. In Christ, the righteousness of God is imputed and the effects of sin can be eliminated (see 2 Corinthians 5:21).

This does not mean that we are without sin or above temptation. It means, "If we confess our sins, He is faithful and just to forgive us our sins and to cleanse us from all unrighteousness" (1 John 1:9, *NKJV*).

> **First born among many brethren** (*prototokon en pollois adelphois*). Christ is 'first born' of all creation (Colossians 1:15), but here he is 'first born from the dead' (Colossians 1:18), the Eldest Brother in this family of God's sons, though "Son" in a sense not true of us. (*Robertson's Word Pictures*)

All who are born again by the Spirit of God and the blood of Jesus are accepted by the Father as coheirs with the Son. We are recipients of the great inheritance God offers His own children, both on the earth and in the promised heaven to come. (*See # 94.*)

202. Deliverer – *Rhoumai*

"And so all Israel will be saved, as it is written: 'The *deliverer* will come from Zion; he will turn godlessness away from Jacob'" (Romans 11:26, *NIV*).

> **Definition:** *Rhoumai* (hroo'-om-ahee) [4506]; middle voice of an obsolete verb, akin to *rheo* (through the idea of a current; compare *rhusis*); to rush or draw (for oneself), i.e. rescue: – deliver (-er). (S)

> **The Deliverer** (*Ho Ruomenos*). Present middle articular participle of *ruomai*, to rescue, to deliver. The Hebrew *Goel*, the Avenger, the Messiah, the Redeemer (Deuteronomy 25:5-10; Job 19:25; Ruth 3:12, 13). Paul interprets it of Jesus as Messiah. (*Word Pictures in the New Testament*)

The story of Ruth illustrates God's redemption. Naomi, Ruth's mother-in-law, found herself in a foreign country through no fault of her own. Naomi's husband and both sons died in the foreign land, and there was no one to go to for help. A widow left in a foreign land suffered and sometimes died if she didn't remarry or find a relative to support her. Naomi's only hope for survival was to find her way to her homeland and pray for a *goel* (redeemer) to come and redeem her.

Boaz was a kinsman of Naomi who could legally deliver her out of poverty and shame. The Hebrew word *goel* is translated "kinsman" (Ruth 2:20), "avenger" (Deuteronomy 19:6) and "redeemer" (Job 19:25). Naomi returned to her native land and people, and did all the things that she should do; but until the redeemer came forward and purchased her inheritance, she was still alienated and without help.

Much like Naomi, we were in bondage to sin and left as orphans in a foreign land. Without a redeemer, we were without hope. We could go to church, do all the right things and work hard as laborers for the kinsman of our souls; but until we allowed the Redeemer to purchase our inheritance, and we entered into a relationship with Him, we were lost. We need a deliverer, and Jesus is the only One who can deliver us out of sin and restore our entire inheritance in God's kingdom. (*See # 50.*)

203. Lord of Both the Dead and the Living – *Kurieuo Kai Nekros Zao*

"For to this end Christ both died, and rose, and revived, that he might be *Lord both of the dead and living*" (Romans 14:9).

> **Definition:** *Kurieuo* (ko-ree-yoo'-o) [2961]; from *kurios*; to rule: – have dominion over, lord, be lord of, exercise lordship over. (S)
>
> *Kai* (kahee) [2532]; apparently, a primary particle, having a copulative and sometimes also a cumulative force; and, also, even, so then, too, etc.; often used in connection (or composition) with other particles or small words: –

and, also, both, but, even, for, if, or, so, that, then, there-fore, when, yet. (S)

Nekros (nek-ros') [3498]; from an apparently primary *nekus* (a corpse); dead (literally or figuratively; also as noun): – dead. (S)

Zao (dzah'-o) [2198]; a primary verb; to live (literally or figuratively): – life (-time), (a-) live (-ly), quick. (S)

My family went through a trial on the day after Christmas in 1997, when our 5-year-old grandson, Derek Anthony Canter, was killed by an automobile. Nobody was charged with negligence or found guilty of foul play in the freak accident; but that gave us little comfort at the time.

On the night of the tragedy my wife, Linda, was crying uncontrollably and I was worried about her. The next morning found Linda quite calm and in control of her emotions. When I asked what had affected her so, Linda answered that she had met God in her prayer time and was assured that Derek was at peace with Jesus.

Our grandson had been playing and running through the yard one moment, and the next moment he was running with Jesus. Jesus is the Lord of both the living and the dead.

Search the Scriptures and you will find that believers do not suffer death in its true meaning. A believer may be separated from this tent of a body that now houses his or her spirit, but true death entails separation from the giver of life, Jesus.

Mark 12:27 reads, "He is not the God of the dead, but of the living" (*NIV*). Jesus was addressing some Sadducees who did not believe in the supernatural. He was proclaiming the reality that all people are eternal beings.

Those who had gone to be with the Lord in years past were as much alive as those still on the earth in Jesus' day. In Romans 14:9, Paul is saying the same thing in another way. Paul is explaining to believers in Rome that life is eternal for those in Christ. Whether the body is alive or dead, the spirit is eternal. Therefore, Jesus is "Lord both of the dead and the living." (*See #10.*)

204. Christ the Power of God – *Christos Dunamis Theos*

"But unto them which are called, both Jews and Greeks, *Christ the power of God*, and the wisdom of God" (1 Corinthians 1:24).

Definition: *Christos* (khris-tos') [5547]; from *Chrio*; anointed, i.e. the Messiah, an epithet of Jesus: – Christ. (S)

Dunamis (doo'-nam-is) [1411]; from 1410; force (literally or figuratively); specially, miraculous power (usually by implication, a miracle itself): – ability, abundance, meaning, might (-ily, -y, -y deed), (worker of) miracle (-s), power, strength, violence, mighty (wonderful) work. (S)

Theos (theh'-os) [2316]; of uncertain affinity; a deity, especially (with *ho*) the supreme Divinity; figuratively, a magistrate; by Hebraism, very: – X exceeding, God, god [-ly, -ward]. (S)

From the Greek word *dunamis* we get the word *dynamite* in English. It speaks of kinetic energy, something that is working right now. Another word translated "power" in the New Testament is *exousia*, which refers to the potential energy of God through Jesus (see Matthew 9:6). Both aspects of His nature are worth looking at in order to understand fully the power and majesty of our Lord and Savior, Jesus Christ.

Jesus is omnipotent (all powerful) just as the Father is omnipotent. According to John's Gospel, Jesus was the creative force through whom God the Father spoke all things into existence (John 1:1-4). Yet, Jesus is the One through whom the Father works out His will on earth. Our responsibility as believers is to allow the *dunamis* of God to flow through us and accomplish His will on earth as it is in heaven. (*See #210.*)

205. Wisdom of God – *Sophia Theos*

"But unto them which are called, both Jews and Greeks, Christ the power of God, and the *wisdom of God*" (1 Corinthians 1:24).

> **Definition:** *Sophia* (sof-ee'-ah) [4678]; from *sophos*; wisdom (higher or lower, worldly or spiritual): – wisdom.
>
> *Theos* (theh'-os) [2316]; of uncertain affinity; a deity, especially (with *ho*) the supreme Divinity; figuratively, a magistrate; by Hebraism, very: – X exceeding, God, god [-ly, -ward].

To those who have not received by faith the offer of eternal life in Christ, Jesus seems to be a fool's hope. But to those who walk in the Spirit, Jesus is the wisdom of God. In Proverbs there is a recurring theme of the wise man and the fool:

"The fear of the Lord is the beginning of knowledge: but fools despise wisdom and instruction" (Proverbs 1:7, *NKJV*).

"For scorners delight in their scorning, and fools hate knowledge" (Proverbs 1:22, *NKJV*).

"The way of a fool is right in his own eyes: but he that hearkeneth unto counsel is wise" (Proverbs 12:15).

"The wise shall inherit glory: but shame shall be the promotion of fools" (Proverbs 3:35).

God's ways are different from our own. A wise person accepts the counsel of God; a fool rejects it.

> "For My thoughts are not your thoughts, nor are your ways My ways," says the Lord. "For as the heavens are higher than the earth, so are My ways higher than your ways, and My thoughts than your thoughts" (Isaiah 55:8, 9, *NKJV*).

(*See #275, #53.*)

206. Lord of Glory – *Kurios Doxa*

"Which none of the princes of this world knew: for had they known it, they would not have crucified the *Lord of glory*" (1 Corinthians 2:8).

231

Definition: *Doxa* (dox'-ah) [1391]; from the base of *dokeo*; glory (as very apparent), in a wide application (literal or figurative, objective or subjective): – dignity, glory (-ious), honor, praise, worship. (S)

Paul defines spiritual wisdom from God's perspective. Religious leaders (the princes of this world) had unwittingly hanged the Lord of lords and King of kings on a cross. They misunderstood Him, thinking He was a rebel and blasphemer. The *New American Bible* translates *princes of this world* as "rulers of this age," indicating that more than just worldly rulers were involved. Leaders in the spiritual realm were involved as well.

But they did not realize that they were playing into the hands of God when they killed His Son. You see, Jesus had to die. In fact, He had to die the exact death that the "rulers of this age" thought they had concocted. His crucifixion and resurrection were the vehicles through which Jesus received His glorified body and overcame death. He defeated all the forces of evil set against Him by Satan.

The rulers of this age. This suggests not only the political leaders of the Jews and Romans under whom Jesus was crucified (cf. Acts 4:25-28) but also the cosmic powers behind them (cf. Ephesians 1:20-23; Ephesians 3:10). *They would not have crucified the Lord of glory*: they became the unwitting executors of God's plan, which will paradoxically bring about their own conquest and submission (1 Corinthians 15:24-28). (*NAB Commentary*).

(*See #32, #87, #91.*)

207. Passover Lamb – *Pascha*

"Get rid of the old yeast that you may be a new batch without yeast—as you really are. For Christ, our *Passover lamb*, has been sacrificed" (1 Corinthians 5:7, *NIV*).

Definition: *Pascha* (1) the paschal sacrifice (which was accustomed to be offered for the people's deliverance of old from Egypt) (2) the paschal lamb, that is, the lamb the Israelites were accustomed to kill and eat on the 14th day of the month of Nisan (the first month of their year) in memory of the day on which their fathers, preparing to depart from Egypt, were bidden by God to slay and eat a lamb, and to sprinkle their door posts with its blood, that the destroying angel, seeing the blood, might pass over their dwellings; Christ crucified is likened to the slain paschal lamb (3) the paschal supper (4) the paschal feast, the feast of the Passover, extending from the 14th to the 20th day of the month Nisan" (*Thayer's Greek-English Lexicon*).

Jesus is our Passover Lamb! Exodus 12 tells of the first Passover. Moses was sent by God to lead the Israelites out of the captivity of Egypt and to the Promised Land that was given to Abraham and his seed. When Pharaoh hardened his heart toward Moses and the Israelites, God demonstrated His superiority over the gods of the Egyptians through the plagues that Moses prophesied.

The last plague visited on Egypt was the death of all the first-born, both of animal and men. Moses was instructed regarding God's provision for deliverance from this plague through the sacrifice of a Passover lamb. The lamb was called this because the angel of death would *pass over* the homes that had the blood of a lamb on the doorposts and lintel of the entrance.

The events that took place on the night of the first Passover offer many implications for the Christian. Notice the angel's utter disregard for who was in the houses. Good and wicked people, men and women, young and old, dark-skinned and light-skinned, rich and poor—all manner of people were in the homes. The only thing that mattered to the angel of death was the blood.

Jesus is our Passover Lamb. His blood was shed that we might apply it to the door posts and lintels of our hearts and receive newness of life. No matter who we are or what we have done, when the blood of Jesus is applied to our lives we are received by the Father. The ground is level at the cross; there is no favoritism with God (Romans 2:11).

Our Passover Lamb was also the Great High Priest who carried His own blood to the throne of God and offered it for the sins of humanity. (*See #175, #244, #264.*)

208. Rock – *Petra*

"And did all drink the same spiritual drink: for they drank of that spiritual *Rock* that followed them: and that *Rock* was Christ" (1 Corinthians 10:4).

> **Definition:** *Petra* (pet'-ra) [4073]; feminine of the same as *petros*; a (mass of) rock (literally or figuratively): – rock. (S)

> **A Spiritual Rock That Followed Them.** The Torah speaks only about a rock from which water issued, but rabbinic legend amplified this into a spring that followed the Israelites throughout their migration. Paul uses this legend as a literary type: he makes the rock itself accompany the Israelites, and he gives it a spiritual sense (*NAB Commentary*).

> **The Rock Was the Christ.** In the Old Testament, Yahweh is the Rock of his people (cf Deuteronomy 32, Moses' song to Yahweh the Rock). Paul now applies this image to the Christ, the source of the living water, the true Rock that accompanied Israel, guiding their experiences in the desert (Exodus 17:1-7; Numbers 20:7-11; Deuteronomy 8:15.) (*NAB Commentary*)

(*See #48, #51, #77, #81, #113, #114, #214.*)

209. Last Adam – *Eschatos Adam*

"And so it is written, The first man Adam was made a living soul; the *last Adam* was made a quickening spirit" (1 Corinthians 15:45).

Definition: *Eschatos* (es'-khat-os) [2078]; a superlative probably from *echo* (in the sense of contiguity); farthest, final (of place or time): – ends of, last, latter end, lowest, uttermost. (S)

Adam (ad-am') [76]; of Hebrew origin [*athoos*]; Adam, the first man; typical (of Jesus) man (as his representative): – Adam. (S)

The imagery here is unmistakable. We were all "in Adam" inasmuch as he was the father of all humanity. What happened to Adam affected all who came after him, because he was the father of the whole human race.

Jesus is the "last Adam." No more provision will be made. Jesus is the final provision of God for the establishing of His kingdom of priests. Adam was made a living "soul," while Jesus came as a "quickening spirit." Soulishness brought Adam down and marked his life as one of sin and failure.

1 Corinthians 15:45. The "last Adam" refers to Christ. Because Christ rose from the dead, he is a life-giving spirit. This means that he entered into a new form of existence. He is the source of the spiritual life that will result in our resurrection. Christ's new glorified human body now suits his new glorified life—just as Adam's human body was suitable to his natural life. When we are resurrected, God will give us a transformed, eternal body suited to our new eternal life (*Life Application Study Bible*).

210. Quickening Spirit – *Zoopoieo Pneuma*

"And so it is written, The first man Adam was made a living soul; the last Adam was made *a quickening spirit*" (1 Corinthians 15:45).

Definition: *Zoopoieo* - (1) to produce alive, to begat or to bear living young (2) to cause to live, to make alive, to give life (a) by spiritual power to arouse and invigorate (b) to restore to life (c) to give increase of life: thus, of physical life (d) used of the spirit, quickening as respects the spirit, endued with new and greater powers of life (3) metaphorically, used of seeds quickened into life, that is, germinating, springing up, growing. (*Thayer's Greek-English Lexicon*)

Pneuma (pnyoo'-mah) [4151]; from *pneo*; a current of air, i.e. breath (blast) or a breeze; by analogy or figuratively, a spirit, i.e. (human) the rational soul, (by implication) vital principle, mental disposition, etc., or (superhuman) an angel, demon, or (divine) God, Christ's spirit, the Holy Spirit: – ghost, life, spirit (-ual, -ually), mind. Compare *psucho*. (S)

Zoopoieo is translated "quickening" in this scripture. It is a reproductive life-form with the power and unction to make more of its own kind. Jesus came that we may have life, abundant life (John 10:10)! But the life Jesus offers must be released to others. It reproduces itself in those willing to listen and receive. The more you give this quickening spirit away, the more you have for yourself! (*See #204.*)

211. Image of God – *Eikon Theos*

"The god of this age has blinded the minds of unbelievers, so that they cannot see the light of the gospel of the glory of Christ, who is the image of God" (2 Corinthians 4:4, *NIV*).

Definition: *Eikon* (i-kone') [1504]; from *eiko*; a likeness, i.e. (literally) statue, profile, or (figuratively) representation, resemblance: – image. (S)

The great lie that we are told in the media and society is that what the world has to offer us is the best. They say it is something we want and need. Jesus and Christianity have been depicted as an undesirous and impotent belief system that limits the rights and joys of those who believe in them.

Christians, however, have better eyesight than that. We see by the light of the gospel of Christ, the very image of God. The Bible and the Holy Spirit define our values and joys. What God offers through Jesus Christ is the true definition of joy and fulfillment in Him. (*See #215.*)

PART 3
The Son of God

His Greek Names in

EPHESIANS – TIMOTHY

---

212. Head of the Church – *Kephale Huper Pas Ekklesia*

"[God] hath put all things under [Christ's] feet, and gave him to be the head over all things to the church" (Ephesians 1:22).

Definition: *Kephale* (kef-al-ay') [2776]; from the primary *kapto* (in the sense of seizing); the head (as the part most readily taken hold of), literally or figuratively: – head. (S)

Huper (hoop-er') [5228]; a primary preposition; "over", i.e. (with the genitive case) of place, above, beyond, across, or causal, for the sake of, instead, regarding; with the accusative case superior to, more than: – (+exceeding, abundantly) above, in (on) behalf of, beyond, by, + very chiefest, concerning, exceeding (above, -ly), for, + very highly, more (than), of, over, on the part of, for sake of, in stead, than, to (-ward), very. In comp. it retains many of the above applications. (S)

Pas (pas) [3956]; including all the forms of declension; apparently a primary word; all, any, every, the whole: – all (manner of, means), alway (-s), any (one), X daily, + ever, every (one, way), as many as, + no (-thing), X thoroughly, whatsoever, whole, whosoever. (S)

Ekklesia (ek-klay-see'-ah) [1577]; from a compound of *ek* and a derivative of *kaleo*; a calling out, i.e. (concretely) a popular meeting, especially a religious congregation (Jewish synagogue, or Christian community of members on earth or saints in heaven or both): – assembly, church. (S)

In Charles Rolls' book *The World's Greatest Name*, he defines Christ as the Head of the Church. When the church is a family, Christ is the Firstborn and His likeness is impressed on the members of the household of faith. When the church is a flock, Christ is the Chief Shepherd, guiding and guarding with sympathy and sufficiency.

When the church is a fellowship, Christ is the bond of peace and basis of brotherhood that unites in worship and witness. When the church is a spotless bride, Christ is the faultless bridegroom; when the church is a body, Christ is the head. When the church is a building, Christ is the foundation on which the living stones are built. When the church is an army, Christ is the captain leading to victory.

Jesus is the vine, we are the branches. He is the Creator, we are the new creation in Christ. He is the head of the church in every aspect of its existence. (*See #217.*)

213. Our Peace – *Hemon Eirene*

"For he is *our peace*, who hath made both one, and hath broken down the middle wall of partition between us" (Ephesians 2:14).

Definition: *Hemon* (hay-mone') [2257]; genitive case plural of *ego*; of (or from) us: – our (company), us, we. (S)

Eirene (i-ray'-nay) [1515]; probably from a primary verb *eiro* (to join); peace (literally or figuratively); by implication, prosperity: – one, peace, quietness, rest, + set at one again. (S)

The "middle wall of partition" separated the rest of the world from the Holy Place in the Temple. Only the Jewish people could go beyond this wall; no Gentile was allowed. At the hour of Christ's death, the thick veil that separated the Most Holy Place (where only the high priest could go) and the Holy Place (or court of the men) was rent (or ripped) in two from the top to the bottom (Mark 15:38).

Christ himself has broken down the wall of partition. Jesus has made the way for every man and woman to enter into the presence of God. The only barrier standing between you and God is your pride. Even sin cannot keep you from the face of the Lord, for He has made provision by His sacrifice for all sin. "By one sacrifice he has made perfect forever those who are being made holy" (Hebrews 10:14, *NIV*). (*See #23, #109.*)

214. Corner Stone – *Akrogoniaios*

"And are built upon the foundation of the apostles and prophets, Jesus Christ himself being the chief *corner stone*" (Ephesians 2:20).

> **Definition:** *Akrogoniaios* (ak-rog-o-nee-ah'-yos) [204]; from *akron* and *gonia*; belonging to the extreme corner: – chief corner. (S)

Some think the building is the church. But the church is not the physical structure; the people themselves make up God's true church. God is building His church in the hearts of faithful people. Jesus is the chief cornerstone of the foundation of that building. The greatest building project of any fellowship is an evangelistic outreach to the lost in the area where the church meets. (*See #48, #51, #77, #81, #113, #114, #208.*)

215. Image of the Invisible God – *Eikon Aoratos Theos*

"Who is the *image of the invisible God*, the firstborn of every creature" (Colossians 1:15).

Definition: *Eikon* (i-kone') [1504]; from *eiko*; a likeness, i.e. (literally) statue, profile, or (figuratively) representation, resemblance: – image. (S)

Aoratos (ah-or'-at-os) [517]; from *a* (as a negative particle) and *horatos*; invisible: – invisible (thing). (S)

Humans have always tried to see God in a tangible way. Religions make statues of their gods and draw or paint likenesses to worship. Paul capitalized on this bit of human nature when he saw an altar with the inscription, "To the Unknown God" (see Acts 17). He told the people that he knew this God intimately, and offered to reveal the character and nature of the one true God to those who would listen.

In Colossians 1:15, Paul says that to know Jesus is to know God. To see Him move in the lives of His followers is to see God. Jehovah appeared to the Israelites on occasions as light, fire, clouds and thunderings; but they were sternly warned against making an image of God. Other nations worshiped idols and images, but the Jews were forbidden to make an image or likeness to worship. Paul proclaimed Jesus to be the image of the invisible God. (*See #211.*)

216. Creator of All Things – *Pas Ktizo Dia Autos*

"For by Him all things were created that are in heaven and that are on earth, visible and invisible, whether thrones or dominions or principalities or powers. All things were created through Him and for Him" (Colossians 1:16, *NKJV*).

Definition: *Pas* (pas) [3956]; including all the forms of declension; apparently a primary word; all, any, every, the whole: – all (manner of, means), alway (-s), any (one), X daily, + ever, every (one, way), as many as, + no (-thing), X thoroughly, whatsoever, whole, whosoever. (S)

Ktizo (ktid'-zo) [2936]; probably akin to *ktaomai* (through the idea of proprietor-ship of the manufacturer); to fabricate, i.e. found (form originally): – create, Creator, make. (S)

> *Dia* (dee-ah') [1223]; a primary preposition denoting the channel of an act; through (in very wide applications, local, causal, or occasional): – after, always, among, at, to avoid, because of (that), briefly, by, for (cause), fore, from, in, by occasion of, of, by reason of, for sake, that, thereby, therefore, X though, through (-out), to, wherefore, with (-in). In composition it retains the same general import. (S)

> *Autos* (ow-tos') [846]; from the particle au [perhaps akin to the base of *aer* through the idea of a baffling wind] (backward); the reflexive pronounself, used (alone or in the comparative *heautau*) of the third person and (with the proper personal pronoun) of the other persons: – her, it (-self), one, the other, (mine) own, said, ([self-], the) same, ([him-, my-, thyself, [your-] selves, she, that, their (-s), them ([-selves]), there [-at, -by, -in, -into, -of, -on, -with], they, (these) things, this (man), those, together, very, which. Compare *hautau*. (S)

Chronological Bibles often begin with John 1:1, 2: "In the beginning was the Word, and the Word was with God, and the Word was God. He was in the beginning with God." Jesus was with the Father before creation, and was the creative force who spoke everything into being. Not only were all things created *by* Jesus, but all things were made *for* Him. He is the epicenter of creation, with worlds revolving around Him and finding their purpose in Him. For His pleasure all things were made.

217. Head of the Body – *Kephale Soma*

"And he is the *head of the body*, the church: who is the beginning, the firstborn from the dead; that in all things he might have the preeminence" (Colossians 1:18).

> **Definition:** *Kephale* (kef-al-ay') [2776]; from the primary *kapto* (in the sense of seizing); the head (as the part most readily taken hold of), literally or figuratively: – head. (S)

> *Soma* (so'-mah) [4983]; from *sozo*; the body (as a sound whole), used in a very wide application, literally or figuratively: – bodily, body, slave. (S)

> **The head of the body** (*he kephale tou somatos*). Jesus is first also in the spiritual realm as he is in nature (vv. 18-20). Paul is fond of the metaphor of the body (*soma*) for believers of which body Christ is the head (*kephale*) as seen already in 1 Corinthians 11:3; 12:12, 27; Romans 12:5. See further Colossians 1:24: 2:19; Ephesians 1:22, 23; 4:2, 15; 5:30. (*Word Pictures in the New Testament*)

Paul frequently uses the metaphor of Christ as the head of His body—the church. I heard Pastor Lonnie Curl Jr. preach a series of messages on the government of the church from a Biblical perspective. He stated that the highest place a pastor holds in a local assembly is a "neck-down" ministry. He was referring to the fact that only Jesus has the right to be the head of the church. No pastor should call himself or herself the head of the church, or take that authority. Jim Jones and David Koresh tried to, and caused those who followed them to fail with them.

Each believer is responsible for knowing the Word of God, and for making spiritual judgments concerning what he or she is being fed. A good pastor holds a position of great influence over the congregation, but no man can take the place reserved only for Jesus, the head of the body, Christ's church. (*See #212.*)

218. Beginning – *Arche*

"And he is the head of the body, the church: who is the *beginning*, the firstborn from the dead; that in all things he might have the preeminence" (Colossians 1:18).

> **Definition:** *Arche* - (1) beginning, origin (2) the person or thing that commences, the first person or thing in a series, the leader (3) that by which anything begins to be, the origin, the active cause (4) the extremity of a thing; used of the corners of a sail (5) the first place, principality, rule, magistracy; used of angels and demons (*Thayer's Greek-English Lexicon*).

Life as a Christian is something like a spiritual game of follow-the-leader. Wherever Jesus goes, we follow.

Everything Jesus accomplished in living on earth was for us. Everything He accomplished through His death was for us. Jesus lived so that we might have life more abundantly (see John 10:10). He was crucified—put to death—and buried so that we might have the power to overcome death (see John 3:16). He was resurrected and He ascended to the Father so that we could have the hope of resurrection (see John 11:25). Jesus received His glorified body so that we too might have the hope of a glorified body (see 1 Corinthians 15:35-49). (*See #261.*)

219. Christ Is All and In All – *Christos Pas Pas*

"There is neither Greek nor Jew, circumcised nor uncircumcised, barbarian, Scythian, slave nor free, but *Christ is all and in all*" (Colossians 3:11, *NKJV*).

> **Definition:** *Christos* (khris-tos') [5547]; from *Chrio*; anointed, i.e. the Messiah, an epithet of Jesus: – Christ. (S)

> *Pas* (pas) [3956]; including all the forms of declension; apparently a primary word; all, any, every, the whole: – all (manner of, means), alway (-s), any (one), X daily, + ever, every (one, way), as many as, + no (-thing), X thoroughly, whatsoever, whole, whosoever. (S)

The message of the gospel is explicit about the lack of favoritism that Jesus demonstrated and required. Paul wrote almost these same words to the Galatian churches in Galatians 3:26-28. To the Romans he wrote, "For God does not show favoritism" (Romans 2:11, *NIV*).

Jesus, the Savior of all the world, offers salvation to all races, creeds, colors, ages and genders (see 1 Timothy 2:4). No social group is more acceptable or more loved by God. He does not prefer anyone or have a single favorite. You are not preferred because of your denomination, how high your steeple is, or how deep the water was when you were baptized. His unconditional love and salvation are offered to all who believe (see Romans 10:9-13).

> The Christian church should have no barriers of nationality, race, education level, social standing, wealth, gender, religion, or power. Christ breaks down all barriers and accepts all people who come to him. Nothing should keep us from telling others about Christ or accepting into our fellowship any and all believers (Ephesians 2:14, 15). Christians should be building bridges, not walls (*Life Application Study Bible*).

Following Christ is presented as a way to please the Father. Emphasis is often placed on obeying a set of rules, giving up a list of unholy activities or beginning a new lifestyle. It is implied that this is the way to earn God's love. While these things are beneficial to a new convert as a way to order his or her life, believers should understand that God's love is not affected or manipulated by such activities or by the lack thereof.

Scripture places emphasis on what God did through Christ as Savior and reconciler, not upon the actions of the people involved in His work. Jesus is the only way to the Father; there is no other. Christ is all and in all. "Be still, and know that I am God; I will be exalted among the nations, I will be exalted in the earth!" (Psalm 46:10, *NKJV*).

220. Lord of Peace – *Kurios Eirene*

"Now the *Lord of peace* himself give you peace always by all means. The Lord be with you all" (2 Thessalonians 3:16).

Definition: *Eirene* (i-ray'-nay) [1515]; probably from a primary verb *eiro* (to join); peace (literally or figuratively); by implication, prosperity: – one, peace, quietness, rest, + set at one again. (S)

This is part of the benediction to the second and last letter that Paul wrote to the church of the Thessalonians. Paul is asking God for the Lord of peace, Jesus Christ, to give and impart His peace to the Thessalonian church always and by all means. This is not the same type or level of peace that the world has to offer, and Paul went to great lengths in his letters to explain God's peace and to impart it to the church through his prayers. Many scriptures refer to peace throughout the Bible. (*See #23, #109, #213.*)

221. Our Hope – *Hemon Elpis*

"Paul, an apostle of Jesus Christ by the commandment of God our Savior, and Lord Jesus Christ, which is *our hope*" (1 Timothy 1:1).

> **Definition:** *Hemon* (hay-mone') [2257]; genitive case plural of *ego*; of (or from) us: – our (company), us, we. (S)
>
> *Elpis* (el-pece') [1680]; from a primary *elpo* (to anticipate, ususally with pleasure); expectation (abstractly or concretely) or confidence: – faith, hope. (S)
>
> **Our hope** (*tes elpidos hemon*). Like Colossians 1:27. More than the author and object of hope, "its very substance and foundation" (Ellicott). (*Word Pictures in the New Testament*)

Hope has always seemed to me to be an abstract thought. You can hope for only what you do not have. Faith is involved in hope, but all hope is not necessarily based on faith. You can hope for good weather even when you do not really believe that good weather is coming. Paul writes to Timothy that the Lord Jesus Christ *is* the hope of Christians. The favor we have been promised with God, through the blood of His Son, Jesus, overwhelms us. Although it may seem unbelievable, all of us should hope for it. I want peace, and to have right standing with the God of this universe . . . knowing that there is nothing in me worthy of such a gift. (*See #25.*)

222. Mediator – *Mesites*

"For there is one God, and one *mediator* between God and men, the man Christ Jesus" (1 Timothy 2:5).

> **Definition:** *Mesites* (mes-ee'-tace) [3316]; from *mesos*; a go-between, i.e. (simply) an internunciator, or (by implication) a reconciler (intercessor): – mediator. (S)

The difference between a mediator and an arbitrator is important. An arbitrator is appointed to settle a dispute, and is given authority to enforce his decisions; a mediator can only suggest a course of action to settle a disagreement. Jesus is a mediator, not an arbitrator. God never takes away your free will to accept or reject His counsel. This does not minimize the results of your actions in response to God's directions and prodding. Humans have the imputed sovereignty to say yea or nay to what God knows is the best course for us to take.

> **1 Timothy 2:5.** We human beings are separated from God by sin, and only one person in the universe is our mediator and can stand between us and God and bring us together again—Jesus, who is both God and man. Jesus' sacrifice brought new life to all people. Have you let him bring you to the Father? (*Life Application Study Bible*).

(*See #238, #242.*)

223. Blessed and Only Potentate – *Makarios Monos Dunastes*

"Which in his times he shall shew, who is the *blessed and only Potentate*, the King of kings, and Lord of lords" (1 Timothy 6:15).

> **Definition:** *Makarios* (mak-ar'-ee-os) [3107]; a prolonged form of the poetical *makar* (meaning the same); supremely blest; by extension, fortunate, well off: – blessed, happy (X -ier). (S)
>
> *Monos* (mon'-os) [3441]; probably from *meno*; remaining, i.e. sole or single; by implication mere: – alone, only, by themselves. (S)
>
> *Dunastes* (doo-nas'-tace) [1413]; from *dunamai*; a ruler or officer: – of great authority, mighty, potentate. (S)
>
> **Who is the blessed and only Potentate** (*Ho makarios kai monos Dunastes*). The happy and alone Potentate. *Dunastes*, old word, in N.T. only here, Luke 1:52; Acts 8:27 (the Eunuch) (*Word Pictures in the New Testament*).

I like the image in the Robertson's phrase, "the happy and alone Potentate." Jesus often spent time alone with His Father in prayer. Even with His disciples, He was alone in many respects. They often had no idea what He was talking about as He taught with parables and allegories. I have heard the phrase, "It is lonely at the top," from people in authority. It seems that the life of authority and responsibility tends to be rather solitary and lonely.

Jesus knew this kind of loneliness, but He did not suffer depression or despair. He was happy while alone and happy in a crowd. As King of kings and Lord of lords, He never allowed Himself to be unapproachable. Realizing the power and anointing He walked in, I am sure that few ever really gave themselves freely in relationship with Him. Jesus appeared to have a close relationship with John, Peter and James, but even these rarely understood Him when He opened His heart to them. Although alone and misunderstood, Jesus was not downtrodden or grief-stricken.

As Christians, we need to reflect this attribute of Christ more in our lives. Many are treated as lepers in the workplace because of their stand for Christ. Many pastors do not have a close friend and confidant they can trust. We often face times of being alone, even as we stand in a crowd of humanity. Let Jesus' joy be your strength. Let the Spirit of the Great "I Am" bless you and keep you, even in the midst of this messed-up world. (*See #145.*)

224. King of Kings – *Basileus Basileuo*

"Which in his times he shall shew, who is the blessed and only Potentate, the *King of kings*, and Lord of lords" (1 Timothy 6:15).

"These shall make war with the Lamb, and the Lamb shall overcome them: for he is Lord of lords, and *King of kings*: and they that are with him are called, and chosen, and faithful" (Revelation 17:14).

> **Definition:** *Basileus* (bas-il-yooce') [935]; probably from *basis* (through the notion of a foundation of power); a sovereign (abstractly, relatively, or figuratively): – king. (S)
>
> **The King of kings** (*ho basileus ton basileuonton*). 'The King of those who rule as kings.' Oriental title (*Word Pictures in the New Testament*).

Many have authority, or rule in one area or another. Some rule over great kingdoms and some over lesser ones. One person may lead a great nation, while another may act as a king in the workplace or the church. But Jesus Christ is the King of kings. Our Lord Jesus is the One who has ultimate rule and authority over all kings and kingdoms.

Bosses who are domineering and difficult to work with may appear as though they are autonomous or sovereign. Leadership in some churches may behave in an authoritative and legalistic manner. Many people do not approve of the president of the United States, or agree with all of his decisions.

There is One in control, however, to whom you can go for loving guidance and protection. As you pray to the King of kings, he often intervenes on behalf of His own. When God allows situations to continue, seemingly unaffected by prayers or petitions, know that He is in control and He will give you peace in the midst of your trials. (*See #38, #74, #225, #265.*)

225. Lord of Lords – *Kurios Kurieuo*

"Which in his times he shall shew, who is the blessed and only Potentate, the King of kings, and *Lord of lords*" (1 Timothy 6:15).

"These shall make war with the Lamb, and the Lamb shall overcome them: for he is *Lord of lords*, and King of kings: and they that are with him are called, and chosen, and faithful" (Revelation 17:14).

> **Definition:** *Kurios* (koo'-ree-os) [2962]; from *kuros* (supremacy); supreme in authority, i.e. (as noun) controller; by

implication, Mr. (as a respectful title): – God, Lord, master, Sir. (S)

"Lord" was a common title in Christ's day. Landowners were called "lord," teachers and rabbis were called "lord," and men of any level of authority would commonly be referred to as "lord" by those subservient to them. There were many lords with diversities of influence. Jesus Christ is the Lord who exercises influence over all other lords. Jesus was Lord of lords in 33 A.D. and He is still Lord of lords today. (*See #38, #74, #224, #265.*)

226. Righteous Judge – *Dikaios Krites*

"Henceforth there is laid up for me a crown of righteousness, which the Lord, the *righteous judge*, shall give me at that day: and not to me only, but unto all them also that love his appearing" (2 Timothy 4:8).

> **Definition:** *Dikaios* (dik'-ah-yos) [1342]; from *dike*; equitable (in character or act); by implication, innocent, holy (absolutely or relatively): – just, meet, right (-eous). (S)
>
> *Krites* (kree-tace') [2923]; from *krino*; a judge (genitive case or specially): – judge. (S)
>
> **The righteous judge** (*ho dikaios krites*). The "just judge," the umpire who makes no mistakes who judges us all (2 Corinthians 5:10) (*Word Pictures in the New Testament*).

I have had the misfortune of being a part of sporting activities where bad calls by the officials decided the game. These bad calls were made by imperfect people who were fallible and should not have been expected to make just calls in every circumstance; but it was hard to deal with these mistakes, nonetheless.

Jesus is the righteous judge. *Dikaios krites* evoke the image of an umpire who is both righteous and infallible. It almost seems sacrilegious to imply that Jesus is like an umpire, but comparisons are striking. An umpire's decision is always the final word. It doesn't matter what your eye saw or what the stop-action camera caught. What the umpire says is the judgment; his opinion is the only one that really matters. When an imperfect umpire makes an imperfect decision and a good manager gets upset, usually all that is accomplished by argument is that the coach is thrown out of the game for his enthusiastic rebuttal.

Jesus has the advantage of knowing not only what we have said and done, He even knows the thoughts and motivations that led us to the word or action. When Jesus passes judgments and makes His decisions, they are without error and above reproach.

Christians have an advantage, however. Jesus is on our side. He wants us to win . . . to attain the goal for which we strive. The Lord is able to pass absolute judgments concerning our failures and shortcomings, but His desire for all of us is to make it to His final "end-zone" or score the final "home-run."

Jesus wants us to come home to Him and bring as many of our loved ones as possible with us. (*See #36, #197.*)

PART 3
The Son of God

His Greek Names in

HEBREWS

---

227. Heir of All Things – *Kleronomos Pas*

"In these last days he has spoken to us by his Son, whom he appointed *heir of all things*, and through whom he made the universe" (Hebrews 1:2, *NIV*).

> **Definition:** *Kleronomos* (klay-ron-om'-os) [2818]; from *kleros* and the base of *nomos* (in its original sense of partitioning, i.e. [reflexively] getting by apportionment); a sharer by lot, i.e. inheritor (literally or figuratively); by implication, a possessor: – heir. (S)

In the Garden of Eden, Adam sold his birthright as the first-born and his enviable position as inheritor of all of God's best creation for a taste of forbidden fruit from the Tree of the Knowledge of Good and Evil. Adam still inherited God's creation, but it was a fallen creation and only a shadow of what God originally had for him (see Genesis 3). In chapter 25, Esau, Jacob's brother, found himself hungry. In his haste to satisfy his hunger, he fool-ishly sold his birthright to his brother for a bowl of red stew (see Genesis 25:29-34).

The first recorded temptation that Jesus faced was one of appe-tite, "If You are the Son of God, command that these stones be-come bread" (Matthew 4:3, *NKJV*). Jesus' response was, "It is written, 'Man shall not live by bread alone, but by every word that proceeds from the mouth of God'" (Matthew 4:4, *NKJV*).

The third temptation was Satan's invitation for Jesus to reject God's inheritance and receive all the kingdoms of this earth by simply worshiping Satan. Jesus knew Himself to be the "heir of all things," therefore He rejected Satan's offer of a kingdom that couldn't last for one He knew was eternal. Although what Jesus inherited cost Him more than what Satan offered would have, the returns far outweighed the costs. (*See #239.*)

228. Brightness of His Glory – *Apaugasma Doxa*

"Who being the *brightness of his glory*, and the express image of his person, and upholding all things by the word of his power, when he had by himself purged our sins, sat down on the right hand of the Majesty on high" (Hebrews 1:3).

> **Definition:** *Apaugasma* (ap-ow'-gas-mah) [541]; from a compound of *apo* and *augazo*; an offflash, i.e. effulgence: – brightness. (S)
>
> *Doxa* (dox'-ah) [1391]; from the base of *dokeo*; glory (as very apparent), in a wide application (literal or figurative, objective or subjective): – dignity, glory (-ious), honour, praise, worship. (S)

Jesus is the brightness of God's glory. We have identified sev-eral ways that God has appeared to humanity through the mani-festation of light. When all of it is summed up, the brightness of God's glory is best expressed in the person of Jesus Christ. He is the sum total of all that God is, including glory.

The brightness of God's glory brings revelation to the mysteries contained in the Old and New Testaments. None of the prophets or laws make sense, until they are seen through the light of who Jesus is. Even the disciples, who had traveled with Jesus and heard Him speak the oracles of God, did not understand Him or His stories until the Holy Spirit came to them.

The brightness of God's glory discloses the dark recesses of the hearts of men and women. Our sins and iniquities are visible to us when Jesus illuminates them. Before the light of Christ was shed upon my heart, I thought I was a good fellow. Once I saw how dark the light of my life was in comparison to the shadow cast by the brilliant presence of Jesus, I was under conviction and ready for repentance.

The brightness of God's glory draws some to Christ and repels others from Him. No one remains unaffected after coming into contact with the piercing brightness of the glory of God as expressed by the person of Jesus Christ. The light of Christ always makes a difference. (*See #79, #271.*)

229. Express Image of His Person – *Charakter Hupostasis*

"[Jesus] being the brightness of [God's] glory and the *express image of His person*, and upholding all things by the word of His power, when He had by Himself purged our sins, sat down at the right hand of the Majesty on high" (Hebrews 1:3, *NKJV*).

> **Definition:** *Charakter* (khar-ak-tare') [5481]; from the same as *charax*; a graver (the tool or the person), i.e. (by implication) engraving (["character"], the figure stamped, i.e. an exact copy or [figuratively] representation): – express image. (S)
>
> *Hupostasis* (hoop-os'-tas-is) [5287]; from a compound of *hupo* and *histemi*; a setting under (support), i.e. (figuratively) concretely, essence, or abstractly, assurance (objectively or subjectively): – confidence, confident, person, substance. (S)

God has been seen by few people throughout all of history. When Moses asked to see God's glory, he was told, "You cannot see My face; for no man shall see Me, and live" (Exodus 33:20, *NKJV*). God hid Moses in the cleft of a rock as He passed by in order to protect Moses from direct contact with the glory of God, for it would have destroyed him. Jesus said, "He who sees Me sees Him who sent Me" (John 12:45, *NKJV*).

Jesus was (and is) the express image of God. "No one has seen God at any time. The only begotten Son, who is in the bosom of the Father, He has declared Him" (John 1:18, *NKJV*). The character and love expressed through the life of Jesus depicts who God is and what He is like.

230. Captain of Salvation – *Archegos Autos Soteria*

"For it became him, for whom are all things, and by whom are all things, in bringing many sons unto glory, to make the *captain of their salvation* perfect through sufferings" (Hebrews 2:10).

> **Definition:** *Archegos* (ar-khay-gos') [747]; from *arche* and *ago*; a chief leader: – author, captain, prince. (S)
>
> *Autos* (ow-tos') [846]; from the particle *au* [perhaps akin to the base of *aer* through the idea of a baffling wind] (backward); the reflexive pronoun self, used (alone or in the comparative *heautau*) of the third person and (with the proper personal pronoun) of the other persons: – her, it (-self), one, the other, (mine) own, said, ([self-], the) same, ([him-, my-, thyself, [your-] selves, she, that, their (-s), them ([-selves]), there [-at, -by, -in, -into, -of, -on, -with], they, (these) things, this (man), those, together, very, which. (S)
>
> *Soteria* (so-tay-ree'-ah) [4991]; feminine of a derivative of *soter* as (properly, abstract) noun; rescue or safety (physically or morally): – deliver, health, salvation, save, saving. (S)

Hardly any leader today performs the way Jesus did. All of the captains I served under in the U.S. Army stayed away from the front lines as much as they could. Others walked point and took the first shot. It was expedient for the captains and for those who fought under their leadership to remain safe and protected by their men so that they could continue to offer their wisdom and leadership throughout the battle.

Jesus never entertained the idea of having others face the foes He was assigned to defeat. He was in the midst of the battle, the point man, being wounded for you and me (see Isaiah 53:5). The Lord of Hosts could have called a legion of angels to fight for Him and take the punishment (see Psalm 91:12), but He chose instead to protect us by offering His own body as a shield. We never deserve such a Captain, but God saw fit for us to receive much more than we have ever earned or are worthy of. *(See #122, #161, #181, #235.)*

231. Merciful and Faithful High Priest – *Eleemon Pistos Archiereus*

"Wherefore in all things it behooved him to be made like unto his brethren, that he might be a *merciful and faithful high priest* in things pertaining to God, to make reconciliation for the sins of the people" (Hebrews 2:17).

> **Definition:** *Eleemon* (el-eh-ay'-mone) [1655]; from *eleeo*; compassionate (actively): – merciful. (S)
>
> *Pistos* (pis-tos') [4103]; from *peitho*; objectively, trustworthy; subjectively, trustful: – believe (-ing, -r), faithful (-ly), sure, true. (S)
>
> *Archiereus* (ar-khee-er-yuce') [749]; from *arche* and *heireus*; the high-priest (literally, of the Jews, typically, Christ); by extension a chief priest: – chief (high) priest, chief of the priests. (S)

The high priest offered sacrifices for the sins of the people on the Day of Atonement and other holy days as prescribed in the law of Moses. The man assigned this position had to be of the tribe of

Levi and of the family of Aaron. The ministry of a priest required him to go to God on behalf of the people of Israel, to intercede for them and plead their case before a holy God. Much ritual and tradition accompanied the performance of the priestly duties.

Jesus was not of the tribe of Levi or of the family of Aaron. Jesus was, and is, a Great High Priest according to the order of Melchizedek. His priesthood was not based on human inheritance, but was a godly appointment. In His mercy, Jesus died for us, offering His own blood for the remission of sin. His faithfulness held Him to the cross when everything within Him wanted to be released from the anguish and end the separation from His Father. Mercy and justice met at the Cross, and the faithfulness of God in Christ brought it together so men and women could have right standing with God the Father. (*See #232, #234.*)

232. Apostle and High Priest of Our Profession – *Apostolos Archiereus Homologia*

"Wherefore, holy brethren, partakers of the heavenly calling, consider the *Apostle and High Priest of our profession*, Christ Jesus" (Hebrews 3:1).

> **Definition:** *Apostolos* (ap-os'-tol-os) [652]; from *apostello*; a delegate; specially, an ambassador of the Gospel; officially a commissioner of Christ ["apostle"] (with miraculous powers): – apostle, messenger, he that is sent. (S)
>
> *Archiereus* (ar-khee-er-yuce') [749]; from *arche* and *hiereus*; the high-priest (literally, of the Jews, typically, Christ); by extension a chief priest: – chief (high) priest, chief of the priests. (S)
>
> *Homologia* (hom-ol-og-ee'-ah) [3671]; from the same as *homologeo*; acknowledgment: – con- (pro-) fession, professed. (S)

We must know and confess what Jesus has said about us. He assures us that we have a vital relationship with Christ. He tells us that through Him, we have a relationship with God. We confess with Him that we are blessed of God. He tells us that God answers our prayers. And because He answers our prayers, God is our healer! (*See #231, #234.*)

233. Builder – *Kataskeuazo*

"For He has been counted worthy of more glory than Moses, by just so much as the *builder* of the house has more honor than the house" (Hebrews 3:3, *NASB*).

> **Definition:** *Kataskeuazo* (kat-ask-yoo-ad'-zo) [2680]; from *kata* and a derivative of *skeuos*; to prepare thoroughly (properly, by external equipment; whereas *hetoimazo* refers rather to internal fitness); by implication, to construct, create: – build, make, ordain, prepare. (S)

Believers make up the body called the church and Jesus is the builder. Preachers excite, teachers educate and deacons serve, but only Jesus can make the people into His church and establish it as His body. "Unless the Lord builds the house, they labor in vain who build it" (Psalm 127:1, *NKJV*). (*See #138.*)

234. Great High Priest – *Megas Archiereus*

"Seeing then that we have a *great high priest*, that is passed into the heavens, Jesus the Son of God, let us hold fast our profession" (Hebrews 4:14).

> **Definition:** *Megas* (meg'-as) [3173]; [including the prolonged forms, feminine *megale*, plural *megaloi*, etc.; compare also *megistos*, *meizon*]; big (literally or figuratively, in a very wide application): – (+fear) exceedingly, great (-est), high, large, loud, mighty, + (be) sore (afraid), strong, X to years. (S)
>
> *Archiereus* (ar-khee-er-yuce') [749]; from *arche* and *hiereus*; the high-priest (literally, of the Jews, typically, Christ); by extension a chief priest: – chief (high) priest, chief of the priests. (S)

All high priests who served Israel prior to the coming of Jesus offered the sacrifices and offerings prescribed by Moses repeatedly for the sins of the people. These sacrifices could never fully atone for their sins, they only covered them up. Sin entered the world through Adam, a man; so sin could only be done away with through the blood of a man, Christ Jesus. God required the offerings made to be unblemished animals, so only a perfect man could legally become a sacrifice acceptable to Him. None had been found worthy to do so until Christ.

The high priest who served the Temple at Jerusalem had only the blood of an animal to offer the Most High God. Jesus, the Great High Priest, brought His own blood to the altar of God, not only for atonement, but also for the remission of sin. The blood of Jesus paid the full price due, and made a way for humankind to have fellowship with the Father. This is redemption. (*See #231, #232.*)

235. Author of Eternal Salvation – *Aitios Aionios Soteria*

"And being made perfect, he became the *author of eternal salvation* unto all them that obey him" (Hebrews 5:9).

> **Definition:** *Aitios* (ah'-ee-tee-os) [159]; from the same as *aiteo*; causative, i.e. (concretely) a causer: – author. (S)
>
> *Aionios* (ahee-o'-nee-os) [166]; from *aion*; perpetual (also used of past time, or past and future as well): – eternal, for ever, everlasting, world (began). (S)
>
> *Soteria* (so-tay-ree'-ah) [4991]; feminine of a derivative of *soter* as (properly, abstract) noun; rescue or safety (physically or morally): – deliver, health, salvation, save, saving. (S)

The salvation Jesus offers is eternal. Those who have truly tasted this gift from God can say with Paul in Philippians 1:6: "Being confident of this very thing, that He who has begun a good work in you will complete it until the day of Jesus Christ" (*NKJV*). If Jesus has begun the work in your life, He can be expected to complete it. (*See #122, #161, #181, #230.*)

236. Forerunner – *Prodromos*

"Where Jesus has entered as a *forerunner* for us, having become a high priest forever according to the order of Melchizedek" (Hebrews 6:20, *NASB*).

> **Definition:** *Prodromos* - a forerunner (a) especially one who is sent before to take observations or act as a spy, a scout, a light-armed soldier (b) one who comes in advance to a place where the rest are to follow" (*Thayer's Greek-English Lexicon*).

> **As a forerunner** *(prodromos)*. Old word used for a spy, a scout, only here in N.T. Jesus has shown us the way, has gone on ahead, and is the surety (*egguos*, Hebrews 7:22) and guarantor of our own entrance later. In point of fact, our anchor of hope with its two chains of God's promise and oath has laid hold of Jesus within the veil. It will hold fast. All we need to do is to be true to him as he is to us (*Word Pictures in the New Testament*).

The Lord Jesus Christ is our forerunner throughout this Christian walk. He told us, "Most assuredly, I say to you, he who believes in Me, the works that I do he will do also; and greater works than these he will do, because I go to My Father" (John 14:12, *NKJV*). As forerunner, Jesus fully expects us to follow His footsteps and allow the Holy Spirit to work through us as He did through Jesus—and even greater works are possible for those who believe! We must get out of the way and allow Him to be God in us and through us. (*See #254, #256, #258.*)

237. Minister of the Sanctuary – *Leitourgos Hagion*

"Now of the things which we have spoken this is the sum: We have such an high priest, who is set on the right hand of the throne of the Majesty in the heavens; a *minister of the sanctuary*, and of the true tabernacle, which the Lord pitched, and not man" (Hebrews 8:1, 2).

> **Definition:** *Leitourgos* (li-toorg-os') [3011]; from a derivative of *laos* and *ergon*; a public servant, i.e. a functionary

in the Temple or Gospel, or (genitive case) a worshiper (of God) or benefactor (of man): – minister (-ed). (S)

Hagion (hag'-ee-on) [39]; neuter of *hagios*; a sacred thing (i.e. spot): – holiest (of all), holy place, sanctuary. (S)

The tabernacle of God is not a building of stones and mortar. The tabernacle of which Jesus is minister is located in the hearts of those who have placed their faith and trust in Him. The church of the Lord Jesus Christ is made up of believers from many local bodies, denominations and social groups. No single group of people has a monopoly on the promises of God, or can expect to have exclusive rights in the kingdom of Heaven.

"Lord, prepare me to be a sanctuary" is a line in a worship chorus we sing from time to time at our church. The prayer asks God to make us pure and holy for Him.

238. Mediator of a Better Covenant – *Mesites Kreitton Diatheke*

"But now hath he obtained a more excellent ministry, by how much also he is the *mediator of a better covenant*, which was established upon better promises" (Hebrews 8:6).

Definition: *Mesites* (mes-ee'-tace) [3316]; from *mesos*; a go-between, i.e. (simply) an internunciator, or (by implication) a reconciler (intercessor): – mediator. (S)

Kreitton (krite'-tohn) [2909]; comparative of a derivative of *kratos*; stronger, i.e. (figuratively) better, i.e. nobler: – best, better. (S)

Diatheke (dee-ath-ay'-kay) [1242]; from diatithemai; properly, a disposition, i.e. (specially) a contract (especially a devisory will): – covenant, testament. (S)

The Old Testament promises a new covenant that is different from the old. Jesus did not come to do away with the old covenant. Rather, He came to fulfill its requirements and usher in a new covenant for all who will receive it by faith.

The old covenant was a covenant of law; the new is a covenant of grace. The old covenant was a list of "thou shalt nots"; while the new is a list of "you shalls." The new covenant is summed up:

> "You shall love the Lord your God with all your heart, with all your soul, and with all your mind." This is the first and great commandment. And the second is like it: "You shall love your neighbor as yourself." On these two commandments hang all the Law and the Prophets (Matthew 22:37-40, *NKJV*).

(*See #222, #242.*)

239. Testator – *Diatithemi*

"And for this cause he is the mediator of the new testament, that by means of death, for the redemption of the transgressions that were under the first testament, they which are called might receive the promise of eternal inheritance. For where a testament is, there must also of necessity be the death of the *testator*. For a testament is of force after men are dead: otherwise it is of no strength at all while the *testator* liveth" (Hebrews 9:15-17).

> **Definition:** *Diatithemi*; from *dia* and *tithemi*; to place separately, i.e. dispose of by a will :- grant(1), granted(1), made(m)(3), make(2)." (*NASB Dictionary*)

All the promises of God find their fulfillment in the death of Christ. While alive, our Lord did many great things; but the promises of His Word were made possible by His sacrificial death. The promises Jesus made were all dependent on the death of the *testator* for their fulfillment. Promises like these:

"Nevertheless I tell you the truth. It is to your advantage that I go away; for if I do not go away, the Helper will not come to you; but if I depart, I will send Him to you" (John 16:7, *NKJV*).

"However, when He, the Spirit of truth, has come, He will guide you into all truth; for He will not speak on His own authority, but whatever He hears He will speak; and He will tell you things to come" (John 16:13, *NKJV*).

"But you shall receive power when the Holy Spirit has come upon you; and you shall be witnesses to Me in Jerusalem, and in all Judea and Samaria, and to the end of the earth" (Acts 1:8, *NKJV*). (*See #227.*)

240. Author of Our Faith – *Archegos Pistis*

"Let us fix our eyes on Jesus, the *author* and perfecter *of our faith*, who for the joy set before him endured the cross, scorning its shame, and sat down at the right hand of the throne of God" (Hebrews 12:2, *NIV*).

> **Definition:** *Archegos* (ar-khay-gos') [747]; from *arche* and *ago*; a chief leader: – author, captain, prince. (S)
>
> *Pistis* (pis'-tis) [4102]; from *peitho*; persuasion, i.e. credence; moral conviction (of religious truth, or the truthfulness of God or a religious teacher), especially reliance upon Christ for salvation; abstractly, constancy in such profession; by extension, the system of religious (Gospel) truth itself: – assurance, belief, believe, faith, fidelity. (S)

Jesus, the source of all faith, offers fullness of joy and eternal life. Everything in the form of godliness, goodness or righteousness is received from God by grace through faith in Jesus. "For by grace you have been saved through faith, and that not of yourselves; it is the gift of God, not of works, lest anyone should boast" (Ephesians 2:8, 9, *NKJV*). Moffatt's translation says that Jesus is the "pioneer of personal faith." (*See #241.*)

241. Perfecter of Our Faith – *Teleiotes Pistis*

"Let us fix our eyes on Jesus, the author and *perfecter of our faith*, who for the joy set before him endured the cross, scorning its shame, and sat down at the right hand of the throne of God" (Hebrews 12:2, *NIV*).

> **Definition:** *Teleiotes* (tel-i-o-tace') [5051]; from *teleioo*; a completer, i.e. consummater: – finisher. (S)

Not only is Jesus the one who begins our faith, He is the one who finishes our faith as well. When you think of it, there is really not anything that the believer can take credit for in this walk of faith, except possibly for getting out of the way and allowing God to have His way in us. This walk truly does not depend upon us, it depends on Jesus, the author and finisher of our faith. (*See #240.*)

242. Mediator of the New Covenant – *Mesites Neos Diatheke*

"To Jesus the *Mediator of the new covenant,* and to the blood of sprinkling that speaks better things than that of Abel" (Hebrews 12:24, *NKJV*).

> **Definition:** *Mesites* (mes-ee'-tace) [3316]; from *mesos*; a go-between, i.e. (simply) an internunciator, or (by implication) a reconciler (intercessor): – mediator. (S)
>
> *Neos* (neh'-os) [3501]; including the comparative *neoteros* (neh-o'-ter-os); a primary word; "new", i.e. (of persons) youthful, or (of things) fresh; figuratively, regenerate: – new, young. (S)
>
> *Diatheke* (dee-ath-ay'-kay) [1242]; from *diatithemai*; properly, a disposition, i.e. (specially) a contract (especially a devisory will): – covenant, testament. (S)

Jesus is not acting as an arbitrator in this situation, He is mediator. Although He has every right to demand actions and decisions from us, He never takes away our free will. He is the mediator of the covenant offered by His blood rather than as an arbitrator. We have already seen what the new covenant is, and covenant of grace, and how it differs from the old, a covenant of law. (*See #222, #238.*)

243. My Helper – *Emoi Boethos*

"So that we may boldly say, The Lord is *my helper,* and I will not fear what man shall do unto me" (Hebrews 13:6).

Definition: *Boethos* (bo-ay-thos') [998]; from *boe* and *theo* (to run); a succorer: – helper. (S)

Jesus is the best friend and helper any person could ever have. Verse 5 says emphatically that God is One who will never leave one of His own without support. *The Amplified Bible* renders the verse, "He (God) Himself has said, I will not in any way fail you nor give you up nor leave you without support. [I will] not, [I will] not, [I will] not in any degree leave you helpless, nor forsake nor let [you] down, [relax my hold on you]—Assuredly not!" (Hebrews 13:5).

You can trust this Helper in any and every situation! Jesus will never ask you to do something that He will not also equip you to do.

PART 3
The Son of God

His Greek Names in

PETER – JUDE

244. Lamb Without Blemish and Without Spot – *Amnos Amomos Aspilos*

"With the precious blood of Christ, as of a *lamb without blemish and without spot*" (1 Peter 1:19, *NKJV*).

Definition: *Amnos* (am-nos') [286]; apparently a primary word; a lamb: – lamb. (S)

Amomos (am'-o-mos) [299]; from *a* (as a negative particle) and *momos*; unblemished (literally or figuratively): – without blame (blemish, fault, spot), faultless, unblameable. (S)

Aspilos (as'-pee-los) [784]; from *a* (as a negative particle) and *spiloo*; unblemished (physically or morally): – without spot, unspotted. (S)

Jesus was the final sacrifice for sin. There is no reason to continue the repetitious killing of lambs, goats and bullocks in or around the Temple in an attempt to atone for the sins of humanity. The final sacrifice has been made by One who went to the altar of His own accord and laid His life down as the final sacrificial Lamb without blemish or spot. The sacrifices offered on our behalf by our Lord and Savior Jesus Christ cannot be improved.

You may be called on to give up many things as you walk this Christian path, but none of them make you more acceptable to God. God sometimes asks you to walk away from something for your own sake. But your sacrifice does not make sin or iniquity pardonable or palatable to a holy God. The blood of Jesus has provided a way into the Holy of Holies. You can have fellowship with the King of kings and Lord of lords. (*See #175, #207, #264.*)

245. Living Stone – *Zao Lithos*

"Coming to Him as to a *living stone*, rejected indeed by men, but chosen by God and precious" (1 Peter 2:4, *NKJV*).

> **Definition:** *Zao* (dzah'-o) [2198]; a primary verb; to live (literally or figuratively): – life (-time), (a-) live (-ly), quick. (S)
>
> *Lithos* (lee'-thos); apparently a primary word; a stone (literally or figuratively): – (mill-, stumbling-) stone. (S)

The church is "built on the foundation of the apostles and prophets, with Christ Jesus himself as the chief cornerstone" (Ephesians 2:20, *NKJV*). The church is not a building made by human hands. Rather, it is a temple where God dwells within the hearts of each living stone that forms its framework.

Jesus is still alive and well in the world today. An obvious sign of life is movement and change. Our Lord is complete and perfect. Jesus does not need to change, nor would He be capable of change. Yet, what we know of our Lord does change because He reveals new things about Himself daily. Jesus is a "living stone;" He moves in the hearts of those who allow Him access to their innermost beings. (*See #48, #351, #77, #81, #113, #114, #208, #214, #246, #247.*)

246. Stone of Stumbling – *Lithos Proskomma*

"Therefore, to you who believe, He is precious; but to those who are disobedient, 'The stone which the builders rejected has become the chief cornerstone,' and 'a *stone of stumbling* and a rock of offense.' They stumble, being disobedient to the word, to which they also were appointed" (1 Peter 2:7, 8, *NKJV*).

Definition: *Proskomma* (pros'-kom-mah) [4348]; from *proskopto*; a stub, i.e. (figuratively) occasion of apostasy: – offence, stumbling (-block, [-stone]). (S)

To those who have received Christ, He is the One who keeps them from falling. To those who have rejected our Lord, He is the stone of stumbling who will be their undoing. You cannot be indifferent about Jesus. Either you accept Jesus as the living stone upon which your life is founded, or you trip and stumble over Him and are counted among those who are offended by God's Rock of Salvation. (*See #48, #51, #77, #81, #113, #114, #208, #210, #214, #245, #247.*)

247. Rock of Offense – *Petra Skandalon*

"Therefore, to you who believe, He is precious; but to those who are disobedient, 'The stone which the builders rejected has become the chief cornerstone,' and 'A stone of stumbling and a *rock of offense.*' They stumble, being disobedient to the word, to which they also were appointed" (1 Peter 2:7, 8, *NKJV*).

Definition: *Petra* (pet'-ra) [4073]; feminine of the same as *petros*; a (mass of) rock (literally or figuratively): – rock. (S)

Skandalon (skan'-dal-on) ("scandal") [4625]; probably from a derivative of *kampto*; a trap-stick (bent sapling), i.e. snare (figuratively, cause of displeasure or sin): – occasion to fall (of stumbling), offence, thing that offends, stumblingblock. (S)

It is interesting to note that the author of this epistle is Simon Peter. When Jesus first met Simon, He called him *Cephas*, a name of Aramaic origin which means "stone" or "small rock."

"And he brought him to Jesus. And when Jesus beheld him, he said, Thou art Simon the son of Jona: thou shalt be called *Cephas*, which is by interpretation, A stone" (John 1:42). Later, Jesus changed Cephas' name to *Petros*, which means "rock." "And I say also unto thee, That thou art Peter *(Petros)*, and upon this rock I will build my church; and the gates of hell shall not prevail against it" (Matthew 16:18).

Peter now reveals Jesus as the rock of offence. He had been offended more than once by the Lord because of his inappropriate reactions to Christ's ministry. Peter had failed to hold up his part of the relationship with Jesus, and had denied even knowing Christ when challenged in the courtyard of the high priest. Peter had been broken by the rock of offence himself and was now a new man, fired by the power of the Holy Spirit. Peter knew that his only hope of living the Christian life was to allow the living stone, Jesus Christ himself, to live His life through him and strengthen him. (*See #48, #51, #77, #81, #113, #114, #208, #210, #214, #245, #246.*)

248. Shepherd and Bishop of Souls – *Poimen Episkopos Humon Psuche*

"For ye were as sheep going astray; but are now returned unto the *Shepherd and Bishop of your souls*" (1 Peter 2:25).

Definition: *Poimen* (poy-mane'); of uncertain affinity; a shepherd (literally or figuratively): – shepherd, pastor. (S)

Episkopos (ep-is'-kop-os) [1985]; from *epi* and *skopos* (in the sense of *episkopeo*); a superintendent, i.e. Christian officer in genitive case charge of a (or the) church (literally or figuratively): – bishop, overseer. (S)

Jesus is the shepherd and bishop (overseer) over our souls. Our Lord and Savior Jesus Christ is personally responsible for getting us, keeping us and bringing us to the Father. The words of Psalm 23 bring clarity to the true meaning behind this revelation of Christ.

Too often this psalm is read only at funerals and memorial services. But it is a psalm of hope and promise from the One in the heavenlies who has charge over us. I challenge you to read Psalm 23 again, as if you have never heard it before, with your mind and heart open to the promises of God. (*See #31, #76, #187, #249.*)

249. Chief Shepherd – *Archipoimen*

"And when the *Chief Shepherd* appears, you will receive the unfading crown of glory" (1 Peter 5:4, *NASB*).

Definition: *Archipoimen* (ar-khee-poy'-mane) [750]; from *arche* and *poimen*; a head shepherd: – chief shepherd. (S)

"Jesus Christ is the chief shepherd of the whole flock and heritage of God. He bought them, and rules them; he defends and saves them for ever. He is also the chief shepherd over all inferior shepherds; they derive their authority from him, act in his name, and are accountable to him at last. This chief shepherd will appear, to judge all ministers and under-shepherds, to call them to account, whether they have faithfully discharged their duty both publicly and privately according to the foregoing directions" (*Matthew Henry's Commentary*). (*See #31, #76, #187.*)

250. Word of Life – *Logos Zoe*

"That which was from the beginning, which we have heard, which we have seen with our eyes, which we have looked upon, and our hands have handled, of the *Word of life*" (1 John 1:1).

Definition: *Logos* (log'-os) [3056]; from *lego*; something said (including the thought); by implication a topic (subject of discourse), also reasoning (the mental faculty) or motive; by extension, a computation; specifically (with the article in John) the Divine Expression (i.e. Christ): – account, cause, communication, X concerning, doctrine, fame, X have to do, intent, matter, mouth, preaching, question, reason, + reckon, remove, say (-ing), shew, X speaker, speech, talk, thing, + none of these things move me, tidings, treatise, utterance, word, work. (S)

Zoe - (1) life (a) the state of one who is possessed of vitality or is animate (b) every living soul (2) life (a) used of the absolute fullness of life, both essential and ethical, which belongs to God, and through him both to the hypostatic "logos" and to Christ in whom the "logos" put on human nature (b) life real and genuine, a life active and vigorous, devoted to God, blessed, in the portion even in this world of those who put their trust in Christ, but after the resurrection to be consummated by new accessions (among them a more perfect body), and to last forever. (*Thayer's Greek-English Lexicon*)

John emphasizes the fact that Jesus was fully human, yet never was anything less than the Son of God. Before the end of the first century, Gnosticism had infected the teachings of certain men who began to doubt and deny that Jesus was really a man. They taught that He was only a spirit come to earth.

John established the fact that Jesus was much more than a spirit. He was seen, heard and touched before His resurrection, as well as after it. (*See #84, #172.*)

251. Advocate – *Parakletos*

"My little children, I am writing these things to you that you may not sin. And if anyone sins, we have an *Advocate* with the Father, Jesus Christ the righteous" (1 John 2:1, *NASB*).

Definition: *Parakletos* - (1) summoned, called to one's side, especially called to one's aid (a) one who pleads another's cause before a judge, a pleader, a counsel for defense, a legal assistant, an advocate (b) one who pleads another's cause with one, an intercessor of Christ in his exaltation at God's right hand, pleading with God the Father for the pardon of our sins (c) in the widest sense, a helper, a succorer, an aider, an assistant; used of the Holy Spirit destined to take the place of Christ with the apostles (after Christ's ascension to the Father), to lead them to a deeper knowledge of the gospel truth, and to give them divine strength needed to enable them to undergo trials and persecutions on behalf of the divine kingdom. (*Thayer's Greek-English Lexicon*)

Advocate *(parakleton).* The Holy Spirit is God's Advocate on earth with men, while Christ is man's Advocate with the Father (the idea, but not the word, in Romans 8:31-39; Hebrews 7:25). As *dikaios* (righteous) Jesus is qualified to plead our case and to enter the Father's presence (Hebrews 2:18). (*Word Pictures in the New Testament*).

Jesus, our advocate, speaks on our behalf to a holy God (our righteous judge). At no time does He pretend that we are without sin or blameless. Our Lord goes to the Father on our behalf with a plea of "guilty as charged."

But the Christian faces the Judge differently than does the rest of the world. Jesus tells the Father, "Lay his or her sin on Me . . . that My child may be made whole." Our Lord Jesus paid the full penalty for sin and transgression, thereby making a way for us to be pardoned by the Judge. (*See #296, #297.*)

252. Only Wise God Our Savior – *Monos Sophos Theos Soter*

"To the *only wise God our Savior,* be glory and majesty, dominion and power, both now and ever. Amen" (Jude 1:25).

Definition: *Monos* (mon'-os) [3441]; probably from *menos*; remaining, i.e. sole or single; by implication mere: – alone, only, by themselves. (S)

Sophos (sof-os') [4680]; akin to *saphes* (clear); wise (in a most general application): – wise. Compare *phronimos.* (S)

Soter (so-tare') [4990]; from *sozo*; a deliverer, i.e. God or Christ: – savior. (S)

There is only one truly wise God and Savior. His name is Jesus Christ, the Anointed One. Jesus is the only way to the Father. Our Lord is the only One in whom salvation is made available and manifest. He is more than another wise man; He is the source of all true wisdom and understanding. All truth must be filtered through who Jesus is, and what He said. Although many teachings and discoveries are being made in the name of science and technology, all such information must be judged by what we know to be absolute truth in the person of Jesus. One such topic would be evolution.

In secular educational facilities in America, evolution is taught as the undisputed, unapproachable, scientific explanation of how life on earth as we know it came into existence. Many teachers of evolution consider the Christian teachings of creation to be a myth, unsupported by any scientific evidence.

Actually, quite the opposite is true. Evolution is a theory and only a theory, unsupported by hard and fast evidence. Not one missing link or the complete skeletal remains of one has ever been found. Bits and pieces of bone have been found and used to recreate what amounts to an artist's concept of what it might have looked like.

But because the "artists" in this case believe in evolution, all such re-creative artistry is done from that mind-set.

Jesus is the only wise God, our Savior. Only in the fullness of His wisdom and grace can other thoughts or revelations make any real sense. (*See #56, #122, #181.*)

The Son of God

His Greek Names in

REVELATION

---

253. Faithful Witness – *Pistos Martus*

"And from Jesus Christ, who is the *faithful witness*, and the first begotten of the dead, and the prince of the kings of the earth. Unto him that loved us, and washed us from our sins in his own blood" (Revelation 1:5).

> **Definition:** *Pistos* (pis-tos') [4103]; from *peitho*; objectively, trustworthy; subjectively, trustful: – believe (-ing, -r), faithful (-ly), sure, true. (S)

> *Martus* (mar'-toos) [3144]; of uncertain affinity; a witness (literally [judicially] or figuratively [genitive case]); by analogy, a "martyr": – martyr, record, witness. (S)

Jesus is a trustworthy witness to the manifold glories of God. In the last book of the Bible, John addresses his writings to the seven churches in Asia. John credits Jesus Christ, the *faithful witness*, with co-authoring this letter; and describes "Him who is and who was and who is to come, and from the seven Spirits who are before His throne" (Revelation 1:4, *NKJV*). John was saying, through his careful presentation of authorship, that this book is not a fairy tale or an allegorical dissertation. John was careful to write down what he saw exactly as he saw it. The writer calls on Jesus himself to verify and testify of the authenticity of the revelation. A witness' function is to testify to what he saw and give credence to the testimony or statements of others. (*See #267*.)

254. First Begotten of the Dead – *Prototokos Nekros*

"And from Jesus Christ, who is the faithful witness, and the *first begotten of the dead*, and the prince of the kings of the earth. Unto him that loved us, and washed us from our sins in his own blood" (Revelation 1:5).

> **Definition:** *Prototokos* (pro-tot-ok'-os) [4416]; from *protos* and the alternate of *tikto*; first-born (usually as noun, literally or figuratively): – firstbegotten (-born). (S)

> *Nekros* (nek-ros') [3498]; from an apparently primary nekus (a corpse); dead (literally or figuratively; also as noun): – dead. (S)

Jesus was not the first to have died and been raised again. But, Jesus was the first to have died and come back with His resurrected body. When Lazarus was brought back to life, he returned with the same body in which he died. After Jesus raised Lazarus, he had to die again, because he still occupied a temporal body with limits on its ability to remain alive.

Jesus' resurrected body was different. His own disciples did not recognize Him until He spoke and the Spirit opened the eyes of their hearts (Luke 24: 13-35). Jesus was able to enjoy a meal (John 21); yet, the risen Christ could enter a sealed building without opening the doors (Luke 24:36). When He ascended to the Father, the disciples saw Him rise to the sky before them. Our Lord truly is the firstborn from the dead in His new glorified body. (*See #40, #256, #258*.)

255. Prince of the Kings of the Earth – *Archon Basileus Ge*

"And from Jesus Christ, who is the faithful witness, and the first begotten of the dead, and the *prince of the kings of the earth.* Unto him that loved us, and washed us from our sins in his own blood" (Revelation 1:5).

> **Definition:** *Archon* (ar'-khone) [758]; present participle of *archo*; a first (in rank or power): – chief (ruler), magistrate, prince, ruler. (S)
>
> *Basileus* (bas-il-yooce') [935]; probably from *basis* (through the notion of a foundation of power); a sovereign (abstractly, relatively, or figuratively): – king. (S)
>
> *Ge* (ghay) [1093]; contracted from a primary word; soil; by extension a region, or the solid part or the whole of the *terrene* globe (including the occupants in each application): – country, earth (-ly), ground, land, world. (S)

Prince means "ruler" or "chief." Christ is ruler over all the kings of the earth. They may not acknowledge Him as sovereign, but that in no way diminishes His authority. He is lord over world leaders, including the United States president and the Chinese rulers. He controls the stock market and the downsizing taking place at your job.

> Rejoice in the Lord always. Again I will say, rejoice! Let your gentleness be known to all men. The Lord is at hand. Be anxious for nothing, but in everything by prayer and supplication, with thanksgiving, let your requests be made known to God; and the peace of God, which surpasses all understanding, will guard your hearts and minds through Christ Jesus (Philippians 4:4-7, *NKJV*).

(*See #131.*)

256. Alpha and Omega – *Alpha Omega*

"I am *Alpha and Omega*, the beginning and the ending, saith the Lord, which is, and which was, and which is to come, the Almighty" (Revelation 1:8).

> **Definition:** *Alpha* (al'-fah) [5655]; See *a*; the first letter of the Greek alphabet, sometimes signifying the value of 1; used as a symbolic letter, with omega (See *omega* meaning the end); alpha and omega became idiomatic for designating the universe and every kind of divine and demonic power: alpha, beginning, first. (S)
>
> *Omega* (o'-meg-ah) [5598]; the last letter of the Greek alphabet, i.e. (figuratively) the finality: – Omega. (S)

Alpha is the first letter in the Greek alphabet, and *Omega* is the last. Jesus Christ is the first and the last of all that is good. He was with God in the beginning (see John 1:1-4), and He will be with the Father when everything else passes away. Our Lord is from everlasting to everlasting. Jesus has no beginning and He will have no end. (*See #40, #254, #258.*)

257. Almighty – *Pantokrator*

"I am Alpha and Omega, the beginning and the ending, saith the Lord, which is, and which was, and which is to come, *the Almighty*" (Revelation 1:8).

> **Definition:** *Pantokrator* (pan-tok-rat'-ore) [3841]; from *pas* and *kratos*; the all-ruling, i.e. God (as absolute and universal sovereign): – Almighty, Omnipotent. (S)

In this passage, Jesus is credited with having "all might" and "all power." He is the all-ruling, almighty, absolute and universally sovereign Omnipotent One. There is no circumstance in your life that Jesus cannot affect by His presence and authority. Jesus Christ is Lord of all! (*See #10, #11, #107, #291.*)

258. First and Last – *Protos Eschatos*

"When I saw him, I fell at his feet as though dead. Then he placed his right hand on me and said: 'Do not be afraid. I am *the First and the Last*'" (Revelation 1:17, *NIV*).

Definition: *Protos* (pro'-tos) [4413]; contracted superlative of *pro*; foremost (in time, place, order or importance): – before, beginning, best, chief (-est), first (of all), former. (S)

Eschatos (es'-khat-os) [2078]; a superlative probably from *echo* (in the sense of contiguity); farthest, final (of place or time): – ends of, last, latter end, lowest, uttermost. (S)

John, the disciple whom Jesus loved (John 21:7), leaned on his friend in the upper room at the Last Supper. John, with James and Peter, traveled with Jesus everywhere the Lord ventured. He was with Jesus at the raising of Jairus' daughter (Mark 5:37), and with Jesus at the transfiguration (Mark 9:2). We see John with Jesus in the Garden of Gethsemane (Mark 14:33).

Even with this level of familiarity, when John saw Jesus glorified in Revelation 1:17, he fell on his face as if dead. To comfort His friend, Jesus identified Himself simply as the *First and the Last.* John immediately knew Him. In his Gospel, John had said that He was with God in the beginning, or *the first* (John 1:1-4). Now John was seeing that He was also *the last.* Bigger than time, Jesus was before time and will live after time has passed away. (*See #40, #254, #256.*)

259. Hidden Manna – *Krupto Manna*

"He that hath an ear, let him hear what the Spirit saith unto the churches; to him that overcometh will I give to eat of the *hidden manna*, and will give him a white stone, and in the stone a new name written, which no man knoweth saving he that receiveth it" (Revelation 2:17).

Definition: *Krupto* (kroop'-to) [2928]; a primary verb; to conceal (properly, by covering): – hide (self), keep secret, secret [-ly]. (S)

Manna - (man'-nah) [3131]; manna = "what is it" (1) the food that nourished the Israelites for 40 years in the wilderness (2) used of the manna was kept in the ark of the covenant (3) symbolically, what is kept in the heavenly temple for the food of angels and the blessed (*Thayer's Greek-English Lexicon*).

God told the church at Pergamos that He would give hidden manna to those who overcame Satan. The manna that fed the Israelites in the wilderness for 40 years was an interesting food source.

Those who ate it never suffered from scurvy, rickets or any other disease that plagues those who fail to eat a balanced diet. The Israelites needed no other nutrients for continued good health. Manna supplied all their vitamins, minerals, carbohydrates and proteins.

In the same way, Jesus provides for all the spiritual needs of Christians who abide in Him. While the manna that fed the Israelites was visible, the hidden manna that Jesus offers is received by faith. The fact that it is not visible in no way affects its ability to sustain the Christian in every way and in every situation. *(See #182, #183.)*

260. Amen – *Amen*

"And unto the angel of the church of the Laodiceans write; These things saith the *Amen*, the faithful and true witness, the beginning of the creation of God" (Revelation 3:14).

> **Definition:** *Amen* (am-ane') [281]; of Hebrew origin [*apeitheia*]; properly, firm, i.e. (figuratively) trustworthy; adverbially, surely (often as interjection so be it): – amen, verily. (S)

Christians typically end prayer with *amen,* meaning "so be it." The word implies trustworthiness and surety in what is said or done. Jesus ended His ministry with "It is finished" (John 19:30).

He is God's "Amen" over all His works on earth. Preachers and teachers proclaim the words of Christ. Prophets preceded and came after Jesus (see Acts 11:27-28).

But no one has a greater word than that spoken to us in God's amen, Jesus. *(See #256, #258.)*

261. Beginning of the Creation of God – *Arche Ktisis Theos*

"And unto the angel of the church of the Laodiceans write; These things saith the Amen, the faithful and true witness, the *beginning of the creation of God*" (Revelation 3:14).

> **Definition:** *Arche* (ar-khay') [746]; from *archomai*; (properly abstract) a commencement, or (concretely) chief (in various applications of order, time, place, or rank): – beginning, corner, (at the, the) first (estate), magistrate, power, principality, principle, rule. (S)

> *Ktisis* (ktis'-is) [2937]; from *ktizo*; original formation (properly, the act; by implication, the thing, literally or figuratively): – building, creation, creature, ordinance. (S)

This does not imply that Jesus was a created being. That would make Him less than God and unequal with the Father. Jesus was God in the beginning (John 1:1-2). He was the speaking force that created the worlds (Genesis 1:3; John 1:3). All things were made through Jesus and all things were made for Him. (*See #218.*)

262. Lion of the Tribe of Judah – *Leon Phule Ioudas*

"And one of the elders saith unto me, Weep not: behold, the *Lion of the tribe of Juda*, the Root of David, hath prevailed to open the book, and to loose the seven seals thereof" (Revelation 5:5).

> **Definition:** *Leon* - (1) a lion (2) a brave and mighty hero; Both Christ and Satan are referred to as a lion, indicating great strength, Satan as a "roaring lion" (1 Peter 5:8) and Christ as 'the Lion of the tribe of Judah' (Revelation 5:5)" (*The New Thayer's Greek-English Lexicon*).

> *Phule* (foo-lay') [5443]; from *phuo* (compare *phullon*); an offshoot, i.e. race or clan: – kindred, tribe. (S)

> *Ioudas* (ee-oo-das) [2455]; of Hebrew origin [*loipon*]; Judas (i.e. Jehudah), the name of ten Israelites; also of the posterity of one of them and its region: – Juda (-h, -s); Jude. (S)

The last recorded words of Jacob to his son, Judah, are: "Judah is a lion's whelp; from the prey, my son, you have gone up. He bows down, he lies down as a lion; and as a lion, who shall rouse him?" (Genesis 49:9, *NKJV*). Jacob went on to say, "The scepter shall not depart from Judah, nor a lawgiver from between his feet, until Shiloh comes" (Genesis 49:10, *NKJV*).

Revelation 5:5 calls Jesus the *Lion of the tribe of Judah* in fulfillment of these words. Shiloh (Jesus) does come, but not just as an earthly leader. Centuries ago, Jesus came as a bondslave and a shepherd. Now our Lord comes as a lion, bold and mighty. (*See #264.*)

263. Conqueror – *Nikao*

"And I saw, and behold a white horse: and he that sat on him had a bow; and a crown was given unto him: and he went forth conquering, and to conquer" (Revelation 6:2).

Definition: *Nikao* (nik-ah'-o) [3528]; from *nike*; to subdue (literally or figuratively): – conquer, overcome, prevail, get the victory. (S)

There is disagreement about this rider on the white horse. Many scholars reject the idea that it is Jesus because of the judgment wrought by the remaining three riders. The rider in Revelation 6:2 is said to be wearing a crown and going out into the world to conquer. I believe it is Jesus, however, and He is going out conquering and to conquer.

We see a rider on a white horse in Revelation 19:11-16, and there has never been a dispute over the identity of this rider. It is obviously Jesus Christ our Lord. "Now I saw heaven opened, and behold, a white horse. And He who sat on him was called Faithful and True, and in righteousness He judges and makes war" (Revelation 19:11, *NKJV*). I urge you to allow the Lord Jesus Christ to conquer every part of you. (*See #38, #74, #224, #225.*)

264. Lamb Slain From the Foundation of the World
– *Arnion Sphazo Katabole Kosmos*

"All who dwell on the earth will worship him, whose names have not been written in the Book of Life of the *Lamb slain from the foundation of the world*" (Revelation 13:8, *NKJV*).

Definition: *Arnion* (ar-nee'-on) [721]; diminutive from *aren*; a lambkin: – lamb. (S)

Sphazo (sfad'-zo) [4969]; a primary verb; to butcher (especially an animal for food or in sacrifice) or (generally) to slaughter, or (specifically) to maim (violently): – kill, slay, wound. (S)

Katabole (kat-ab-ol-ay') [2602]; from *kataballo*; a deposition, i.e. founding; figuratively, conception: – conceive, foundation. (S)

Kosmos (kos'-mos) [2889]; probably from the base of *komizo*; orderly arrangement, i.e. decoration; by implication, the world (in a wide or narrow sense, including its inhabitants, literally or figuratively [morally]): – adorning, world. (S)

Most of the believers John was writing to were converted Jews. They had many traditions, including the ceremonial offerings and sacrifices ordered by Moses. The most common sacrifice was a lamb. Each animal had to be perfectly normal, unmarked and without blemish.

The messianic Jew understood exactly what John meant. This name established the fact that our Lord's sacrifice was not an afterthought of God. Jesus came to earth to die. He could not complete His work until He was sacrificed exactly as the prophets had foretold through the centuries.

Jesus knew the work He had to do. When He chose Judas He knew that this was the one who would betray Him.

The Romans and the Jewish council had a gruesome task to perform, but perform it they must if the law and the prophets were to be fulfilled. The life, death, resurrection and ascension of Jesus were all according to God's plan. (*See #175, #207, #244.*)

265. King of Saints – *Basileus Ethnos*

"And they sing the song of Moses the servant of God, and the song of the Lamb, saying, Great and marvellous are thy works, Lord God Almighty; just and true are thy ways, thou *King of saints*" (Revelation 15:3).

> **Definition:** *Basileus* (bas-il-yooce') [935]; probably from *basis* (through the notion of a foundation of power); a sovereign (abstractly, relatively, or figuratively): – king. (S)
>
> *Ethnos* (eth'-nos) [1484]; probably from *etho*; a race (as of the same habit), i.e. a tribe; specially, a foreign (non-Jewish) one (usually by implication, pagan): – Gentile, heathen, nation, people. (S)

In "the Song of the Lamb," the name *King of Saints* appears. The Israelites sang the song of Moses after they crossed the Red Sea. The saints singing the song of the Lamb are victorious over the beast and his mark.

These saints are standing on what appears to be a sea of glass mingled with fire. A multitude of overcomers have just witnessed a great deliverance from the evil beast and his system. Jesus is the king and only sovereign whom they will worship and follow obediently. (*See #38, #224, #225.*)

266. Lord God Omnipotent – *Kurios Theos Pantokrator*

"And I heard as it were the voice of a great multitude, and as the voice of many waters, and as the voice of mighty thunderings, saying, Alleluia: for the *Lord God omnipotent* reigneth" (Revelation 19:6).

> **Definition:** *Pantokrator* (pan-tok-rat'-ore) [3841]; from *pas* and *kratos*; the all-ruling, i.e. God (as absolute and universal sovereign): – Almighty, Omnipotent. (S)

The omnipotence of God is one of His great attributes. There is nothing God cannot do; He is all-powerful. No created being shares in God's omnipotence. He alone has that kind of authority and majesty. All of the attributes and characteristics of the Father, Son and Holy Spirit are alike. They may have different functions and names, but they are of one nature and being. The Father is omnipotent, as is the Son and the Holy Spirit.

Satan is not omnipotent! Nor are demons in and around our world. Only God has this fullness of power and authority. There is no place where Jesus is not sovereign, nothing He cannot affect or use for his glory. Jesus said, "All power has been given to me in heaven and on earth" (Matthew 28:18). (*See #10, #11, #107, #257, #291.*)

267. Faithful and True – *Pistos Alethinos*

"Now I saw heaven opened, and behold, a white horse. And He who sat on him was called *Faithful and True*, and in righteousness He judges and makes war" (Revelation 19:11, *NKJV*).

Definition: *Pistos* (pis-tos') [4103]; from *peitho*; objectively, trustworthy; subjectively, trustful: – believe (-ing, -r), faithful (-ly), sure, true. (S)

Alethinos (al-ay-thee-nos') [228]; from *alethes*; truthful: – true. (S)

Jesus is faithful and true by His very nature. Instead of when it is convenient or easy, our Lord is faithful to His Word at all times. Jesus is faithful and true to Himself, His Word, His Father and His church at all times. (*See #253.*)

268. Word of God – *Logos Theos*

"He is dressed in a robe dipped in blood, and his name is the *Word of God*" (Revelation 19:13, *NIV*).

Definition: *Logos* (log'-os) [3056]; from *lego*; something said (including the thought); by implication a topic (subject of discourse), also reasoning (the mental faculty) or motive; by extension, a computation; specifically (with the article in John) the Divine Expression (i.e. Christ): – account, cause, communication, X concerning, doctrine, fame, X have to do, intent, matter, mouth, preaching, question, reason, + reckon, remove, say (-ing), shew, X speaker, speech, talk, thing, + none of these things move me, tidings, treatise, utterance, word, work. (S)

Theos (theh'-os) [2316]; of uncertain affinity; a deity, especially (with *ho*) the supreme Divinity; figuratively, a magistrate; by Hebraism, very: – X exceeding, God, god [-ly, -ward]. (S)

The gospel writer identifies Jesus as the Word who was with God in the beginning and who is God now (John 1:1-4). Here he goes a step farther in labeling Jesus as the "Word of God." He is not just any word, He is the spoken word of God.

At our Lord's baptism and at the Transfiguration, Father God spoke to give glory and credibility to His Son. God communicates with believers by His Holy Spirit. But Jesus is the "Word of God."

Most of the New Testament occurrences of God's speaking concern Jesus' communicating with His followers. (*See #84, #172, #250, #268.*)

269. Tabernacle of God – *Skene*

"And I heard a loud voice from heaven saying, 'Behold, the *tabernacle of God* is with men, and He will dwell with them, and they shall be His people. God Himself will be with them and be their God" (Revelation 21:3, *NKJV*).

Definition: *Skene* (skay-nay') [4633]; apparently akin to *skeuos* and *skia*; a tent or cloth hut (literally or figuratively): – habitation, tabernacle. (S)

The *tabernacle,* or tent of God, is with men. We are His dwelling place. I have seen the outer skin of Boy Scout tents glow at night as they protected the boys within. This is the way the world should see Christians. The body is just a tent containing the life and Spirit of Christ. We too should appear to glow with the revealed presence of the Lord in our lives. (*See #270.*)

270. Temple – *Naos*

"But I saw no temple in it, for the Lord God Almighty and the Lamb are its *temple*" (Revelation 21:22, *NKJV*).

> **Definition:** *Naos* (nah-os') [3485]; from a primary *naio* (to dwell); a fane, shrine, temple – shrine, temple. Compare *hieron*. (S)

There will be no sun or moon to light the new city of Jerusalem. The glory of God will illuminate it and the Lamb will be its light. It will be the fulfillment of all of the types and shadows of the Old and New Testaments.

All that Moses understood in his vision of the Tabernacle; and all that David and others saw in the building of the Temple will be made complete when God dwells in His people as a mighty city called the New Jerusalem. No longer will a veil separate God's people from His presence. And nothing within the Temple will defile or cause an abomination. There will be no lies or deceit.

Most of us would probably have felt uncomfortable in the Temple of David or Herod, because of the formalities and the legalistic worship. We are spoiled by our access to God through His presence as we worship and fellowship with Him. In New Jerusalem, there will be an even greater manifestation of the presence of God, and a more intimate fellowship with the Lord. This is a place I will gladly call home! (*See #269.*)

271. Bright and Morning Star – *Lampros Proinos Aster*

"I Jesus have sent mine angel to testify unto you these things in the churches. I am the root and the offspring of David, and the *bright and morning star*" (Revelation 22:16).

Definition: *Lampros* (lam-pros') [2986]; from the same as *lampas*; radiant; by analogy, limpid; figuratively, magnificent or sumptuous (in appearance): – bright, clear, gay, goodly, gorgeous, white. (S)

Proinos (pro-ee-nos') [4407]; from *proi*; pertaining to the dawn, i.e. matutinal: – morning. (S)

Aster (as-tare') [792]; probably from the base of *stronnumi*; a star (as strown over the sky), literally or figuratively: – star. (S)

This name always reminds me of a picture of the planet Venus on a cool, clear morning. No other object in the sky, besides the moon, is quite as bright or steady. The morning star does not twinkle or shimmer; its light is steady and sure. This is a picture of the gentle presence of Jesus in the city of God.

The light and presence of our Lord will be steady and sure. It will be a comfort to all who are within. The light of the morning star is not overwhelming, either. Instead, it is a gentle light that brings comfort and peace.

Jesus is both David's 'Root' and 'Offspring.' As the Creator of all, Jesus existed long before David. As a human, however, he was one of David's direct descendants (see Isaiah 11:1-5; Matthew 1:1-17). As the Messiah, he is the "bright Morning Star," the light of salvation to all (*Life Application Study Bible*).

(See #2, #63, #121, #173, #184.)

PART 4

THE HOLY SPIRIT

PART 4
The Holy Spirit

His Hebrew Names in the
OLD TESTAMENT

---

272. Spirit of God – *Ruwach 'Elohiym*

"And the earth was without form, and void; and darkness upon the face of the deep. And the *Spirit of God* moved upon the face of the waters" (Genesis 1:2).

> **Definition:** *Ruwach* (roo'-akh) [7307]; from *ruwach*; wind; by resemblance breath, i.e. a sensible (or even violent) exhalation; figuratively, life, anger, unsubstantiality; by extension, a region of the sky; by resemblance spirit, but only of a rational being (including its expression and functions): – air, anger, blast, breath, X cool, courage, mind, X quarter, X side, spirit ([-ual]), tempest, X vain, ([whirl-]) wind (-y). (S)
>
> *'Elohiym* (el-o-heem') [430]; plural of *elowahh*; gods in the ordinary sense; but specifically used (in the plural thus, especially with the article) of the supreme God; occasionally applied by way of deference to magistrates; and sometimes

as a superlative: – angels, X exceeding, God (gods)- dess,
-ly), X (very) great, judges, X mighty. (S)

All of the Trinity were present and involved in the creation. We have already seen how Jesus, as the Word of God, spoke forth in the creation process (John 1:1-4). But before the Word spoke, the Spirit of God had brooded. What God created, He thought about first and carefully considered every aspect. Creation did not just evolve by chance. God purposed that it should be just as it is.

The Spirit of God still broods over His creation today. The physical world as we know it has been fashioned and is complete, but God is still about the business of building His church. The Spirit of God is watching over that work today. This "holy wind" of God reaches into the most remote areas of earth; yet fills our hearts and brings comfort and counsel to all believers. (*See #1*.)

273. Spirit of the Lord – *Ruwach Yehovah*

"And the *Spirit of the Lord* came upon him, and he judged Israel, and went out to war: and the Lord delivered Chushan-rishathaim king of Mesopotamia into his hand; and his hand prevailed against Chushan-rishathaim (Judges 3:10).

Definition: *Ruwach* - a wind, breath, a mind, a spirit (*The New Thayer's Greek-English Lexicon*).

Yehovah - Jehovah (Yahweh) "the existing One"; the proper name of the one true God; unpronounced except with the vowel pointings (*Thayer's Greek-English Lexicon*).

The Spirit of Yahweh came on Othniel, the first man to lead Israel after the death of Joshua (Judges 3:10). He received power and wisdom to lead the people. They had intermarried with the pagans who inhabited Canaan before them, and the Lord was angry. When the people cried to the Lord, He chose Othniel to judge them and lead them in war. Othniel became a mighty warrior and cunning leader.

The phrase, "The Spirit of the Lord came upon him," was also spoken of the judges Gideon, Jephthah, and Samson, among others. It expresses a temporary and spontaneous increase of physical, spiritual, or mental strength. This was an extraordinary and supernatural occurrence to prepare a person for a special task. The Holy Spirit is available to all believers today, but he will come upon believers in an extraordinary way for special tasks. We should ask the Holy Spirit's help as we face our daily problems as well as life's major challenges. (*Life Application Study Bible*)

(*See #3, #4, #5.*)

274. Holy Spirit – *Qodesh Ruwach*

"Cast me not away from thy presence; and take not thy *holy spirit* from me" (Psalm 51:11).

> **Definition:** *Qodesh* (ko'-desh) [6944]; from *qadach*; a sacred place or thing; rarely abstract, sanctity: – consecrated (thing), dedicated (thing), hallowed (thing), holiness, (X most) holy (X day, portion, thing), saint, sanctuary. (S)
>
> *Ruwach* (roo'-akh) [7307]; from *ruwach*; wind; by resemblance breath, i.e. a sensible (or even violent) exhalation; figuratively, life, anger, unsubstantiality; by extension, a region of the sky; by resemblance spirit, but only of a rational being (including its expression and functions): – air, anger, blast, breath, X cool, courage, mind, X quarter, X side, spirit ([-ual]), tempest, X vain, ([whirl-]) wind (-y). (S)

David sinned when he slept with Bathsheba and had her husband killed (see 2 Samuel 11). After Nathan confronted him with his sin (chapter 12), the king of Israel wrote this tender psalm of praise and worship, acknowledging the character and long-suffering of God. At times like these one usually feels farthest from God, but David understood that God did not jump in and out of him every time he failed.

The Holy Spirit is a person, equal with the Father and the Son. He brings conviction of sin to the reprobate. After one receives salvation, the Spirit keeps the believer from sin or reminds him or her of God's commandments concerning it. No one can walk the

Christian path without the Holy Spirit's direction and empowerment. May you be assured of the presence of the Holy Spirit in your life. (*See #281, #282.*)

275. Spirit of Wisdom – *Chokmah*

"And the spirit of the Lord shall rest upon him, the *spirit of wisdom* and understanding, the spirit of counsel and might, the spirit of knowledge and of the fear of the Lord" (Isaiah 11:2, *NKJV*).

> **Definition:** *Chokmah* (khok-maw') [2451]; from *chakam*; wisdom (in a good sense): – skilful, wisdom, wisely, wit. (S)

> **Wisdom:** 1. The power of true and right discernment; also, conformity to the course of action dictated by such discernment. 2. Good practical judgment; common sense (*Standard College Dictionary*).

Wisdom is a gift of the Spirit in 1 Corinthians 12. "And there are diversities of activities, but it is the same God who works all in all. But the manifestation of the Spirit is given to each one for the profit of all: for to one is given the word of wisdom through the Spirit, to another the word of knowledge through the same Spirit" (1 Corinthians 12:6-8, *NKJV*).

Romans 8:9 tells us that the Holy Spirit is in every believer. To have the "spirit of wisdom" from God would mean that you have discernment and true direction within you for all the events of life. This name of God reminds me of Psalm 1.

> Blessed is the man who walks not in the counsel of the ungodly, nor stands in the path of sinners, nor sits in the seat of the scornful; but his delight is in the law of the Lord, and in His law he meditates day and night.

> He shall be like a tree planted by the rivers of water, that brings forth its fruit in its season, whose leaf also shall not wither; and whatever he does shall prosper. The ungodly are not so, but are like the chaff which the wind drives away. Therefore the ungodly shall not stand in the

judgment, nor sinners in the congregation of the righteous. For the Lord knows the way of the righteous, but the way of the ungodly shall perish (Psalm 1:1-6, *NKJV*).

This psalm says that the blessing of God is with the believer who seeks godly counsel. A Christian should seek counsel from the Spirit within first, then from those who know God, are filled with His Holy Spirit and are living in a proper relationship with Him. (*See #205, #275, #276, #279; #53.*)

276. Spirit of Understanding – *Biynah*

"And the spirit of the Lord shall rest upon him, *the spirit of* wisdom and *understanding*, the spirit of counsel and might, the spirit of knowledge and of the fear of the Lord" (Isaiah 11:2).

> **Definition:** *Biynah* (bee-naw') [998]; from *biyn*; understanding: – knowledge, meaning, X perfectly, understanding, wisdom. (S)

> **Understanding:** 1. The act of one who understands, or the resulting state; comprehension. 2. The power by which one understands. 3. The sum of the mental powers by which knowledge is acquired, retained, and extended; the power of apprehending relations and making inferences from them" (*Standard College Dictionary*).

Godly understanding is godly comprehension. Often we are accosted by confusing problems and unclear circumstances that throw us into moments of disorientation and confusion. God promises a "spirit of understanding" for clear and direct comprehension of the problem. This enables the believer to get to the heart of a matter and make godly decisions. (*See #99.*)

277. Spirit of Counsel – *'Etsah*

"And the spirit of the Lord shall rest upon him, the spirit of wisdom and understanding, the *spirit of counsel* and might, the spirit of knowledge and of the fear of the Lord" (Isaiah 11:2).

> **Definition:** '*Etsah* (ay-tsaw') [6098]; from *ya' ats*; advice; by implication, plan; also prudence: – advice, advisement, counsel (l- [or]), purpose. (S)

Available counselors include psychiatrists, psychologists, even psychics. Psalm 1 admonishes us to receive counsel only from a godly person. Situations can so confuse that one feels totally overwhelmed and unable to determine the proper direction. Pray for God to manifest His spirit of counsel within you. Should doubt remain, seek the counsel of a godly man or woman. God has gifted some with great wisdom in counseling. The pastor of your church should be the first person you go to.

Always check out the counsel you are given. Make sure it does not contradict the Word of God. Godly counsel never contradicts Biblical truth. Not only Jim Jones, but others like him have used their positions of authority as pastor or spiritual authority to lead their flocks astray. (*See #106, #286.*)

278. Spirit of Might – *Gebuwrah*

"And the spirit of the Lord shall rest upon him, the spirit of wisdom and understanding, the *spirit of* counsel and *might,* the spirit of knowledge and of the fear of the Lord" (Isaiah 11:2).

> **Definition:** *Gebuwrah* (gheb-oo-raw') [1369]; feminine passive participle from the same as *gibbowr,* force (literally or figuratively); by implication, valor, victory: – force, mastery, might, mighty (act, power), power, strength. (S)

The best illustration I could think of concerning this manifestation of the Spirit is taken from the life of the apostle Peter. In Matthew's account of the trial of Jesus, Peter is shown to have been afraid of a servant girl, among others, and the story of his betrayal is told (Matthew 26:69-75). This was done after Peter had spent three years with Jesus and had been part of the closest group of our Lord's disciples.

Later, Peter is a bold witness before the scribes, Pharisees and Sadducees who were at the temple on the Day of Pentecost (Acts 2:14-47). In the Holy Spirit, Peter is gifted with a tremendous spirit of might to stand boldly and proclaim the gospel message. As a result 3,000 souls were added to the kingdom by the preaching of one sermon that day. (*See #10, #11, #15, #90, #257, #291.*)

279. Spirit of Knowledge – *Da'ath*

"And the spirit of the Lord shall rest upon him, the spirit of wisdom and understanding, the spirit of counsel and might, the *spirit of knowledge* and of the fear of the Lord" (Isaiah 11:2).

> **Definition:** *Da' ath* (dah'-ath); from *yada'*; knowledge: – cunning, [ig-] norantly, know (-ledge), [un-] awares (wittingly). (S)

> **Knowledge:** 1. A result or product of knowing; information or understanding acquired. . . . 4. A sure conviction; certainty. 5. The act, process, or state of knowing; cognition (*Standard College Dictionary*).

Knowledge is also a gift of the Spirit in 1 Corinthians 12:1-11. A word of knowledge by the Spirit of God is a supernatural knowing of something that could not have been known by natural means. By such supernatural means Jesus knew that Lazarus would die and be raised again by Him (see John 11:11).

This spirit of knowledge worked in Peter when he passed the lame man at the Temple's gate Beautiful. Jesus must have passed this lame man many times as He entered the Temple, and it is reasonable to assume that Peter and John had passed him at other times. Peter was given supernatural knowledge at that specific time that God would heal the man through him (see Acts 3:6).

Like Jesus and the Father, the Holy Spirit is the same yesterday, today and forever. A spirit of knowledge is available to each believer as the Spirit manifests it within. Do not hold back from believing what He has spoken and promised in His Word. In Jesus' day, He was limited in His own hometown by the people's lack of faith (Matthew 13:58). Do not let this be the epitaph of your life concerning the promises of God. (*See #293.*)

280. Spirit of the Fear of the Lord – *Yir'ah Yehovah*

"And the spirit of the Lord shall rest upon him, the spirit of wisdom and understanding, the spirit of counsel and might, the *spirit of* knowledge and of *the fear of the Lord*" (Isaiah 11:2).

> **Definition:** *Yir'ah* (yir-aw') [3374]; feminine of *yare'*; fear (also used as infinitive); morally, reverence: – X dreadful, X exceedingly, fear (-fulness). (S)

It is difficult to comprehend the absolute holiness of God and our subsequent unworthiness before Him. When Isaiah saw the Lord, he could only say, "Woe is me, for I am undone! Because I am a man of unclean lips, and I dwell in the midst of a people of unclean lips: for my eyes have seen the King, the Lord of Hosts" (Isaiah 6:5, *NKJV*).

John the Revelator had a similar experience when he beheld Jesus in his vision of heaven and the future of the church (Revelation 1:17). We should have a holy fear of God. The Lord loves us, but He is still awesome, and we should be fearful of standing before Him in our own strength.

"The fear of the Lord is the beginning of wisdom, and the knowledge of the Holy One is understanding" (Proverbs 9:10, *NKJV*).

"In the fear of the Lord there is strong confidence, and His children will have a place of refuge. The fear of the Lord is a fountain of life, to turn one away from the snares of death" (Proverbs 14:26, 27, *NKJV*). (*See #19, #54.*)

PART 4
The Holy Spirit

His Greek Names in the
NEW TESTAMENT

---

281. Holy Ghost – *Hagios Pneuma*

"Now the birth of Jesus Christ was on this wise: When as his mother Mary was espoused to Joseph, before they came together, she was found with child of the *Holy Ghost*" (Matthew 1:18).

Definition: *Hagios* (hag'-ee-os) [40]; from *hagos* (an awful thing) [compare *hagnos, thalpo*]; sacred (physically, pure, morally blameless or religious, ceremonially, consecrated): – (most) holy (one, thing), saint. (S)

Pneuma (pnyoo'-mah); from *pneo*; a current of air, i.e. breath (blast) or a breeze; by analogy or figuratively, a spirit, i.e. (human) the rational soul, (by implication) vital principle, mental disposition, etc., or (superhuman) an angel, demon, or (divine) God, Christ's spirit, the Holy Spirit: – ghost, life, spirit (-ual, -ually), mind. (S)

In the King James version of the Bible this name is often used for the Holy Spirit. The translators were trying to describe what the Greek words *Hagios Pneuma* represented. The name describes the Holy Spirit as a holy wind, or the breath of God. Some would explain this phenomenon as a ghost-like manifestation of the Spirit of God. (*See #274, #282.*)

282. Holy Spirit – *Hagios Pneuma*

"Now the birth of Jesus Christ was as follows: After His mother Mary was betrothed to Joseph, before they came together, she was found with child of the *Holy Spirit*" (Matthew 1:18, *NKJV*).

"Holy Spirit" is the term used by most contemporary translators when describing the third person of the Trinity. Jesus gives perhaps the best description of the Spirit when He spoke to Nicodemus in John 3. In verse 8, Jesus likened the Spirit to a wind that cannot be seen or fully described, but nonetheless is present and manifested by sound and movement.

HOLY SPIRIT or **HOLY GHOST**. The mysterious third Person of the Trinity through whom God acts, reveals His will, empowers individuals, and discloses His personal presence in the Old and New Testament.

Old Testament. The term "Holy Spirit" in the Old Testament is found only in Psalm 51:11; Isaiah 63:10, 11. References to the spirit of God, however, are abundant. In one sense the Spirit of God is depicted as a mighty wind, Hebrew using the same word *ruach* for wind, breath, and spirit. Of the eighty-seven times that the Spirit is described as wind, thirty-seven describe the wind as the agent of God, mostly baneful, and ever strong and intense.

New Testament. A watershed in biblical history occurred at the event of Jesus' baptism when He was anointed by the Spirit of God (Luke 3:22). Luke has more references to the Holy Spirit than do the other synoptic accounts. This can be accounted for by Luke's theological interests which are extended in the Acts of the Apostles, which has been rightly named "The Acts of the Holy Spirit" because of the prominence given to the Spirit.

All apostolic writers witnessed to the reality of the Spirit in the church; however, Johannine theology is rich in its doctrine of the Spirit. In the Gospel of John, the Spirit possesses Christ (John 1:32, 33); is indicative of the new birth (John 3:1-16); will come upon Jesus' departure (John 16:7-11); and will endow the believer after the resurrection (John 20:22). The Christian community is anointed by the Spirit (1 John 2:20); and the Spirit assures the believer of the indwelling presence of Jesus (1 John 3:24). In the prophetic Book of Revelation, John, in Old Testament fashion, depicted himself as a prophet inspired by the Spirit. (*Holman Bible Dictionary*)

(*See #274, #281.*)

283. Dove – *Peristera*

"When He had been baptized, Jesus came up immediately from the water; and behold, the heavens were opened to Him, and He saw the Spirit of God descending like a *dove* and alighting upon Him" (Matthew 3:16, *NKJV*).

Definition: *Peristera*, (per-is-ter-ah') [4058]; of uncertain derivative; a *pigeon* :- dove, pigeon. (S)

In Genesis 1:2, the Spirit of God is likened to a bird brooding, or hovering, over the surface of the waters. In Genesis 8:10, 11, the dove is sent out by Noah to search for dry land. When the dove returned with an olive sprig in its beak, Noah knew that land was nearby. Artists depict the Holy Spirit as a dove in many religious works. It is symbolic of the Holy Spirit and commonly used to represent the third person of the Trinity. The dove is a symbol of peace and tranquility to men and women all over the earth.

It is interesting to note that this image of the Spirit descending like a dove and lighting on Jesus at His baptism was used in all four Gospels. Few accounts of Jesus' life are as well documented, or described by all the witnesses in the same language.

284. Comforter – *Parakletos*

"And I will pray the Father, and he shall give you another *Comforter*, that he may abide with you for ever" (John 14:16).

"But the *Comforter*, which is the Holy Ghost, whom the Father will send in my name, he shall teach you all things, and bring all things to your remembrance, whatsoever I have said unto you" (John 14:26).

> **Definition:** *Parakletos* (par-ak'-lay-tos) [3875]; an intercessor, consoler: – advocate, comforter. (S)

The translators for the *King James Version* of the Bible used the word "comforter" to describe the Greek word *parakletos*. A *paraklete* is one who stands alongside another. In this way God comforts the believer by sending His Holy Spirit to stand alongside us. The comfort we feel knowing God is with us is a tangible manifestation of His presence within the life and ministry of all believers. (*See #285, #286.*)

285. Helper – *Parakletos*

"And I will pray the Father, and He will give you another *Helper*, that He may abide with you forever" (John 14:16, *NKJV*).

"But the *Helper*, the Holy Spirit, whom the Father will send in My name, He will teach you all things, and bring to your remembrance all things that I said to you" (John 14:26, *NKJV*).

The translators of the *New King James Version* of the Bible, as well as many other modern-language translations, used the word "helper" to describe the *parakletos* whom the Father would send. The Holy Spirit is thus seen as One who will come alongside each believer and help him or her live this Christian life. We are not asked to live a pure life by our own power; God helps us by sending the Holy Spirit to live out His life through us. (*See #284, #286.*)

286. Counselor – *Parakletos*

"I will ask the Father, and he will give you another *Counselor* to be with you forever" (John 14:16, *NIV*).

"The *Counselor*, the Holy Spirit, whom the Father will send in my name, will teach you all things and will remind you of everything I have said to you" (John 14:26, *NIV*).

When the translators of the *New International Version* of the Bible came to the word *parakletos*, they described Him as a "Counselor." Isaiah 11:2 presents us with a picture of a "Spirit of Counsel" coming from the Godhead. This is the person of the Holy Spirit dwelling within each believer, giving understanding of the mysteries and ways of God. (*See #107, #284, #285.*)

287. Spirit of Truth – *Pneuma Aletheia*

"Even the *Spirit of truth*, whom the world cannot receive, because it seeth him not, neither knoweth him: but ye know him; for he dwelleth with you, and shall be in you" (John 14:17).

Definition: *Aletheia*, (al-ay'-thi-a) [225]; (*alethes*); truth: - true, × truly, truth, verity. (S)

The Holy Spirit is the spirit of truth. There can be no deceit or lies coming from God. "For what if some did not believe? Will their unbelief make the faithfulness of God without effect? Certainly not! Indeed, let God be true but every man a liar. As it is written: 'That You may be justified in Your words, and may overcome when You are judged'" (Romans 3:3, 4, *NKJV*).

The following chapters teach these truths about the Holy Spirit: he will be with us forever (John 14:16); the world at large cannot accept him (John 14:17); he lives with us and in us (John 14:17); he teaches us (John 14:26); he reminds us of Jesus' words (John 14:26; John 15:26); he convicts us of sin, shows us God's righteousness, and announces God's judgment on evil (John 16:8); he guides into truth and gives insight into future events (John 16:13); he brings glory to Christ (John 16:14). The Holy Spirit has been active among people from the beginning of time, but after Pentecost (Acts 2) he came to live in all believers. Many people are unaware of the Holy Spirit's activities, but to those who hear Christ's words and understand the Spirit's power, the Spirit gives a whole new way to look at life" (*Life Application Study Bible*).

288. Spirit of Life – *Pneuma Zoe*

"There is therefore now no condemnation to them which are in Christ Jesus, who walk not after the flesh, but after the Spirit. For the law of the *Spirit of life* in Christ Jesus hath made me free from the law of sin and death" (Romans 8:1, 2).

Definition: *Zoe* (*dzo-ay*) [2222]; life (literally or figuratively): – life (-time). (S)

This Spirit of life is the Holy Spirit. He was present at the creation of the world (Genesis 1:2), and he is the power behind the rebirth of every Christian. He gives us the power we need to live the Christian life (*Life Application Study Bible*).

We looked at the *zoe* life that God offers through Jesus. This is the life He has and is by His very nature. When a person receives Jesus, the Spirit of Christ comes in and lives out God's own life in and through the person. This spirit of life, called eternal life, is more than just an endless number of days on earth and in heaven. The spirit of life offers believers a quality of life in this world far better than what the world offers. (*See #192, #195.*)

289. Eternal Spirit – *Aionios Pneuma*

"How much more shall the blood of Christ, who through the *Eternal Spirit* offered Himself without spot to God, purge your conscience from dead works to serve the living God?" (Hebrews 9:14, *NKJV*).

> **Definition:** *Aionios*, (ahee-o'-nee-os) [166]; from *aion*; perpetual (also used of past time, or past and future as well) :- eternal, for ever, everlasting, world (began). (S)

The Holy Spirit is an eternal spirit. In Genesis 1:2, this Spirit hovered, or brooded, over the waters of God's creation. In Revelation 22:17, the same Spirit joins with the bride in saying "come" to all who hunger and thirst after the Lord. The *eternal Spirit* of God is going about endlessly offering hope and salvation to a dying world. (*See #68, #108.*)

290. Spirit of Grace – *Pneuma Charis*

"How much more severely do you think a man deserves to be punished who has trampled the Son of God under foot, who has treated as an unholy thing the blood of the covenant that sanctified him, and who has insulted the *Spirit of grace?*" (Hebrews 10:29, *NIV*).

> **Definition:** *Charis* (khar'-ece) [5485]; from *chairo*; graciousness (as gratifying), of manner or act (abstract or concrete; literal, figurative or spiritual; especially the divine influence upon the heart, and its reflection in the life; including gratitude):– acceptable, benefit, favor, gift, grace (-ious), joy, liberality, pleasure, thank (-s, -worthy). (S)

The grace of God is the undeserved, unmerited gift of God, whereby He sent His only begotten Son to die for those who hated Him. The Spirit of grace defines the ongoing work of the Holy Spirit, in continually interceding on behalf of an undeserving world that always strives with God. We need such a Spirit.

In the context of this passage, the writer of Hebrews addressed believers who wanted to continue the blood sacrifices ordered by the law of Moses. Jesus was the final sacrifice for all sin, and no valid reason for the Temple sacrifices now exists. When a believer tries to become acceptable to God by giving things up (making sacrifices), he or she is still trampling the Spirit of grace underfoot. Jesus offered the final sacrifice for all sin, for all time. No additional sacrifice can cause God to love you more or make you more acceptable in His sight.

God loves you because He is love, and because He created you and me to be the objects of that great love. Thank God, through the Spirit of grace, he loves the unlovable and forgives the unforgivable.

PART 5

GOD'S ATTRIBUTES

PART 5

The Names for
GOD'S ATTRIBUTES

To describe a Red Delicious apple, you may use adjectives that correspond with the name. The ripened fruit is red and delicious. You may also use descriptive words that are not a part of the official name. You can say the meat of the fruit is white, juicy, sweet and crunchy, if eaten at certain time. The green fruit can be sour, bitter and hard. Then overripe fruit becomes soft and pulpy, and can be discolored.

We have been looking at the names of God disclosed in His Word. Now we look at other descriptive words that help us understand the nature and character of our God. Some of these words are written in the Bible, others never appear in it. Yet, all of them can be useful in our search for revelation and understanding.

291. Omnipotent – *Pantokrator*

"And I heard as it were the voice of a great multitude, and as the voice of many waters, and as the voice of mighty thunderings, saying, Alleluia: for the Lord God *omnipotent* reigneth" (Revelation 19:6).

> **Definition:** *Pantokrator* (pan-tok-rat'-ore) [3841]; from *pas* and *kratos*; the all-ruling, i.e. God (as absolute and universal sovereign): – Almighty, Omnipotent. (S)

Omnipotent means God is all-powerful. "Who hath measured the waters in the hollow of his hand, and meted out heaven with the span, and comprehended the dust of the earth in a measure, and weighed the mountains in scales, and the hills in a balance? Who hath directed the Spirit of the Lord, or being his counsellor hath taught him? With whom took he counsel, and who instructed him, and taught him in the path of judgment, and taught him knowledge, and shewed to him the way of understanding?" (Isaiah 40:12-14).

> Sovereignty and omnipotence must go together. One cannot exist without the other. To reign, God must have power, and to reign sovereignly, He must have all power. And that is what omnipotent means, having all power. God possesses what no creature can: an incomprehensible plentitude of power, a potency that is absolute. (*The Knowledge of the Holy*)

(*See #10, #11, #107, #257, #266.*)

292. Omnipresent – *(Implied)*

"Where can I go from your Spirit? *Where can I flee from your presence?* If I go up to the heavens, you are there; if I make my bed in the depths, you are there. If I rise on the wings of the dawn, if I settle on the far side of the sea, even there your hand will guide me, your right hand will hold me fast" (Psalm 139:7-10, *NIV*).

God is always present; He is everywhere at the same time.

> Few other truths are taught in the Scriptures with as great clarity as the doctrine of the divine omnipresence. Those passages supporting this truth are so plain that it would take considerable effort to misunderstand them. They declare that God is immanent in His creation, that there is no place in heaven or earth or hell where men can hide from His presence. They teach that God is at once far off and near, and that in Him men move and live and have their being. And what is equally convincing is that they everywhere compel us to assume that God is omnipresent to account for other facts they tell us about Him. For instance, the scriptures teach that God is infinite. This means that His being knows no limits. Therefore there can be no limit to His presence; He is omnipresent. (*The Knowledge of the Holy*)

(*See #45.*)

293. Omniscient – *(Implied)*

"O Lord, *you have searched me and you know me.* You know when I sit and when I rise; you perceive my thoughts from afar. You discern my going out and my lying down; you are familiar with all my ways. Before a word is on my tongue you know it completely, O Lord. You hem me in—behind and before; you have laid your hand upon me" (Psalm 139:1-5, *NIV*).

Omniscient means God is *all-knowing.* There is nothing we can do or say that He does not know.

> To say that God is omniscient is to say that He possesses perfect knowledge and therefore has no need to learn. But it is more: it is to say that God has never learned and cannot learn. Could God at any time or in any manner receive into His mind knowledge that He did not possess and had not possessed from eternity, He would be imperfect and less than Himself. (*The Knowledge of the Holy*)

(*See #9, #279.*)

294. Immutable – *(Implied)*

"God is not a man, that he should lie; neither the son of man, that he should repent: hath he said, and shall he not do it? or hath he spoken, and shall he not make it good?" (Numbers 23:19).

"Jesus Christ the same yesterday, and to day, and for ever" (Hebrews 13:8).

Immutable means that God is *unchanging.*

> To say that God is immutable is to say that He never differs from Himself. For a moral being to change it would be necessary that the change be in one of three directions. He must go from better to worse or from worse to better; or, granted that the moral quality remain stable, he must change within himself, as from immature to mature or from one order of being to another. It should be clear that God can move in none of these directions. His perfections forever rule out such possibility. God cannot change for the better. Since He is perfectly holy, He has never been less holy than He is now and can never be holier than He is and has always been. Neither can God change for the worse. Any deteriorations within the unspeakably holy nature of God is impossible." (*The Knowledge of the Holy*)

295. Holy – *Qadowsh*

"Exalt the Lord our God and worship at his holy mountain, *for the Lord our God is holy*" (Psalm 99:9, *NKJV*).

> **Definition:** *Qadowsh* (kaw-doshe') [6918]; or *qadosh* (kaw-doshe'); from *qadash*; sacred (ceremonially or morally); (as noun) God (by eminence), an angel, a saint, a sanctuary: – holy (One), saint. (S)

To call God holy is to refer to Him as *separate* from His creation and *pure* in all His ways. This quality in His person and in His influence makes Him unique and supreme.

Until we have seen ourselves as God sees us, we are not likely to be much disturbed over conditions around us as long as they do not get so far out of hand as to threaten our comfortable way of life. We have learned to live with unholiness and have come to look upon it as the natural and expected thing. We are not disappointed that we do not find all truth in our teachers or faithfulness in our politicians or complete honesty in our merchants or full trustworthiness in our friends. That we may continue to exist we make such laws as are necessary to protect us from our fellow men and let it go at that. Holy is the way God is. To be holy He does not conform to a standard. He is that standard. He is absolutely holy with an infinite, incomprehensible fullness of purity that is incapable of being other than it is. Because He is holy, His attributes are holy; that is, whatever we think of as belonging to God must be thought of as holy. (*The Knowledge of the Holy*)

(*See #20, #124.*)

296. Just – *Dikaios*

"*God is just*: He will pay back trouble to those who trouble you" (2 Thessalonians 1:6, *NIV*).

Definition: *Dikaios* (dik'-ah-yos) [1342]; from *dike*; equitable (in character or act); by implication, innocent, holy (absolutely or relatively): – just, meet, right (-eous). (S)

As the just One, God cannot overlook sin. All sin is an abomination in His eyes and is punishable by death.

The Christian philosopher and saint, Anselm, Archbishop of Canterbury, sought a solution to the apparent contradiction between the justice and the mercy of God. 'How dost Thou spare the wicked,' he inquired of God, 'if Thou art all just and supremely just?' Then he looked straight at God for the answer, for he knew that it lies in what God is. Anselm's findings may be paraphrased this way: God's being is unitary; it is not composed of a number of parts working harmoniously, but simply one. There is nothing in His justice which forbids the exercise of His mercy.

To think of God as we sometimes think of a court where a kindly judge, compelled by law, sentences a man to death with tears and apologies, is to think in a manner wholly unworthy of the true God. God is never at cross-purposes with Himself. No attribute of God is in conflict with another. A simpler and more familiar solution for the problem of how God can be just and still justify the unjust is found in the Christian doctrine of redemption. It is that, through the work of Christ in atonement, justice is not violated but satisfied when God spares a sinner. (*The Knowledge of the Holy*)

(*See #251, #297.*)

297. Merciful – *Rachuwm*

"(For the Lord thy God is a *merciful* God;) he will not forsake thee, neither destroy thee, nor forget the covenant of thy fathers which he sware unto them" (Deuteronomy 4:31).

Definition: *Rachuwm* (rakh-oom') [7349]; from *racham*; compassionate: – full of compassion, merciful. (S)

The unfathomable mercy of God is incomprehensible to us.

Mercy is an attribute of God, an infinite and inexhaustible energy within the divine nature which disposes God to be actively compassionate. If we could remember that the divine mercy is not a temporary mood but an attribute of God's eternal being, we would no longer fear that it will someday cease to be. Mercy never began to be, but from eternity was; so it will never cease to be. It will never be more since it is itself infinite; and it will never be less because the infinite cannot suffer diminution. Nothing that has occurred or will occur in heaven or earth or hell can change the tender mercies of our God. Forever His mercy stands, a boundless, overwhelming immensity of divine pity and compassion. (*The Knowledge of the Holy*)

(*See #251, #296.*)

298. Faithful – *'Aman*

"Thus saith the Lord, the Redeemer of Israel, and his Holy One, to him whom man despiseth, to him whom the nation abhorreth, to a servant of rulers, Kings shall see and arise, princes also shall worship, because of the *Lord that is faithful*, and the Holy One of Israel, and he shall choose thee" (Isaiah 49:7).

> **Definition:** '*Aman* (aw-man') [539]; a primitive root; properly, to build up or support; to foster as a parent or nurse; figuratively to render (or be) firm or faithful, to trust or believe, to be permanent or quiet; morally to be true or certain; once (Isaiah 30:21; interchangeable with '*aman*) to go to the right hand: – hence, assurance, believe, bring up, establish, + fail, be faithful (of long continuance, stedfast, sure, surely, trusty, verified), nurse, (-ing father), (put), trust, turn to the right. (S)

God is faithful in all He does. He will perform everything He has promised and will not fail us in any measure.

> In studying any attribute, the essential oneness of all the attributes soon becomes apparent. We see, for instance, that if God is self-existent He must be also self-sufficient; and if He has power He, being infinite, must have all power. If He possesses knowledge, His infinitude assures us that He possesses all knowledge. Similarly, His immutability presupposes His faithfulness. If He is unchanging, it follows that He could not be unfaithful, since that would require Him to change. (*The Knowledge of the Holy*)

"Let your character or moral disposition be free from the love of money [including greed, avarice, lust, and craving for earthly possessions] and be satisfied with your present [circumstances and with what you have]; for He (God) Himself has said, I will not in any way fail you nor give you up nor leave you without support. [I will] not, [I will] not, [I

Will] not in any degree leave you helpless nor forsake nor let [you] down [relax My hold on you]! [Assuredly not!]" (Hebrews 13:5, *Amp.*). (*See #17.*)

299. Transcendent – (Implied in Exodus 3:6; Isaiah 6:5; Daniel 10:7; Acts 9:3-7)

> When we speak of God as transcendent we mean of course that He is exalted far above the created universe, so far above that human thought cannot imagine it. (*The Knowledge of the Holy*)

Many Scriptures illustrate the transcendence of God. He is far superior to His creation; and when people come in contact with the transcendent God, they are changed forever. Look at these reactions when people saw the Lord in His glory.

1. Moses saw God in the burning bush on the mountain. After hearing God speak, Moses hid his face, because he was afraid to look upon the Lord.

> Moreover he said, I am the God of thy father, the God of Abraham, the God of Isaac, and the God of Jacob. And Moses hid his face; for he was afraid to look upon God (Exodus 3:6).

2. Isaiah walked freely with kings during his lifetime. He held favor with many influential Jews. Yet, when the prophet came in contact with the Lord of Hosts, he found himself totally inadequate to speak on his own. He could only talk of his filth and unworthiness:

> Then said I, Woe is me! for I am undone; because I am a man of unclean lips, and I dwell in the midst of a people of unclean lips: for mine eyes have seen the King, the Lord of hosts (Isaiah 6:5).

3. Daniel saw many visions, but when he saw the glorious man in chapter 10, he found himself quickly left alone by

those who had accompanied him. They were afraid of the dreadful God they beheld, and Daniel was left shaken and in a weakened state:

> And I Daniel alone saw the vision: for the men that were with me saw not the vision; but a great quaking fell upon them, so that they fled to hide themselves. Therefore I was left alone, and saw this great vision, and there remained no strength in me: for my comeliness was turned in me into corruption, and I retained no strength (Daniel 10:7, 8).

4. When Saul of Tarsus made his way to Damascus to persecute the Christians, he met the Christ and was knocked from his horse. The sight of the Lord in His glory blinded Saul and left his fellow travelers speechless:

> And as he journeyed, he came near Damascus: and suddenly there shined round about him a light from heaven: and he fell to the earth, and heard a voice saying unto him, Saul, Saul, why persecutest thou me? And he said, Who art thou, Lord? And the Lord said, I am Jesus whom thou persecutest: it is hard for thee to kick against the pricks. And he trembling and astonished said, Lord, what wilt thou have me to do? And the Lord said unto him, Arise, and go into the city, and it shall be told thee what thou must do. And the men which journeyed with him stood speechless, hearing a voice, but seeing no man (Acts 9:3-7, *NKJV*).

5. When the apostle John sat with Jesus during the Last Supper it was obvious that he felt at ease with the man he knew so well. John 13:23-25 says that John leaned against Jesus' breast when he asked the Lord who it was that would betray Him. A different story is told when John sees Jesus on the Isle of Patmos as he received the revelation of Jesus Christ.

> And when I saw Him, I fell at His feet as dead. But He laid His right hand on me, saying to me, "Do not be afraid; I am the First and the Last. I am He who lives, and was dead, and behold, I am alive forevermore. Amen.

And I have the keys of Hades and of Death" (Revelation 1:17, 18, *NKJV*).

In the upper room, John was fellowshiping the Son of God during His incarnation. On Patmos, John saw Jesus after His glorification. O, that we could only see Jesus as He truly is— Son of God, Son of Man; Lord of lords and God of gods. Jesus is the great "I AM," transcendent in splendor and holy in presence.

300. Sovereign – *Shalliyt*

"He was driven away from people and given the mind of an animal; he lived with the wild donkeys and ate grass like cattle; and his body was drenched with the dew of heaven, until he acknowledged that the Most High God is *sovereign* over the kingdoms of men and sets over them anyone he wishes" (Daniel 5:21, *NIV*).

> **Definition:** *Shalliyt* (Aramaic) (shal-leet') [7990]; corresponding to *shalliyt*; mighty; abstractly, permission; concretely, a premier: – captain, be lawful, rule (-r). (S)

The sovereignty of God describes His awesome power and control of creation. Nothing in all creation can take one out of His hands. He has absolute authority and reigns supremely. Although God is omnipotent, omniscient, omnipresent and has all authority, He has chosen to give humans a certain measure of free will and choice on earth. He does not intervene in every situation, but He waits on us to release His Spirit as we pray.

Issues concerning the sovereignty of God and the resulting confusion about our part in God's creation, about evangelism and about the resulting salvation has been the focus of a lot of debate. Yet, I know that one day we will know all of these things perfectly; for "Now we see but a poor reflection as in a mirror; then we shall see face to face. Now I know in part; then I shall know fully, even as I am fully known" (1 Corinthians 13:12, *NIV*).

Until then, God instructs us to love one another and not let such disputes cause bitterness or separation between believers. (*See #22, #29, #59, #199.*)

301. Triune – (*Implied*)

Then cometh Jesus from Galilee to Jordan unto John, to be baptized of him. But John forbad him, saying, I have need to be baptized of thee, and comest thou to me? And Jesus answering said unto him, Suffer it to be so now: for thus it becometh us to fulfil all righteousness. Then he suffered him. And *Jesus*, when he was baptized, went up straightway out of the water: and, lo, the heavens were opened unto him, and he saw the *Spirit of God* descending like a dove, and lighting upon him: and lo *a voice from heaven*, saying, This is my beloved Son, in whom I am well pleased (Matthew 3:13-17).

Our God is a triune being. He is made up of three distinct Persons: the Father is God; the Son is God; and the Spirit is God (see Genesis 1:26; Matthew 3:13-17). We still recite these words from the Nicene Creed, which was written in A.D. 318:

> I believe in one Lord Jesus Christ, the Only-begotten Son of God, begotten of Him before all ages, God of God, Light of Light, very God of very God, Begotten, not made, being of one substance with the Father, by whom all things were made;" and "I believe in the Holy Spirit, the Lord and giver of life, which proceedeth from the Father and of the Son, who with the Father and Son together is worshiped and glorified.

The mystery of the trinity is understood only by faith. (*See #1, #62, #52.*)

302. Good – *Towb*

The Lord is good to all: and his tender mercies are over all his works" (Psalm 145:9, *NKJV*).

> **Definition:** *Towb* (tobe) [2896]; from *towb*; good (as an adjective) in the widest sense; used likewise as a noun, both in the masculine and the feminine, the singular and the plural (good, a good or good thing, a good man or woman; the good, goods or good things, good men or women), also as an adverb (well): – beautiful, best, better, bountiful, cheerful, at ease, X fair (word), (be in) favour, fine, glad, good (deed, -lier, -liest, -ly, -ness, -s), graciously, joyful, kindly, kindness, liketh (best), loving, merry, X most, pleasant, + pleaseth, pleasure, precious, prosperity, ready, sweet, wealth, welfare, (be) well ([-favored]). (S)

We serve a good God!—a comforting affirmation—acknowledges the fact that His goodness constitutes the condition of our highest good. He has made human nature in such a way that our best and noblest good can only be found in relation to Him.

> When Christian theology says that God is good, it is not the same as saying that He is righteous or holy. The holiness of God is trumpeted from the heavens and re-echoed on the earth by saints and sages wherever God has revealed Himself to men; however, we are not at this time considering His holiness but His goodness, which is quite another thing. The goodness of God is that which disposes Him to be kind, cordial, benevolent, and full of good will toward men. He is tender-hearted and of quick sympathy, and His unfailing attitude toward all moral beings is open, frank, and friendly. By His nature He is inclined to bestow blessedness and He takes holy pleasure in the happiness of His people. (*The Knowledge of the Holy*)

SUBJECT INDEX

*A topic is keyed to the Bible study where it is discussed.
The number(s) following the topic is/are not the page(s) but
the Bible study number(s) for that subject. For example,* Aaron's
Rod, 110 *means Bible study number 110, not page 110.*

Subject Index

Subject Index

NAMES OF GOD INDEX

The names and attributes of God are keyed to the Bible study number for that name. For example, Advocate, 219 means Bible study number #219, not page 219.

Names of God Index

Names of God Index

T

U - V

W

Some trust in chariots, and some in horses: but we will remember the name of the Lord our God (Psalm 20:7).